WITHDRAWN

HARVARD LIBRARY

WITHDRAWN

Realism in Religion

REALISM IN RELIGION

A Pragmatist's Perspective

ROBERT CUMMINGS NEVILLE

Cover art: Beth Neville

Published by
STATE UNIVERSITY OF NEW YORK PRESS, ALBANY

© 2009 State University of New York

All rights reserved

Printed in the United States of America

No part of this book may be used or reproduced in any manner whatsoever without written permission. No part of this book may be stored in a retrieval system or transmitted in any form or by any means including electronic, electrostatic, magnetic tape, mechanical, photocopying, recording, or otherwise without the prior permission in writing of the publisher.

For information, contact State University of New York Press, Albany, NY
www.sunypress.edu

Production, Laurie Searl
Marketing, Fran Keneston

Library of Congress Cataloging-in-Publication Data

Neville, Robert C.
  Realism in religion : a pragmatist's perspective / Robert Cummings Neville.
       p. cm.
  Includes bibliographical references and index.
  ISBN 978-1-4384-2825-3 (hardcover : alk. paper)
  1. Religion. 2. Realism. 3. Pragmatism. I. Title.
  BL51.N445 2009
  210—dc22
                                                                2009000586

10 9 8 7 6 5 4 3 2 1

For Hermann Deuser,
friend

Contents

Preface — xi

Introduction — 1

PART I. REALISM AND TRUTH

One — Theologies of Identity and Truth: Legacies of Barth and Tillich — 9

Barth and Tillich on Theology: Narrative and System
Legacies of Narrative and System
Truth, Identity, and Authority

Two — Truth in Theology — 23

Four Roots of the Evasion of Truth, and their Antidotes
Liberal Theology as a Near Miss
Theology as Symbolic Engagement
Metaphysics for Theology

Three — Realism and Contextualization — 35

Postliberalism and Theological Inquiry
Religious Symbols: Engagement
Religious Symbols: Interpretation

        All Truth Is Contextual
        The Comparative Context for Religious Truth

FOUR   How to Read Scriptures for Religious Truth   57

        Scriptures for Engagement
        Imaginative Differences
        Strategies of Symbolic Interpretation
        Criteria for Reading Scriptures for Truth

FIVE   Systematic Theology in a Global Public   73

        System and Its Public: Three Values
        Truth and Realism
        Minimizing Arbitrariness
        Vulnerability in a Global Public

PART II. REALISM IN PRAGMATISM

SIX   A Peircean Theory of Religious Interpretation   89

        Engagement and Reference
        Reference and Apophatic Theology
        Meaning and Truth
        Interpretation

SEVEN   The Contributions of Charles S. Peirce
        to Philosophy of Religion   109

        The Evolutionary Weight of Religion
        Contributions to Theology
        Comparative Theology
        The Importance of Erudition

EIGHT   Intuition: A Platonizing of Pragmatism   123

        Intuition and Immediate Unity
        A Theory of Harmony
        Judgment and Interpretation
        Intuition and Plato's Divided Line

Nine Whitehead and Pragmatism — 153

*The Entangled Legacies of Pragmatism and
    Process Philosophy*
Tensions regarding Time and Continuity
Eternity and Time
Creation, Eternity, Time, and Continuity

Ten Philosophy of Nature in American Theology — 165

Jonathan Edwards
Ralph Waldo Emerson
The Pragmatists
Alfred North Whitehead

PART III. REALISM IN RELIGION AND METAPHYSICS

Eleven Concepts of God in Comparative Theology — 177

Conceptions of God in Comparison
Theoretical Issues in Comparison
Observations about Ultimacy
*An Hypothesis about the Respect in which
    Concepts of Ultimacy Interpret Reality*

Twelve Some Contemporary Theories of Divine Creation — 191

Classifications of Conceptions of God
Process Theology
Ground-of-Being Theologies
Piety and Conceptions of God

Thirteen Descartes and Leibniz on the Priority of Nature versus Will in God — 203

Texts and Arguments
Transcendence and Immanence
Tillich and Hartshorne as Descartes and Leibniz
Experience and Reason

FOURTEEN	The Metaphysical Sense in Which Life Is Eternal	213

Introduction: Immortality and Eternal Life
Time and Eternity: A Metaphysical Analysis
Eternity in the Divine Life of God
Eternity and Time in Human Life

NOTES	227
INDEX	251

Preface

To discover in one's late sixties that one's early instincts were fruitful is a considerable comfort in the face of the discomforts of that age. I began my career in the 1960s when most philosophers in American and Britain believed in the "linguistic turn," to use Richard Rorty's phrase, which meant that philosophy and theology talk about talking about things, not about the things themselves. Against this, my instincts were for a realism in epistemology and metaphysics, and for an appreciation of the American pragmatists as creative, anti-Kantian realists. At that time, the pragmatists were generally considered to be amateur philosophers, not professionally precise like the Anglo-American analytic philosophers, nor professionally profound like the Continental philosophers. Over the years, my instincts have been rewarded, negatively by the various moves of both analytic and Continental philosophies and theologies toward greater realism and, positively, by the handiness of pragmatically inspired realism for thinking through all sorts of problems Kantian foundationalism said we cannot think.

The chapters in this volume began as essays for various occasions or publications, but exhibit a strong continuity of theme regarding realism in religion. They have been rewritten considerably for this volume to eliminate repetition and provide continuity. Nevertheless, the remaining flavor and style reflect their original contexts. The first two chapters were public talks, and reflect the informal accessibility of that genre. The first, "Theologies of Identity and Truth: Legacies of Barth and Tillich," was the presidential address for the American Theological Society, delivered in April 2006, at the annual meeting in Princeton Theological Seminary, under the title, "Two Dimensions of Religious Belief." Most of the second chapter, "Truth in Theology," was the Armstrong Lecture for 2004 at Kalamazoo College, given at the invitation of Professor and Dean of the Chapel Gary Dorrien, with that title. Other material in chapter 2 began as a talk at the Highlands Institute and published as "Naturalism and Supernaturalism in American Theology" in *American Journal of Theology and Philosophy* 26/1&2 (January-May 2005), pp. 78–84. Most of chapter 3 originated as a lecture at Wolfgang Goethe University at Frankfurt and was subsequently published in *Neue Zeitschrift Fuer Systematische Theologie und Religionsphilosophie*, 44 (2002), pp. 71–88, with the appropriately Germanic title, "Contextualization and the Non-obvious Meaning of Religious Symbols: New Dimensions to the Problem of Truth." Chapter 4, "How To Read Scriptures for Religious Truth," came from an article by that name published in a volume in honor of the late Anthony Saldarini, *When Judaism and Christianity Began: Essays in Memory of Anthony F. Saldarini*, edited by Alan J. Avery-Peck, Daniel Harrington, and Jacob Neusner, volume 2, pp. 601–621 (Leiden/Boston: Brill, 2004). Chapter 5 began as a lecture entitled "On the Conditions for Systematic Theology in a Global Public" that was given at a conference at Frankfurt University and published in *Religious Apologetics—Philosophical Argumentation*, edited by Yossef Schwartz and Volkard Krech (Tuebingen: Mohr Siebeck, 2004), pp. 9–24. "A Peircean Theory of Religious Interpretation," chapter 6, began as an essay in *Pragmatism and Religion* (Urbana, IL: University of Illinois Press, 2003), edited by Stuart Rosenbaum. From *Pragmatism and Religion: Classical Sources and Original Essays*. ©2003 by the Board of Trustees of the University of Illinois. Used with permission of the University of Illinois Press. Chapter 7, "The Contributions of Charles S. Peirce to Philosophy of Religion" was originally published in *Cognitio—Rivista de Filosofia* 2 (2001) 134–46, both in English and in Portuguese translation. Chapter 8, "Intuition: A Platonizing of Pragmatism," is one of the earliest of my papers, published simply as "Intuition" in *International Philosophical Quarterly* 7 (December 1967), 556–590; at the time I did not realize how much Peirce's pragmatism already was Platonized, reacting against his explicit attack on intuition. Still, the chapter makes a valid point of extension of Peirce's theory, I believe, and has been modified only to update footnotes and add continuity to other chapters here. Chapter 9, "Whitehead and Pragmatism," began as an essay by that title in *Whitehead's Philosophy: Points of Connection*, edited by Janusz A. Polanowski and Donald W. Sherburne (Albany: State University of New York Press, 2004). Chapter 10, "Philosophy of Nature in American Theology," was originally published in an earlier version with that title in a Festschrift for Hermann Deuser, *Theologie Zwischen Pragmatismus and Existenzdenken*, edited by Gesche Linde, Richard Purkarthofer, Heiko Schulz, and Peter Steinacker (Marburg: N. G. Elwert, 2006).

Chapter 11 began as "The Role of Concepts of God in Cross Cultural Comparative Theology" in *Philosophy of Religion for a New Century: Essays in Honor of Eugene Thomas Long*, edited by J. Hackett and J. Wallulis (Netherlands: Kluwer Academic Publishers, 2004), pp. 243–259. Chapter 12 first was an address given at the Metaphysical Society of America in March 2006, at the Catholic University of America, under the title, "Some Contemporary

Theories of Divine Creation." Chapter 13, the oldest essay in the book, was originally published as "Some Historical Problems about the Transcendence of God," in *The Journal of Religion* 47/1 (January 1967), pp. 1–9, and is included here following the chapter on the metaphysics of eternity to show how the debate between Descartes and Leibniz can be adjudicated with a similar metaphysical realism. Chapter 14 was an address at the University of Frankfurt for a Studientag celebrating the sixtieth birthday of Hermann Deuser in February 2006. I thank the journals, publishers, and editors for permission to use previously published material.

Although most of these essays have been rewritten to provide continuity and minimize repetition, this still is a book of essays from different contexts. Instead of a single treatment of each major theme, as would be appropriate for a monograph, the basic themes recur here in different contexts and forms. Each is accessible, as befits a lecture, and cumulatively they provide nuances of detail that would be impossible in a massive treatment with one plot-line. These essays embody a system, which is not a single rational structure but rather an examination of a cluster of related themes from many different angles. See the discussion of Peirce's claim that a good argument is not like a chain of links but rather like a rope made of many short strands twisted together and against one another. Notions such as truth, interpretation, engagement, ultimacy, God, and comparison appear in many different contexts of discussion here, each time with a new twist.

To have been in the academic world as long as I, is inevitably to have piled up a mountain of debts too voluminous to enumerate. In this place I want to acknowledge my debt to people and institutions who have invited me to speak. With only two exceptions, chapters 8 and 13, every chapter here began as a lecture. Hopefully, the necessity of writing so as to be understood on first hearing makes this book more accessible than my more numbingly nuanced monographs. I want also to acknowledge three partners in the general inquiry into pragmatism and religions. One is Wesley J. Wildman, my good friend and colleague in theology at Boston University. We have worked together often and have taught each other enough that sometimes it is difficult to say which idea originated with whom. The second is Jay Schulkin, a profound friend for very many years, who is a philosophical pragmatist and a prolific scientist, embodying the ideals of inquiry defended here. The third is Hermann Deuser, to whom I am grateful for our many conversations that lie behind most of the chapters of this book, and for his enduring, growing friendship. He is the professor of philosophy of religion and systematic theology at Frankfurt and was the moving force behind the invitations for two of the lectures from which these chapters come, 3 and 5. Moreover, chapter 10 originated as a surprise Festschrift contribution celebrating his sixtieth birthday, and that chapter begins by indicating his contributions to the topics that occupy this volume. Chapter 14 began as a lecture on the occasion of the presentation of that Festschrift and was delivered between sets of music played by his theology department rock band! Who but Hermann Deuser could inspire a tribute mixing rock music and arcane metaphysics in equal measure? If the concluding chapter of this book ends with sermonic rhetoric, it is because he inspired the metaphysical muse to dance. In humble gratitude and awe, I dedicate this volume to him. I thank my wife, Beth Neville, for the art that adorns the cover of this volume. Her art has been on the covers of most of my books, and often on the inner pages. Our long partnership has many facets, and this is one of the most publicly delightful.

Introduction

Charles S. Peirce (1839–1914), the founder of American Pragmatism, often blamed philosophy's mistakes and most of the world's ills on nominalism. Against all forms of nominalism, he asserted what he called "Scotistic realism," lauding the medieval philosopher/theologian Duns Scotus.[1] Peirce did not contrast realism with idealism; in fact he was something of an idealist as well as a realist. Rather he contrasted it with the nominalistic view that only singular individuals exist and that general terms have no objective reference. He emphasized habit and tendency as more highly evolved aspects of reality than singularity. Although the argument in favor of realism in this volume goes far beyond what Peirce explicitly considered, particularly in its application to theology, it follows out his initial skepticism about nominalism and its baleful influences, and develops realism in several directions suggested by him. Peirce should not be noted as a champion of realism without also acknowledging the contributions of his junior colleague, Alfred North Whitehead (1859–1941), who showed how realistic metaphysics, including philosophical theology, is possible by doing it. Whitehead was an avowed Platonist, whereas Peirce spoke more appreciatively of Aristotle; chapter 8 here is my first attempt to combine Peirce's pragmatic fallibilism with Whitehead's Platonic intuitionism. Although Whitehead is not generally regarded as a pragmatist, his way of doing metaphysics fits neatly in the pragmatic view that metaphysics is hypothetical, and his own metaphysics serves many of the same purposes as Peirce's, with far more detail and precision. Peirce and Whitehead both died in the first half of the twentieth century. The struggle between realism and nominalism in religion intensified in the second half.

Nominalism has many forms, not only the medieval view that only particular things exist and that all general terms refer only to ways in which we think about particulars. In the mid and late twentieth century American theology took a great interest in narrative form. A story, of course, supposes its subject to be a singular history. The claim that reality is mainly narrative is nominalistic. Perhaps mostly influenced by Karl Barth, many Christian and Jewish theologians construed narrative as the basic frame within which to understand their religion—a story of God as creator and redeemer of the world, including human history. In 1974, Hans W. Frei, one of my most influential teachers, published *The Eclipse of Biblical Narrative* in which he noted that the demystification of literal theological readings of biblical history resulted in failed attempts to base theology on "realistic" historiography and historicist understandings of theology itself.[2] He argued instead for a narrative approach to theology inspired by Karl Barth. His title turned out to be ironic, because his book focused Barthian theology on narrative as never before, quite the opposite of an eclipse. Chapter 1 here explores the contrast between Barthian narrative theology and Tillich's realistic "systematic theology" (a term of contempt for Barth). The attraction of narrative theology is the ease with which it serves the search for religious identity—you too can play a part in the divine narrative. But because narrative theology cannot be realistic enough, it sacrifices strong justifications to be true.

The case for the importance of truth in theology, over against the use of religious belief to define identity, is not an easy one to make, although it would seem to be obvious. Here the question of realism versus nominalism takes a slightly different form. If the only real things are bare particulars, and general terms refer to our thinking rather than to real things, then theology has little of interest to say about reality. Put another way, our general interpretations of the meanings and values of things in religious matters do not refer to real things. Rather, they refer to our language about things, the language by which we live, or so it is said from the nominalist side. Chapter 2 explores some of the issues in affirming a realistic theology as true of the world, and discusses why so many liberal theologies that were aware of problems of realistic reference were near misses. It then sketches an approach to theology called "symbolic engagement" that will be elaborated in subsequent chapters, and it concludes with the introduction of a conception of metaphysics that shows how religiously important things can be aspects of reality, not merely of language or conceptuality. That conception of metaphysics is developed in many of the later chapters.

The nominalistic view that theology is about our language or conceptuality rather than its purported real subjects has been given great precision by Frei and his colleague, also my teacher, George Lindbeck, known together with their followers as the "Yale School" of theology. For them, the religious realities are not what they seem but rather are the deep structure or grammar of religious communities as cultural/linguistic systems. Theology is less like philosophy, aiming to refer to God and all that depends therefrom, than it is like a social science uncovering the deep structure of a community's ideal practice. The great strength of this approach is its sensitivity to the contextuality of theology. Theological assertions are always made only in concrete contexts, and both their meanings and truth might vary when removed to other contexts. The difficulty with this approach is that theological claims seem to be incapable of referring to what they intend, but rather only to the deep structure of the way a community uses the language of reference. Chapter 3 argues that the vital contextualism of the Yale School can be maintained within a theological approach that still is realistic in its reference to the ultimate realities that are theology's ostensible subjects. The realism of symbolic reference is defended with some technical distinctions from Peirce that will be further elaborated in chapter 6.

For Frei and many others, the test case for realism in theology is not so much in the reference of general theological concepts such as God, creation, and redemption, but in the reference of scripture. Obviously, the spiritual meaning of scripture is not often literal, but it does attempt to say something religiously important about reality and our place in it. So chapter 4 applies and elaborates some of the arguments of the preceding chapters to scriptural understanding, carrying out theology as symbolic engagement with respect to a specific genre of symbols. The theory of reference, distinguishing iconic, indexical, and conventional reference, is expressed more technically than discussions in earlier chapters, and later chapters will add even more detail.

If properly realistic, theology attempts to say what is true of religious realities. It employs symbols and concepts and these of course always have a history. Theology should not be caught within the symbol systems of one or a few communities, however, because presumably all religious with deep reflective traditions have grappled with the religious realities. To make a case for a religious claim, as chapter 3 argues, requires dealing with alternative claims and their cases. Often the languages of different religions are so incommensurate that it is impossible to tell whether they are talking about the same thing, or, contrary-wise, whether they seem to be talking about the same thing when they are not. With its realistic commitments, therefore, theology needs a base in comparative theology to create the global public necessary for making its cases. Chapter 5 explores this in some detail, and later chapters elaborate and illustrate the theory of comparison.

Because the approach to theology advocated in the first five chapters is based on Peirce's pragmatism and other sources, that debt needs to be spelled out. Although earlier chapters mention elements of Peirce's theory, chapter 6 lays it out directly, distinguishing issues of meaning, context, and reference in his general theory of interpretation. Of particular note is his theory of indexical reference, in which causal contact is established by the interpreter and the interpretation's object. By virtue of indexical reference we can understand how concrete symbolic interpretations actually engage the world in fallible, corrigible ways. This is the theoretical heart of "theology as symbolic engagement." Chapter 7 goes on to elaborate a number of the consequences of Peirce's theory for religion and religious inquiry. They amount to a presentation of religious inquiry that is thoroughly empirical, without being reductionistic as in most sciences of religion.

The pragmatic approach to inquiry, including religious or theological inquiry, argues that all knowing is interpretation. Moreover, one knows the meaning of an interpretation by interpreting it again, and then again, and so on indefinitely. A standard criticism of pragmatism is that all knowledge is postponed until the infinite long run, which never comes. Pragmatists answer this criticism with their theory of belief, which is that beliefs are guiding principles (Peirce's term) for habitual actions, and that interpretations stop when the actions they guide become unproblematic. They might be made problematic subsequently, but by and large we live and act within habitual assumptions about the world. As Dewey pointed out, experience is mainly a matter of enjoying or suffering what is real, only rarely wondering what in fact is real. Yet something unsatisfactory lurks in this kind of argument for unproblematic habit, namely, the unexplained immediate sense that we directly engage the objects of our interpretation. The engagement is mediated by interpreting signs, of course. But what accounts for the unity of the interpretive act that embraces both the object of interpretation and the interpreter? Peirce had argued against intuition as a cognition "in immediate relation to its object" (Kant's phrase). Then there must be some other form of intuition that allows for a mediated immediacy, something Dewey documented so well in his notion of experience as art. Chapter 8 is my youthful technical defense of intuition as "fourthness" in Peirce's philosophy, a point Peirce should have learned from Plato. The intentional character of the religious experience of ultimate realities depends on something like this kind of intuition, which is the ground for experiential realism.

Pragmatism has been closely associated with process theology and philosophy in late twentieth century discussions. I am convinced that the way forward in the twenty-first century is to find legacies in both. Chapter 9 details a number of close connections and interesting differences between Whitehead and pragmatism. I have to say, however, that the arguments in this book are far less dependent on Whitehead's specific metaphysics than those in much of my earlier work. For me, at least, pragmatism is the more enduring and fruitful legacy, it seems. Chapter 12 explicitly argues against Whitehead's theology.

The American theological scene does not first become interesting with the philosophical contributions of Peirce and Whitehead. On the contrary, Jonathan Edwards, in the early eighteenth century, introduced notions that became great themes in American theology, including in pragmatism and process theology. These include realism in theological reference, realism in theological knowledge of nature as revealing the ultimate, realism regarding value being resident in things, and aestheticism in experience as the means by which interpreters recognize real value. These are all anti-nominalist themes, and are explored briefly in chapter 10, which, as noted in the preface, began as a Festschrift contribution for Herman Deuser, Germany's most acute theological interpreter of American philosophical and hermeneutical theology.

Having reflected on the pragmatic historical roots of a realistic theology of symbolic engagement, it is appropriate to address some of the most pertinent theological issues. Chapter 11 addresses a specific question with a theology of world religions, namely, how conceptions of God fare when employed cross-culturally. I argue there that comparison can be fair and still normative, and explore the role of comparative treatments of the problem of the one and the many as one criterion for assessing theologies in comparative perspective. Chapter 12 divides conceptions of God into those of a determinate being and those of God as ground of being. It argues for the latter, and claims that a theology of creation *ex nihilo* explains this best, an old theme of mine. My theory of creation *ex nihilo* claims that God's nature as God is the result of the act of creation; a medieval way of saying this is to affirm with Duns Scotus that God's will precedes God's nature, in contrast to Thomas Aquinas for whom the converse precedence obtained. In modern thought, Descartes held to something like the Scotistic position whereas Leibniz held to something like Thomas'. So chapter 13 places the debate between God as a being and God as ground of all being in an early modern historical context, attributing the former view to Leibniz and the latter to Descartes. Because of the close connection between them, some clarity is brought to the debate about whether God is a being with a nature who creates on the basis of that nature, Leibniz' view, or whether God is the ground for all natures, all intelligibility, and all value, which thus depend on the divine creative will. Descartes' hypothesis of the priority of divine will to divine nature is defended, which is not so far from the famous claims on the matter by Duns Scotus, the realist. Chapter 14 pulls together many of the themes of creation *ex nihilo* to elaborate a theory of time and eternity in reference to human life, with special emphasis on eternity. Contrary to the usual analogy for understanding God, according to which God is like temporal human beings but somewhat above time, it argues with contrarian vigor that temporal human life should be understood on the analogy of the eternal God. We discover who we are only in God.

PART I

Realism and Truth

ONE

Theologies of Identity and Truth

Legacies of Barth and Tillich

AT THE PRESENT TIME in our profession, a seeming incommensurable tension exists between what some call "identity theologies" and theologies that aim first to make a case for the truth about the theological topic and then to make religious identity contingent on that discovery.[1] This tension is by no means new. When theology is practiced by people who belong to religious communities, it nearly always has played a dual role—that of defining and refining the identity of the community and that of inquiring into what is true, usually about a problem that has come up within the community. In principle, of course, no theologian especially attentive to the identity dimension of religious belief would want to employ beliefs that were not also true on their own. By the same token, few theologians especially attentive to the truth dimension of belief would deliberately ignore for long the practical implications of belief for the identities of believers. Nevertheless, in our time these two dimensions of religious belief have come into very serious tension. This tension is high not only in Christian theology but in the theological traditions of all the world religions at this time. Reflect with me, if you will, on some aspects of this tension, which I will discuss mainly in reference to the Christian case.

BARTH AND TILLICH ON THEOLOGY: NARRATIVE AND SYSTEM

The two great giants of Protestant Christian theology of the twentieth century, Karl Barth and Paul Tillich, famously agreed that theology is for the sake of the Church. The first sentences of Barth's *Church Dogmatics* are: "As a theological discipline, dogmatics is the scientific test to which the Christian Church puts herself regarding the language about God which is peculiar to her. Dogmatics is a theological discipline. But theology is a function of the Church."[2] The first sentences of Tillich's *Systematic Theology* are: "Theology, as a function of the Christian Church, must serve the needs of the Church. A theological system is supposed to satisfy two basic needs: the statement of the truth of the Christian message and the interpretation of this truth for every new generation."[3] Barth and Tillich differed widely on the public to be engaged by theology, which is not identical with the public each meant to serve with his theology.

For Barth, "The subject of theology is the history of the communion of God with man and of man with God. This history is proclaimed, in ancient times and today, in the Old and New Testaments."[4] He also added the creeds and confessions of the Church as sources for the understanding of the great Christian narrative, and of course engaged in an extremely rich dialogue with many elements of the Christian tradition. His intent was to flesh out in exquisite detail the grand narrative of God's creation and redemption of the world in Jesus Christ. The form of theology for Barth was ultimately narrative, and the public for that theology consisted of those interested in that narrative, affirmatively or critically. Like Mozart, whose music he adored, Barth told his story with consummate complex artistry, and many people discovered themselves and their religious identity within his narrative. The force of his theology was that it gave Christian identity to those who found themselves within his story; the negative force of his theology was that those Christians who did not find themselves identified within his narrative were dismissed by many of his followers as not Christians. The force of Barth's theology in both positive and negative respects was very powerful indeed in American Protestant theological education after World War II.

For all its beauty, Barth's theology was seriously arbitrary. From the outside, it simply did not engage the stories of the Buddhists and Hindus, Confucians and Daoists, and hardly the Jews and Muslims. From their standpoint, Barth's story looks both parochial and uninteresting except as perhaps giving clues for understanding colonialism. From the inside, Barth's story is felt by those who identify with it to be God's revelation, not a human creative invention at all. Nevertheless, it had a very Reformed Protestant orientation, especially in comparison with John Milbank's slightly variant Anglican-Thomistic story. Variant Roman Catholic and Orthodox stories also flourish, often without insistence on strict narrative form. The Dispensationalist story, made popular by the "Left Behind" series of books, is even more strictly narrative in form than Barth's story. My point is that narrative, as a conceptual and literary form, lends itself to the arbitrariness of the narrator's own stresses and internal interpretations, even when the main characters and events are shared with alternative narratives.

To seek a non-narrative path for ascertaining the truth of a narrative is possible. Nineteenth century Christian historians tried to subject Christian narratives to non-narrative scientific history; twentieth century Christian fundamentalists tried to subject them to a non-narrative literal reading of the Bible. Both are fruitless attempts and Barth declined both. Immediately and also in the long run, the power in Barth's theology derives in large measure from the aesthetic beauty of its narrative, given the biblical, creedal and confessional base from which it is drawn. Most of my students today are uncomfortable with the authoritative status of the Bible, being aware of the wide variety of interpretations possible, and they quickly historicize the creeds and confessions. Many of them prefer the aesthetic imaginative narratives of Tolkien or Rowling that present Christian story themes in which they can find identity without embarrassing tethers to Bible, creed, or official theology. Few of these students would say that Tolkien or Rowling are theologians, only that they provide stories within which they can find their Christian identity. For Barth, the theological public he engaged in telling his story consisted of those who accepted his biblical and traditional sources and were willing to struggle with him for how to tell the story.

For Tillich, by contrast, the narrative associated with Christianity was relatively suppressed in favor of the form of system for theology. In a passage immediately preceding my last quotation from Barth on theology as history, Barth said,

> Is not the term 'Systematic Theology' as paradoxical as a 'wooden iron'? One day this conception will disappear just as suddenly as it has come into being. Nevertheless, even if I allow myself to be called and to be a 'Professor of Systematic Theology,' I could never write a book under this title, as my great contemporary and colleague Tillich has done! A 'system' is an edifice of thought, constructed on certain fundamental conceptions which are selected in accordance with a certain philosophy by a method which corresponds to these conceptions. Theology cannot be carried on in confinement or under the pressure of such a construction.[5]

The reason for this, Barth went on to say, is that theology is the *narration of a history* given in the Bible, etc. What Barth said about systematic theology would be quite acceptable to Tillich, I think, so far as it went. It failed to point out that the "fundamental conceptions," "philosophy," and "method" are themselves internal to the theological system for Tillich, and therefore in need of critical elaboration and defense as one proceeds.

The implication of systematic form for Tillich was that he had to engage as within his theological public any thinker, position, or discipline that had something to say on the topics within the system. Philosophy is clearly important, and not only with regard to method. He had to defend his conception of God as fundamental ontology, his conception of the human condition in terms of philosophical anthropology, his interpretation of the Christian narrative in terms of philosophy of history, and so forth. Tillich began philosophically pretty much where Barth began, with the Western tradition read through the problematics of German idealism, Kierkegaard, and crisis existentialism. As his career progressed, however, he was driven to wider philosophical publics that strayed from the historical connections between Christianity and German idealism. Much of twentieth century existentialism was directly atheistic. Sartre had an elaborate idea of God he was convinced does not exist. For Tillich, systematic theology needed to engage the world of secular atheism. Systematic theology's anthropology had to engage scientific psychology, especially psychoanalysis.

For Tillich, the pervasive, if crumbling, languages and images of the Christian narrative obscured the religious realities. The critical imagination of art was required to break through to revelatory truth. The power in Tillich's systematic theology was not its aesthetic coherence but rather its insistence on theology reaching out to any domain of inquiry that might bear upon the systematic topics. Tillich's vision was a powerful motivator in the development of religious studies in the United States, because all the many disciplines in that amorphous field can be relevant to the systematic questions. Tillich himself did not pursue all these disciplines, of course, but toward the end of his life he was moving to develop a theology of other religions, engaging directly in dialogue with Buddhists.

From our perspective, Tillich's system turns out to be extremely leaky. On the one hand, the "eternal truths" of the Christian kerygma, that he advertised as being a solid abutment of the bridge of correlation, have been relativized, historicized, and rendered ambiguous in comparison with the so-called eternal truths of other religions, and indeed of the secular aesthetic vision. On the other hand, the systematic engagements of public domains of theological discourse extending beyond the Christian theological circle has opened sluice-gates to alien seas, and we cannot tell whether it is so-called Christian truth that is washing out or an overwhelming wave of new and barely digestible material racing in. The neat world of German culture, including theology, the anti-establishment arts of the Weimar Republic, and existentialist culture that bounded Tillich's formative years, was exploded by the Second World War. In America Tillich was adopted by the experientialist Methodists whose Boston Personalism then was falling by the wayside because of its implausible idealism. Tillich's combination of rationalism and pietism provided a new language for old Methodist themes. How much of this he understood, I hesitate to say.

The leakiness of Tillich's system, including its readiness for cooptation by sophisticated American pietism, committed it inexorably to the dimension of truth in theology, not identity. Who knows where Tillich and the Tillichians would end up if they were to fan out steadily in all the directions that require cases to be made for Christian claims? One of Tillich's principal legacies is the legitimation of the view that one's religious identity ought to follow one's pursuit of truth, wherever that might lead. This, of course, makes him supremely suspect to Barthians for whom Christian identity is secured immediately with the telling of the story.

Barth, by contrast, with his relatively water-tight story, was committed inexorably to the identity dimension of religious belief. If a Buddhist, say, or a secular person, would challenge the importance of Jesus Christ for Barth, the Barthian answer would not be the making of a case that respects the context, texts, and arguments of the other. It would be to say they simply do not fit the Christian story. Barth, of course, would never suggest that his own dogmatic story is not true, that it is merely a story with aesthetic attractiveness, or that it fails to define the only identity that really counts for human beings. For him it is the revealed word of God that he merely retold in ways relevant for his time.

LEGACIES OF NARRATIVE AND SYSTEM

The oddly parallel careers of Barth and Tillich symbolize the roots of the divergence of identity theologies of religious belief from theologies that make identity contingent upon the outcome of inquiry regarding the truth of theological beliefs. My teachers, Hans Frei and George Lindbeck, took the Barthian trajectory to its next logical step in what has been called the theology of the Yale School. Implicitly admitting the arbitrariness of Barth's story, and drawing on long experience of inter-religious dialogue, they define theology as the exploration of the deep grammar of religious communities as cultural/linguistic systems. The critical edge of theology is the sorting of faithful identity within each community, and theology draws as much on social sciences that adduce the subtleties of community life as upon philosophy that might seek some external reference beyond the community. Each community has its own theology. The Yale School clearly aims theology at the identity dimension of religious belief.

John Milbank and the Radical Orthodox theologians take a more aggressive apologetic approach to identity theology. Claiming that the older theologies had been shaken by the social sciences that represent them as relativized to their social circumstances, class, and so forth, the Radical Orthodox argue that the social sciences themselves are strongly arbitrary in being historically located. If the social sciences can be arbitrary, then so can Christian theology, and Radical Orthodoxy asserts what it represents as the orthodox, that is, Thomistic-Anglican, theology with radical affirmation. Like Barth's theology, Radical Orthodoxy has a clear-edged beauty to it, and defines identity for those who accept it.[6] From Barth through Lindbeck and Milbank, and many other contemporary Protestant identity theologians such as Stanley Hauerwas, Christian identity has somewhat sharp boundary conditions and criteria, though different ones for different theologians.

For the heirs of Tillich, sharp boundary conditions and criteria for Christian identity are much harder to come by. Although there is a Tillich Society associated with the American Academy of Religion, like the Barth Society, few orthodox Tillichians follow the master. Rather, his influence has been multivalent. For instance, probably the closest followers of his ontology of the ground of being for which he is famous are Mary Daly and Rosemary Ruether, extraordinary feminists whose work would have baffled him and who would give him the same low marks for his personal treatment of women that they would give Barth.

Generalizing his own ground-of-being ontology beyond the tradition of German idealism that shaped it, many contemporary theologians take Tillich to legitimate contemporary developments of Neo-Platonic and other ideas of the fullness of being beyond determinate being. My own ground-of-being theology focuses on the act that creates determinate being rather than on any antecedent fullness, so that I would say that the ground is nothing unless it grounds something, and that its whole nature comes from the grounding act.[7] Chapters 12, 13, and 14 below will elaborate this distinction in detail. Tillich is rather vague about the distinction between full and *ex nihilo* grounds.

My colleague, Wesley Wildman, elaborates a distinction between ground-of-being theologies as a class and the class of theologies that conceive God as a determinate being of some kind.[8] Whereas Tillich's insistence on the God beyond god led him to reject all conceptions of God as determinate, except through symbolic participation, nevertheless the metaphysical weight of his theology has given significant support to process theology, the most prominent determinate-being metaphysical theology of our time. Tillich was no match for Whitehead when it comes to precise metaphysics, particularly metaphysics that unites the sciences and arts as Whitehead's does. But Tillich brought to philosophical theology a depth of reflection in the Christian tradition, a serious appropriation of the philosophical as well as ecclesiological dimensions of that tradition, and seriousness about personal and communal piety that was not easily registered among the early Whiteheadians. Process theology has engaged these elements of Tillich to its great profit.

Tillich's concern for human nature, and his openness to existential psychoanalysis, have been influential in the development of pastoral care and counseling, pastoral psychology, and more generally in theological anthropology. Rejecting biblical language per se, Tillich led the way to finding anthropological language from literary and visual arts as well as psychology, sociology, and anthropology, and then relating these conceptions back to biblical themes. Tillich was one of the founders, if not the principal founder, of what we now know as "religion and the arts," and he understood that. His concern that theology engage the physical sciences has promoted the science and religion discussions, and with an alternative in that debate to the theologies of God as a determinate entity; Tillich would be surprised so see how far this dialogue as gone.

One of the influences I most appreciate myself is his suggestion that religious believers participate in the religious object through symbols, albeit broken symbols. Although he thoroughly absorbed Bultmann's demythologizing of the level of first naiveté, he pointed to a much more positive engagement with ultimate concerns and their objects. Connecting his concerns with religious symbols to the pragmatic semiotic tradition of Peirce and Dewey leads in a fruitful direction toward a theology that enlivens a critical appropriation of religious language for an apophatic ground-of-being theology for which little if anything can be said literally about a divine nature.

Another theological project that draws heavily from Tillich's influence, which he only slightly engaged toward the end of his life, is interfaith comparative studies. Because he paired issues of ontological ultimacy with issues of anthropological ultimate concern, his ideas are ideally ready to relate to religions of South and East Asia that focus on the human condition as the way to ultimacy. Because of his conception of God as ground of being transcending any determinate entity, his ideas are ready to relate to those religions for whom the ultimate is nonpersonal and for whom the thought of divine action within the world is superstitious. Theologians who are committed to conceptions of a finite God capable of playing roles within the world find it a nice irony that, in the long Christian-Buddhist dialogue of the Cobb-Abe Group, now in its fourth decade, the Buddhist Masao Abe is the Tillichian.

Tillich's systematic ideas have funded the contemporary theological projects of religious feminism, theological ontology and metaphysics, theology and psychology both theoretical and practical, religion and the arts, natural sciences and religion, social science studies of religion, theological semiotics, comparative theology, and I could extend the list past your patience. My point is that each of these areas and others in which Tillich has been influential has developed its own programmatic concerns for truth, its own plausibility conditions, and its own modes of inquiry. Sometimes these different theological projects learn from each other and sometimes not. Their modes of inquiry are constantly changing and relating to new areas of experience, new instruments of study, and new ideas. In no way could Tillich's original sense of theological system, expressed in the first part of his *Systematic Theology*, begin to integrate these diverse theological projects. The questions of truth, the plausibility conditions, and the modes of inquiry are simply too diverse and independent, even though each of these theological projects has something to say about classical theological issues such as the nature of God, the soul, sin, salvation, faithful community life, and so forth. Hardly anyone would undertake the task of developing a theological system encompassing enough and sufficiently tolerant of internal differences to integrate these projects in ways by which they all can learn from one another and by which the whole can guide comprehensive religious life.

Imagine now the contrast between Barth's heirs, focusing theology around Christian identity, and Tillich's heirs, focusing theology in different ways according to all the directions in which theology can go to learn and be corrected. From the standpoint of Tillich's heirs, if I might use that label for the motley array of projects, the identity theologians have drifted very far from the issues of truth precisely because they do not enter into the different modes of inquiry, plausibility conditions, and even senses of truth that are involved in making good cases for claims. From the standpoint of Barth's heirs, the theologies pursuing truth in all directions simply have insufficient unity to articulate Christian identity in any helpful way. From the standpoint of Tillich's heirs, Christian identity must be, and rightfully is, a piecemeal thing because it depends on the outcomes of critical inquiry in each of the theological projects. From the standpoint of Barth's heirs, if theology goes off on the pursuit of truth in a motley array of incommensurate projects, then some other discipline, say, Theologie (pronounced as in German), needs to say what Christian identity is in order to serve the Church. This Theologie must rest on some authority such as Barth's claim to have the one and only real revelation, or the Yale School's claim that the deep grammar of a cultural/linguistic community is its own authority, or Radical Orthodoxy's claim that since all positions are somewhat arbitrary, it is fine to assert your own.

The two dimensions of religious belief, belief as establishing religious identity and belief as the truth claims of inquiry that in turn establish identity, are thus institutionalized in tension with each other in the current theological situation. I have told the story in terms of recent classic Protestantism that can relate to the debates between Barth and Tillich. By loosening the metaphors we can see how conservative Evangelicalism reflects the tension between its defense of a particular culture and the varied modes of truth seeking, from fundamentalist biblical literalism to charismatic pneumatology. In many places Christian Unitarianism explicitly eschews the project of caring for religious identity. Within Roman Catholicism, the openness to truth-seeking in the secular world, from other Christians, and from other religions, that characterized the immediate results of the Second Vatican Council, stands in tension with a reaction to limit the results of inquiry to what is compatible with the identity of the Magisterium. Orthodoxy has not gone as far as either Catholicism or Protestantism in following truth-seeking inquiry wherever it goes; nevertheless, the growing presence of Orthodoxy in cultures other than those of Eastern Europe untethers the authority for defining Orthodox identity from its traditional cultural base, and wide-ranging truth-seeking will be needed to formulate identity in strange lands. Judaism in America is witnessing a resurgence of traditional practices for the sake of identity, pushing against the almost scientific truth-seeking orientation of Reform Judaism.

Now it would be foolish to try to make the distinction between two dimensions of religious belief, and the theologies they enjoin, do too much work to explain the world situation in religion. But it is apparent that the recent modernization of vast areas of the world has raised problems for traditional religious identity in Hindu, Buddhist, and Confucian/Daoist lands. Moreover, the Enlightenment elements of modernization have provoked truth-seeking projects that often are perpendicular to traditional practices and ideas. Theologians within all these traditions have to cope with the challenges of identity and truth-seeking in religious matters under conditions exacerbated by colonialism and anti-colonialism, the continuing conflict between Muslim and Christian civilizations, and the meteoric explosion of the Indian and Chinese economies contrasted with seemingly intractable poverty and disorder in Africa. The world situation regarding religions and religious cultures is extraordinarily volatile now, and the tension I have been describing is not a settling factor.

TRUTH, IDENTITY, AND AUTHORITY

I am reasonably certain that nearly everyone here believes that I have made an artificially wide distinction between the identity dimension and truth dimension of religious belief. Few who are engaged in the theological projects I have labeled as identity theologies or truth-seeking theologies think that they fail to honor the other. There is also some uneasiness, I suspect, about my labels as such, since truth-seeking is a bit more honorific than identity-seeking, like apple pie. Nevertheless, the tension between these two often leads to dismissal of others in dialogue so that learning is blocked arbitrarily. Those in the truth-seeking projects often dismiss the identity theologians for putting the cart before the horse, with willful arbitrariness. Those in the identity theologies often dismiss the others as not being within the theological circle, not being Christians. Permit me to make some suggestions to remedy such uncharitable dismissals.

First, we can all admit that religious belief does have both dimensions, intellectual and performative. Religious beliefs are not only like the announcement of conclusions of research projects: they include something of a commitment to act in accordance with them, often a deep existential commitment. Thus to believe something in theology is not just to assert a truth claim but to act performatively, giving oneself the identity of living out the consequences of the belief. On the other hand, no religious belief is only performative, with no intellectual content. Perhaps we approach this extreme when someone, say, believes that Jesus Christ is Lord solely in order to be saved. The performance is the act of belief that accomplishes the salvation, allegedly. The person believes, not because the person has reasons to think that it is true that Jesus Christ is Lord, but because believing that is salvific. Nevertheless, at least a modicum of intellectual content is present, no matter how primitive the person's ideas about Jesus, Lordship, and salvation are. Intellectual content is present whenever it is possible that the belief is mistaken, say, if John the Baptist, Caesar, or Buddha, is Lord. Given that both the intellectual and performative dimensions are present in religious belief, theology has a commitment to the integrity of both, and we should be uneasy when one overwhelms the other.

Second, having said this, we can distinguish between inhabiting a religious identity and practicing theology. In Augustine's conversion, he read the passage where Paul said to "put on Jesus Christ," and Augustine put on the Christian identity, like a Roman boy putting on the clothing of an adult citizen. This involved changing his social life, putting away friends and lovers, and taking on a new social life framed by the Church; it also involved taking on Christian intellectual practices, including theological ideas. Yet inhabiting a Christian identity gave Augustine the freedom to think theologically with such originality that he radically transformed the Christian theological heritage. Not only did he add new elements and drop out others, but he reordered theological priorities. This is to say, his theology significantly transformed Christian identity, both for him and for his successors. Of course, not everyone's theological inquiry will be compatible with manageable changes in the inhabited religious identity. Augustine had the advantages of being a bishop and being enormously persuasive. Others might have been rejected from the community as heretics, or have chosen to leave because they decided that Buddha in fact is the Lord. Nevertheless, the religious commitment to a way of life such as Christianity is a different thing from theological commitments to religious beliefs, though related.

Third, religious identities are neither theologically nor morally neutral. In our time Christian identity has been cited as reason to go to war for no other good reason, to denigrate non-Christians, and to abuse women, ethnic minorities, and homosexuals, all of which suggest that something is wrong with that identity. Christian identity has been cited as reason to reject science about scientific matters and to censure art without any other good reason to do so. Therefore, I believe that truth-seeking is the humble way to appropriate religious identity critically, for religious identities need correction as we discover that our conceptions of identity are mistaken. Not to do so is a sacrilege because it demeans the God before whom we seek truthful religious identities for ourselves and our communities. Religious communities shaped by particular identities need to seek out correction, even when that runs the risk of altering them significantly.

Fourth, two kinds of authority should be recognized. Authority within truth-seeking inquiry lies in the plausibility conditions, the modes of inquiry, and the logic of the kinds of truth involved. This kind of authority is diverse, contextual, and usually in the process of being questioned and refashioned. The integrity of this authority lies in faithfulness to the vulnerability of truth-seeking to be corrected. The other kind of authority lies in the investment individuals and communities have in their religious identity. At the very least, this is the authority of will that commits to the identity. Usually also this authority is vested in the scriptures, traditions, experience, and reason, to use the Wesleyan Quadrilateral, by which a community has shaped itself critically through history and continues to govern itself at the present, including its current debates. Sometimes, the authority of religious identity rests in the conviction that the identity and community expressing it is directly shaped by God. Of course, the nature of these senses of authority is complex and subject to much debate. My point is that the authority of the truth dimension is different from the authority of the identity dimension. To assert the authority of religious identity over processes of serious theological inquiry perverts the inquiry and renders the religious identity invulnerable to correction in the issue in question. To assert the authority of truth-seeking in its many modes over religious identity is to confuse the hypothetical and self-correcting character of intellectual authority for the existential commitments of religious identity. Religious identity is how we seek to live truthfully before God.

Fifth, the two authorities can come into conflict, and often have. Most of us can remember our adolescent selves saying some identity-affirming formula, such as the Apostle's Creed, with our fingers crossed because we knew we did not believe the whole creed as we understood it intellectually then. When the truth authority and the identity authority come into conflict, many different outcomes are possible. A change in religious identity can be chosen based on new understanding. One can continue to participate as loyal critical opposition in a community with a religious identity with whose theology one disagrees in certain points. One can continue to participate while accepting a marginalized role for one's theology. One can opt out of the religious identity and its community entirely, joining another, or joining none. One can deny entirely the existential importance of religious identity, thinking instead that one will be a connoisseur of religious inquiries and their tentative truths. Conflicts of these authorities need not be limited to the problems of individuals: communities can fight over changing their religious identity, groups can excommunicate one another within a community, different communities can be pitted against one another despite a common heritage, and religion itself can be attacked for causing more social and personal harm than good. These and other outcomes are possible because neither the authority of the truth dimension nor that of the identity dimension takes precedence over the other.

Sixth, because neither kind of authority takes precedence over the other, the resolution of their conflicts is subject to neither authority alone or together but to something else. In order to address serious conflicts between these authorities we need slightly to transcend, and slightly to relativize, both the truth dimension and the identity dimension of religious belief. The very tentativeness of honest truth-seeking makes it perpetually underdetermined for the task of fixing religious identity. Religious identity in the sense I have traced from Barth and Tillich is an identity based on beliefs with consequences for practice, an identity that can be given either by a narrative saga of creation and redemption or by a system of doctrines expressing truths in historical contexts. A more profound sense of religious identity, however, consists in the characters we give ourselves as we decide how to respond to conflicts between these, and perhaps other, kinds of authority. Whereas religious identity, in the sense that is shaped by narrative or systematic beliefs, is existential in that it involves commitment to a somewhat integrated way of life, religious identity in this other sense is ontological because it is how we make ourselves up in the most important matters. Ontological religious identity might be taken very seriously, wrestling through issues of truth and issues of affiliation in the dark night of the soul. Or, ontological religious identity might happen by default, as when one gives up on the demands of truth or the demands of a religious identity that involves a pattern for loyalty and life. Even if we let things go by default, however, we are still responsible for the making up of our ontological religious identity. All of us, I'm sure, are working on optimal compromises of our respect for the authority of truth, understood according to the lay of our contemporary theological landscape, and for the authority of the religious identity based on beliefs to which we seek to be faithful and committed.

The sermon is the genre of religious thinking in which the truth and identity dimensions of religious belief are in tension, week by week, text by text, topic by topic. This is especially so in a university church where the professional inquirers are in the pews, bent on discovering and practicing true religious identity as Christians, and where the peoples of other faiths listen on the radio. The humility of the preacher comes from knowing that the truth and identity dimensions of the sermon do not always work out in harmony, and that the art of the sermon is to balance these with prudence. Even though you can subscribe to online sermon outlines and illustrations, no rule exists for achieving this balance. At best you can appeal to the charity of the congregation to work through the conflicts, step by step, with good will and respect.

This is how I would close this chapter, to appeal for good will and respect among those who understand that our theological situation has institutionalized divisions between those committed to the truth dimension of religious belief and those committed to the identity dimension. Of course I myself believe that *theology* should never compromise the truth dimension and that my affinities are with the heirs of Tillich rather than Barth. I believe that any Christianity-alone theology is too narrow when we live next door to Buddhists, Hindus, and Confucians. But when personal or communal life comes to address the conflicts between the truth and identity dimensions of belief, theology is only one of the inputs. What else is needed for the decisions that determine our ontological religious identity is not always apparent to theologians.

TWO

Truth in Theology

THE ANALYSIS OF THE relations between identity theology and truth-oriented theology begun in the previous chapter can now be developed with a different slant. In the time of Thomas Aquinas, Christians were presumed to believe certain doctrines because they had reason to think the doctrines were true, not because believing them was part of their identity as Christians. The scholastics gave closely reasoned defenses of their theologies, working patiently to untangle confusions and find relevant evidence. When they argued with Jews and Muslims, they gave reasons for the positions and arguments against their opponents, never thinking to say "as Christians we believe *x*." Why does it seem so odd today to ask what is true theologically, and then encourage Christians to believe it for that reason? Can we get behind the split illustrated by Barth and Tillich in the previous chapter?

In the first segment of my remarks, let me single out four important historical/philosophical events that help explain our situation, although these are not the only relevant factors. With regard to each of the four I shall offer an antidote, as it were, that lays the foundation for the articulation of a new program for appreciating and approaching truth in theology. The second segment of my argument is to review the failure of liberal theology, especially in America, to keep the question of truth in focus. The third segment sketches the program in theology that I advocate that brings the question of truth front and center, which I call "theology of symbolic engagement." Finally, I shall conclude with a discussion of metaphysics and theology.

FOUR ROOTS OF THE EVASION OF TRUTH, AND THEIR ANTIDOTES

The first historical/philosophical event was the Protestant Reformation insistence on *sola scriptura*, scripture alone, as the resource needed for theological knowledge with salvific import. With the invention of printing and the emergence of widespread literacy, common people could have access to saving knowledge without the necessary intervention of priests and a hierarchical teaching establishment, although the Reformed Churches were not without the hierarchies of mediation. One of the problems, however, was that the Bible was couched in cultural assumptions of the first century and earlier that were very different indeed from the cultural assumptions of the sixteenth century, and the Reformers did not always keep their attention on this fact. They did not know how to cope with the divergence in cultural worldviews that they barely could acknowledge. This resulted, first, in a subsequent split between the official theological traditions of Protestantism and the emerging modern philosophical tradition that worked so closely with science. That split remains today. The unacknowledged difference in cultural worldview resulted, second, in a confused scramble to force modern Christians to live with the assumptions of the first century, among the more conservative groups, or to reinterpret the Bible to make it coherent with modern cultural assumptions, among the more liberal ones.

A remedy is well-known for the confusions of trying to live by a biblical norm when the Bible's cultural assumptions are so different from one's own culture. The remedy is hermeneutics, the study of the meaning of a text in the context of its original authors and audiences as different from but related to the interpreter's context, which has different assumptions. When people are aware of the differences between the assumptions they can control for the authority of the claims made on behalf of the norms. To put the point in plainer terms, instead of reading our own cultural assumptions into the Biblical texts, which distorts the texts and asks the Bible to answer questions with which it never deals, we can trace the historical development of Christianity from its beginnings to our times. We can ask how it acquired new meanings and let old concerns drift away. We can take the imaginative task of seeking the mind of Christ for our new situation to be the enormous and risky job it is. Hermeneutics can be used to let any religious tradition recover the meaning and possible validity of its ancient texts, not only the Christian.

The second historical/philosophical event that undermined the quest for truth in theology was the philosopher Immanuel Kant's devastating critique of a certain kind of metaphysics. Until Kant's time theologians, Christian and otherwise, had assumed that some kind of real, if partial, knowledge could be had of God and of the fundamental traits of the world, including human life. In the *Critique of Pure Reason* Kant argued, to the contrary, that we know things only as they appear to us, as structured by our cognitive apparatus. We do not know things in themselves. Moreover, the only things we know with certainty are the things that derive from our cognitive apparatus itself, because we know that appearances must conform to them. All knowledge, Kant thought, had to be based on certainty regarding its foundations. A pious

Christian, Kant thought that he eliminated theoretical knowledge of God to make room for faith. But faith is no substitute for truth in theology because one can have faith in anything one chooses. The rejection of foundationalist metaphysics not only removed theoretical knowledge of God. It also removed the possibility of the philosophical framework that allowed the Christian theological symbols to be put in context; it rejected any kind of philosophical cosmology, and so the whole edifice of the Christian worldview (and Jewish worldview for that matter) was swung out into the realm of pious fideism without serious cognitive tethers.

The answer to Kant's anti-metaphysical position came from the American pragmatists in the ninteenth and early twentieth centuries. Charles Peirce, the first and probably most brilliant of them, argued that metaphysics like science is hypothetical. Metaphysical theories are large hypotheses about the foundational matters of reality, including God. But they are not certain. They are as good as the arguments for them, and the philosophical tradition of the West has brought the main metaphysical positions into complex and careful dialogue with one another. Since Peirce's time the metaphysics of South and East Asian traditions have been added to the dialogue. The formal virtue of a good metaphysical hypothesis is that it is vulnerable to correction. Basic hypotheses are the guiding principles we live by, and so we are never without some metaphysics in our cultural and personal bones, whether we want it or not: the question is always how the metaphysics in our mental muscles can be improved. Kant's arguments against metaphysics do not have anything to say against this pragmatic conception of metaphysics, and so it is possible to think once again metaphysically about God and divine things. Whitehead's great contribution to truth in theology was to produce a theological metaphysics of great genius: *esse* proves *posse*. This is so even if Whitehead's metaphysics is mistaken, for its correction would be an improved metaphysics.

The third historical/philosophical event was the development of a distinctly anti-supernaturalist worldview among educated people in the eighteenth and nineteenth centuries, aided by Kant's careful delineation of what can be known objectively by science. The argument about miracles was the most famous controversy in the eighteenth century but by the nineteenth the whole biblical worldview of spirits, angels, and the geography of heaven had become implausible to many theologians. The result was that many leading thinkers were anxious to abandon all those symbols as having any kind of cognitive value, looking to the moral teachings of the Bible as the central defining Christian core.[1]

Two remedies are available to respond to the rejection of supernaturalist elements in Christian theology. One is the development of naturalistic metaphysical theories that account for the grand themes of creation, sin, and redemption. The pragmatists, again, were the leaders in this naturalizing of Christianity (and Judaism), and they have been joined by the process philosophers who probably are better at abstract naturalistic metaphysics.

More influential by far than either pragmatism or process theology has been the demythologizing theology of Rudolf Bultmann and his school. The demythologizers eliminated the need for supernaturalism, which they called myth, by translating the religious or spiritual points of the Bible into modern, mainly existential, philosophy.[2] The limit of naturalistic metaphysics and demythologizing, however, is that both ways we lose the rich symbolism and language of the Bible and the liturgical traditions of Christianity. The danger is that the modern philosophical vocabularies are not up to the deep resonances of those symbols.

Therefore the second remedy needed is for a semiotic theory that shows how those deep symbols have a truth that is not the same as the kind of truth in which the symbols mirror what they symbolize. As Paul Tillich said, true religious symbols make us participate in the realities they symbolize, without saying that the realities are just like what the symbols suggest.[3] For instance, we symbolize approaching God with an upward movement toward the heavens. Some of the ancients actually believed that God is up there beyond the circling stars, whereas we know that outer space does not have a special place for God; the symbolism of ascent does not have to be taken literally. Fortunately, Peirce and the pragmatists provide just the right sort of semiotic theory necessary for us to recover, not abandon, the classic symbols, interpreted as relevant and salvific for our time.[4] I shall return to this point in greater detail shortly.

The fourth historical/philosophic event that has made it hard to believe in truth in theology is that the nineteenth century attempt to redefine Christianity in terms of morals rather than metaphysics collapsed in three ways. First, that liberal movement had attempted to search the Bible for the historical figure of Jesus who was believed to have advocated the moral life of high civilization. Unfortunately, historical research made that hard to believe; Jesus was less about morals than about the eschaton and the coming of God's Kingdom. Second, after the high sounding platitudes about moral life and high civilization, very serious disagreements about the content of morality exist, all sides of which can find biblical support. Instead of Christian high civilization supporting the move to theological morals, that civilization simply came apart in the European wars of the nineteenth and twentieth centuries. Christendom collapsed, and with it the confident vision of Christian morals. Third, Christianity as morals is simply banal. Why do you need Christianity for the moral life? Or for moral wisdom? Perhaps Jesus contributed some moral insight, but no more than Socrates, Moses, Mohammed, Confucius, or the Buddha. Isn't morality binding on nonreligious people just as much as religious ones? So if moral ideals and energy are all that religion contributes to the moral obligations of human beings, dump the religions. Not only is there little call for theological truth, there is little call for the bother of theology of any sort.

The remedy for the failure of the project of re-transcribing Christianity as moral life is simply to find a deeper reality for Christianity. That is difficult to do with the resources of classic liberalism. I think of classic Christian liberalism as the attempt to modernize biblical culture without serious hermeneutics, to reject foundationalist metaphysics as Kant said, without the pragmatic alternative of metaphysics as non-foundational hypothesis, to reject supernaturalism without a semiotics that allows us to recover the classical symbols of the Bible and Christian traditions, and to redefine Christianity in moral terms that will simply not bear the weight of religious life and belief. It was liberalism that led to the situation where it is odd to seek for profound truth in theology, and in reaction stimulated the Christian identity theologies that seem to be asserting truth but in ultimately arbitrary ways.

LIBERAL THEOLOGY AS A NEAR MISS

Liberalism in American theology has been a near miss. Surely something is fundamentally correct in its insistence that religion, Christianity in most cases, needs to live in the terms of the contemporary world. Without that, religious sensibility and theology exist in a realm disconnected from real life and its deepest imagination, a criticism easily made against most forms of fundamentalism. To live in the terms of the modern world does not mean agreeing with its values or fundamental categories. Liberalism since the nineteenth century, from Schleiermacher and Ritschl onward, has been preoccupied with moral criticism and the transformation of the world into the Kingdom of God, to use one of the common symbols. Whatever its critical stance, liberalism has insisted on engaging the contemporary world on the world's own terms.

The liberal theology of the nineteenth and early twentieth centuries, however, was overwhelmed by the Neo-Orthodoxy of Karl Barth and his colleagues, which said that the contemporary world needs to be confronted in the terms of the Bible. More particularly, Barth and his followers defined reality in terms of the creative and redemptive role of Jesus Christ, construed in a Christocentric theological affirmation and elaborated through the narrative of the Bible. Although this biblical-language perspective resonated with *sola scriptura* Reformation theology and offered a strong bulwark against the cultural Nazification of German Christianity, it found little engagement with the sciences and arts of the twentieth century, and little with the moral and political issues beyond defense of the primacy of Christianity. Barth's theology has a kind of internal aesthetic beauty and drama. It presents an inviting worldview that people can enter, rather like Tolkien's world of Middle Earth, as remarked in the previous chapter. People can imagine that they live in that world. But that imagination misleads them in the way they engage the real world and its religious, moral, political, and philosophical issues. From today's perspective, Barth's worldview is beautiful but arbitrary. Yet it won out over the earlier liberal projects.

Gary Dorrien has beautifully chronicled and interpreted this liberal movement in America, and its failure.[5] He distinguishes three main schools in the late nineteenth and early twentieth centuries: at Union Theological Seminary in New York, at the University of Chicago, and at Boston University.

The liberals at Union Theological Seminary embraced modernism with enthusiasm, including modernism's commitment to science, naturalism, and the rejection of supernaturalism; their hallmark was a Ritschlian and Harnackian reinterpretation of Christianity as an essentially moral movement, with the contemporary tasks for religion being progressive advances toward embodying the Kingdom of God on Earth. As mentioned, however, scholarship on the historical Jesus did not support their view that Jesus was a moral visionary, but rather a kind of eschatological extremist. The optimism of moral progressivism for Christianity was shattered by World War I and buried by World War II.

The Chicago school up through Henry Nelson Wieman emphasized the modernism in a pragmatic mode, insisting that theology be scientific, almost a social science. This left very little of the distinctive Christian heritage in play, and Wieman himself gradually drifted away from even the claim to be Christian. The collapse of progressivistic moral optimism negatively affected the Chicago school, but the greater failure of the Chicago school was religious boredom and banality.

The Boston University personalists were enthusiastic modernists like the other liberals, with a strong commitment to moral progressivism. Their strongly idealistic personalistic metaphysics allowed them access to the supernaturalism of a transcendent personal God; the emphasis on persons gave them a sharp edge in defining moral directions. But the metaphysical idealism was simply unconvincing in the twentieth century and so the defense of the transcendent personal God collapsed. The emphasis on persons was so individualistic that it could not accommodate widespread recognition of the social and natural embeddedness of human beings, or any kind of ecological sensibility.

No wonder, then, that Barthianism was attractive. It provided needed acknowledgment of human sinfulness, a first-order justification to use all the supernaturalistic symbols of the Christian tradition, and the confidence that human failures in morals, politics, and rational modern religion are ultimately unimportant because God is the only real agent in the cosmos. The ironic flip-side of Barth's infamous claim that religions are cultural and that Christianity is not a religion, and is above culture, is that Barth's Christianity is not much relevant to culture and to the religious dimensions of individuals' investments in culture. Contrary to Barth's intent, I believe, his theology is curiously irrelevant to how we should live in the world. Its virtue is in telling us what we should believe in church, as if belief were the be-all and end-all of Christian life. Barth's is the paradigmatic Christian-identity theology.

Three neo-liberal movements reacted to this irrelevance, the Christian Realism led by Reinhold Niebuhr, the ontological Protestantism of Paul Tillich, and the process philosophy deriving from Alfred North Whitehead.[6]

Niebuhr thematized the sinfulness of human beings and their social structures, insisting that Christians be realistic in dealing with this. Counter the Barthians, he dismissed Christocentric triumphalism and called on Christians to dirty their hands in the ambiguities and compromises of seeking the most nearly just path in a field of universally mixed options.

With this Tillich agreed but added a profound ontology of God as creator or Ground of Being. Moreover, Tillich was a brilliant apologist who was able to use modern, existentialist, language to reconstruct many of the fundamental classical Christian symbols. In contrast to the earlier liberals who were rather willing to abandon much of classical Christianity, and to Niebuhr who was not profound on the topic, Tillich devised a neo-liberal theology that laid claim to inherit the ancient kerygma and Reformation position as much as Barth's theology, and to embrace Catholic culture as well.

Whitehead's process philosophy was explicitly designed to provide a new metaphysical interpretation of late-modern science as well as a Victorian conception of civilized religion. Followers such as Charles Hartshorne, John B. Cobb, Jr., Schubert Ogden, Lewis S. Ford, David Griffin, and Marjorie Suchocki developed his views into detailed theological statements in the Christian tradition. Delwin Brown, Joseph Bracken, S.J., and others have a looser process orthodoxy.

Though advances on the earlier liberalisms, these neo-liberalisms are still near misses. Niebuhr's great book was called *The Nature and Destiny of Man*, and his theology was conspicuously skimpy on God. Tillich was truly profound, original, and still classical on God, but did not develop the implications of his apologetic conception of reason and culture. He failed to see that his theory provided a playing field in which other religions as well as Christianity and secularism make equal claim for authority and the right to be respected. His assertion of the priority of the Christian kerygma seems arbitrary in the context of his theory, and his claims for the ontological historicity of Jesus the New Being are not warranted by his ontological grounding. Process theology makes the greatest rapprochement with science but abandons the central Christian doctrines of creation and the transcendent infinity of God in order to maintain human freedom and make God seem moral by human standards. Moreover, its Christology lets Jesus be no more than a model person with a vision of the Kingdom, rather like the early liberal positions that were embarrassed by the eschatological elements revealed by historical research.

THEOLOGY AS SYMBOLIC ENGAGEMENT

As an advance beyond the liberal and neo-liberal positions, confirming their best elements but retrieving also the special qualities of Christianity in a public that includes the other religions, I propose what I call a theology of symbolic engagement. This can be understood as having four levels: imaginative, interpretive, systematic, and practical, and I shall discuss each one in a moment.[7] Theology of symbolic engagement is based on a pragmatic semiotic theory according to which symbols engage us with reality. Without the symbols, we miss the aspects of reality they would symbolize. Language itself is a family of codes of symbols that allow us to engage most practical aspects of life. Specific constructions within language articulate the basic dimensions, such as economics, politics, the arts, friendship and family. Nature itself is a language when we have ways to symbolize it, and we construct much of our world with our architecture, decoration, calendars, schedules, dances, and music. The symbols in all these domains are conventional in that they have arisen through human invention. But they are rarely fictitious: they allow us to discriminate what we would not engage without them. The rough lines of human symbolism have evolved through very pragmatic feedback. The symbols of religions are the ways by which people engage the ultimate dimensions of life and reality.

At the imaginative level, therefore, theology of symbolic engagement lifts up the great symbols that witness to the faith and asks whether, how, in what contexts, and for whom those symbols are engaging. The early liberals may have thought that most of the classical symbols no longer engage modern people with the basic realities, that they lack contemporary significance. The Barthians proved that wrong, however, and the evangelical right continues to do that today by the very popularity they give those old symbols. Because the early liberals dropped most of the classical symbols such as the atonement, Jesus as cosmic Christ, as Second Person of the Trinity, and so forth, the religion they offered had very little to engage people with the ultimate realities. Tillich's genius was to understand two aspects of this. First, those old symbols engaged people with ultimately important things, and modern apologetics needs to get at those ultimately important things through reinterpretation of the classic symbols. Second, Tillich knew that engagement itself is not enough: the Nazis demonstrated that religious symbols can engage people demonically, and so the issue beyond engagement is whether an engaging symbol is true. Part of the imaginative level of theology of symbolic engagement is the cultural criticism of the symbols that do engage, a way in which Tillich's strategy of testing engagement was different from Barth's strategy of cultural disengagement. Whether one's symbols engage at all is a matter of imagination; whether they do so truly is a matter of interpretation, which is the second level of symbolic engagement.

Interpretation asserts engaging symbolic expressions as true and assesses the case for their truth. Truth is not only the mirroring of the form of things in the mind, as Aristotle thought. More basically, it is the carrying across of what is important in the reality interpreted from the reality into the interpreter in the respects in which the interpreting symbols stand for the reality. We are accustomed to think that our interpretations describe their objects, and often they do, perhaps always in some sense. Description is iconic: it refers to its object with the assumption that the object is like what the description says. But interpretations are true if they carry across what is important even though the object does not mirror the reality, as is the case with all metaphoric thought. Many religious symbols are obviously false in a descriptive sense, for instance that God is a big man in the sky; but thinking of God that way sometimes picks up on what is important that would be lost thinking of God other ways.

The question of truth is empirical: does what is important in the object get carried across? To answer that means understanding the logic of the symbols themselves, the senses in which they refer to their objects, the contexts of interpretation, the purposes involved, and the readiness of the individual interpreters to use those symbols. A symbol that is true for one person in one context might carry across something false and demonic for someone else in that context, or even for the same person in another context. The interpretive level of theology of symbolic engagement examines the logical, referential, purposive, contextual, and personal conditions for theological interpretations to answer the empirical question of whether what is important is carried across. With respect to the classical Christian symbols, it is clear that our situation is so different from the ancients that some of the symbols must be radically reconstructed for them to carry across for us what they conveyed to the ancients. In this sense, theology of symbolic engagement elaborates Tillich's apologetics; unlike Tillich, however, it can use the old symbols themselves so long as their reinterpretation is made clear. Because this part of theology is empirical, it can be applied to any religion, and can be practiced by theologians from any traditions who take the time to learn the symbols, context, and personalities involved. Interpretive theology can be cross-cultural and comparative.

The third level of symbolic engagement is the systematization of interpretations to provide fairly comprehensive worldviews and to make that system of interpretation vulnerable to correction from whatever sources might correct it. The second level of interpretations can be so idiosyncratic and diversely contextual as to disallow interpretations to correct one another and add up to a cumulative theological approach to ultimate matters; it might not allow for much summary statement of what Christian theology is, or Jewish, Muslim or Buddhist theology, for that matter. If different interpretations are true for different people in different contexts with different purposes, this might be such a radical contextualism that communal and even personal life might be impossible. The building of a theological system is not the assembly of a set of consistent and coherent propositions about every theological topic. It is rather a systematic understanding of the connections between different contexts, purposes, readiness of individuals to employ the symbols, symbol systems, and kinds of reference so that it is possible to see just why a theological interpretation is true in one context but false in another. With this kind of understanding in hand, it is possible to come at questions of truth from as many angles as can be imagined. System allows individual interpretive claims to be vulnerable for correction from a broad public.

The vulnerability of a theological system does not consist only in opening itself to charges of inconsistency. Perhaps even more importantly it consists in seeking out sources of correction and enrichment. Permit me to call attention to at least four such sources, not all of which are commonly sought in contemporary theology. One source for correction and enrichment, obviously, is the religious tradition itself, with its practices and intellectual self-understanding. All theologians are anxious to appeal to and learn from their traditions. A second source for correction and enrichment is the arts, broadly considered. Art, like religion, often deals with ultimate matters. Sometimes art uses the symbols of religion, as in traditional religious art; but often it creates its own symbols. Art is an ongoing poesis of the imagination and has much to teach theology. "Theology and the arts" is a field of theological inquiry that has not developed yet to a point of maturity. A third source for correction and enrichment is the physical and social sciences. Until the Protestant Reformation, theology was in close contact with the sciences, making scientific knowledge internal to theology itself, as in the work of Thomas Aquinas. As mentioned earlier, the Reformation insistence on biblical language and the imaginative worldview that went with it alienated theology from science, which has been seen to be a problem for theology ever since. No reason for this alienation exists, unless one is unable to develop a metaphysics that unites biblical symbols with contemporary scientific knowledge, a point to which I shall return. A fourth source for systematic correction in theology is the practical disciplines such as law, business, education, and the like, all of which touch on ultimate matters and whose practice involves self-corrective feedback. Theology has been slow to learn from these practical disciplines, saving perhaps that of being a church bureaucrat. Systematic theology is the dialectical thinking that can bring the imaginative witnesses and interpretive claims of the religious tradition into fruitful, critical, and ampliative dialogue with the arts, sciences, and metaphysics to develop a comprehensive theology that corrects itself in the best possible ways.

The fourth level of theology of symbolic engagement is the practical reason that determines how to live on the basis of the theology of the imaginative witness or revelation level, the critical interpretive level, and the systematic level. Superficially this might mean how to shape communities and ethical lives as informed by the interpreted witness of the faith. More profoundly, it has to do with how to become the people who engage reality with the whole of the faith's theology as the engaging symbol. It means living authentically as a Christian, or a Jew, Muslim, Buddhist, or whatever pattern of life for ultimate matters is expressed in the theology to live by. The function of intellect is to guide life, as we Platonists and pragmatists say, and the function of theology is to guide life in living before the ultimate. Moreover, only within authentically engaged theological informed life is the symbolic engagement thick enough to be pragmatically corrected or affirmed. The best long run test of a theology, like testing the spirits by their fruits, is living with the theology as the guiding principle.

METAPHYSICS FOR THEOLOGY

Theology of symbolic engagement needs a metaphysics that expresses ultimacy and its connections with the natural and social world, and how these can be referred to by religious symbols at all levels. With a proper hermeneutics of the ancient symbols, recognizing the differences and similarities between their original worldview and ours, metaphysics is the discipline that can explain what is real relative to what, and in what sense. Metaphysics thus supplies a crucial interpretive understanding of theological claims at all levels. This metaphysics needs to engage science as well as process metaphysics does. It needs also to serve as a basis for comparison among religious traditions with radically different symbol systems. Moreover this metaphysics needs to give expression to how the arts and practical disciplines such as law and economics can carry across ultimate matters. The metaphysics for theology of symbolic engagement need not make any supernatural claims, although it might show how certain supernatural symbols function truly to carry across what is important for some people in some contexts. Theology of symbolic engagement needs to develop its semiotic theory of interpretation as well as its practices of practical reason. Most especially, theology of symbolic engagement needs to embrace the practices of religious communities and individuals, for only there are instances of first-order theological truth to be found. A frequent fault of the earlier liberalism was an embarrassment at the ways religious people behave, with a consequent distancing so that the theologians could not tell whether an actual religious interpretation were true or not. The Chicago school in particular was famous for focusing so much on method that it was never used.

Theology of symbolic engagement inherits early liberalism's embrace of the modern world, its sciences and arts. It can employ the classical symbols shown to be so powerful by the Barthian revolution but without making them a literal story. It recognizes the depths of human depravity that Niebuhr showed to be correctly conveyed by the classical doctrines, and affirms with Tillich the existential significance of living theologically. Like process theology it recognizes the ontological commitments of science and embraces a metaphysics that reflects this, enlarging it to reflect the truth about ultimate things in the arts and practical disciplines.

The empirical character of theology of symbolic engagement leads to the acknowledgment that the theological public consists of thinkers from all religions and the secular world who are interested in the outcome of the discussions and have their own approaches, traditions, and symbols to contribute. Theology of symbolic engagement is a liberal theology that engages the world on its own terms, with vulnerability to a global public and dependence on the resources of the sciences, arts, and practical disciplines as well as religious traditions. At the same time, unlike many earlier liberalisms, it practices and accounts for personal and communal life before God as made possible in the revelatory symbols that get at ultimacy.

THREE

Realism and Contextualization

POSTLIBERALISM AND THEOLOGICAL INQUIRY

GEORGE LINDBECK'S landmark book, *The Nature of Doctrine: Religion and Theology in a Postliberal Age*, has taught many lessons, some perhaps not anticipated by its author.[1] The one that I take most to heart is that religious doctrines, and many other religious symbols, often are not descriptive in ordinary senses and that they are seriously misinterpreted if taken to be descriptive. The doctrine of the ascension of Christ, for instance, is not really about Jesus rising into the stratosphere.

Another lesson is that Lindbeck's cultural/linguistic analysis of doctrine as the grammar underlying the practice of a community of faith (to summarize his complex position roughly) leads many to believe that doctrines so interpreted are therefore neither true nor false. Indeed, some go so far as to hold that Lindbeck's position legitimates any doctrinal affirmations whatsoever because doctrines are merely descriptive of the underlying grammar of some actual community's practice. Theology, on this interpretation of Lindbeck, is transformed to church history or congregational studies.[2] The conclusion that any community's doctrines are valid for that community comes from the negative implication that theology can have no normative thrust other than discerning when a community is being faithful to its basic grammar. That is, Lindbeck's rejection of conservative propositional theology and also of liberal experiential/expressivist theology leaves no normative context for criticizing a "postliberal community" and its doctrines. This is surely not what Lindbeck intended with his theory of doctrine.[3] What went wrong with his theory, or the reception of it, to allow theology to be reduced to social science?

The key question is what happens to theology on Lindbeck's analysis. For both propositional theologians and the experiential/expressivists, theology is the analysis, development, and defense of doctrines. The "defense" part makes theology a normative discipline in both cases. Does theology become merely the explication of the cultural/linguistic grammar of some community's faith on the postliberal view affirmed by Lindbeck?[4] That is the crucial assumption made by people who say theology can only work within a community's deep grammatical assumptions without questioning them. But I believe that Lindbeck would hold to a broader construal of theology than this, one that would allow *The Nature of Doctrine* to be construed as a theology book itself. I shall sketch out such a broader conception of theology and then present a theory of the interpretation and truth of religious matters that affirms his emphasis on truth in the context of practice but also allows clearly for theology as normative inquiry.

Theology, I propose, in both its deepest and broadest senses is *inquiry into the truth about religious matters*. Set aside for the present the question as to what counts as religious; later chapters will address the question with a theory of ultimacy, defined technically in terms of what I call finite/infinite contrasts. Let us reflect on the inquiry part. Lindbeck's chief focus is to show that the place to look for religious matters is in religious people and communities. If doctrines are studied theologically without seeing how they function in practice, the theology will not see the real thing. Such is the force of Lindbeck's polemic against propositional theology for being too abstract and experiential/expressive theology for being too individualistic, interior, and isolated from cultural practice. His polemic could be directed with equal force against Biblical scholars who do not treat their texts as located in communal practice, or against Christian ethicists who do not do the same. So, theological inquiry surely includes the analysis of how doctrinal and other symbolic assumptions and affirmations function in concrete religious practice. I shall argue shortly that concrete practical location, in some community or other, is actually necessary in order to be able to say whether a doctrine or affirmed symbol is true or false: truth or falsity is a function of interpretive location, among other things.

Theological inquiry also includes philosophical and interdisciplinary analyses of the nature of religion. That is the topic of *The Nature of Doctrine*. Philosophy of religion is thus a proper part of theology because careful judgments about truth and falsity in religious matters cannot be made without addressing the crucial issues about the nature of religion. Lindbeck's philosophy of religion is notable for its interdisciplinary use of anthropological resources.

Closely related, theological inquiry needs to come to terms with semiotics, the study of how signs and symbols refer, have systematic meaning, and are interpreted in various contexts. The semiotics of religious symbols is particularly interesting because so many of the basic symbols have built-in apophatic elements: In the Christian tradition all the major theologians have known that God is not a being just like other beings, not purposeful just like human agents, or rational in a human sense, though perhaps a little like each of these. The semiotics of religious symbols might be viewed as another part of philosophy of religion, alongside the analysis of religion, but also as a proper part of theology which needs to understand the ways by which its symbols interpret their subject matter in order to judge how they might be true or false.

Finally, theology includes the study of religious symbols themselves, understood in terms of their semiotic settings and in terms of their various roles within religious practice. Lindbeck focused on *doctrines* as a particular kind of complex religious symbol that has a special function within religious communities to articulate the grammar of cultural/linguistic life. One might also study whole theologies, which have a different kind of focus and are addressed not only to religious communities but to communities of scholars that might extend beyond the religion, as Thomas Aquinas addressed the *Summa contra Gentiles* to the Muslims. One might further study more particularized symbols such as the cannibalistic imagery of the Christian Eucharist, eating the flesh and blood of the community's founder. Crucial to inquiry into all sorts of religious symbols is their study in comparative perspective, relating them to symbols of other religious traditions functioning in different ways in other religious communities; so, one might study the Mahayana Buddhist bodhisattva Guanyin, so like "the friend we have in Jesus."

This program for theology is not innocent. First, it has a naturalistic philosophic base, one that puts Lindbeck's appeal to the social sciences in a better light than that in which it is seen by those who think he has betrayed transcendent reference. The naturalistic causal theory of interpretation and truth treats symbols as means to engage their objects rather than to substitute for and distance them. Second, the theory of interpretation, developed from insights of Charles Sanders Peirce, the founder of American Pragmatism, identifies many more sites of contextualization in religious claims than mere location within a practicing community. Theology needs to specify these sites when it asks the question of truth because it needs diverse criteria that respect the array of contextualizations.

RELIGIOUS SYMBOLS: ENGAGEMENT

Religious symbols, including doctrines, generally have been viewed two ways. According to one way, they are substitutes for the real things, representations of objects that cannot quite be present on their own. On this view, religious symbols stand between us and the divine as some kind of boundary, perhaps as an impediment. From this some people conclude that religious life needs to transcend the symbols, to get around them through mystical or other means such as faith.

The symbols themselves are recognized as cultural, historically relative, projections of finite human images onto an infinite reality, "social constructions of reality," to use the phrase of sociologists of knowledge such as Peter

Berger and Thomas Luckmann.[5] Thinkers hostile to normative religion have taken this view of religious symbols to mean that they are *mere* projections, fictitious social constructions of reality arising out of human need and fear. The name of Feuerbach is associated with this response, though all the hermeneuts of suspicion such as Freud, Marx, and maybe even Nietzsche, have held to this line. It is fair to say that the vast majority of academics and intellectuals in the United States outside the narrow field of theology assume that religious symbols are mere human projections and have no real referents, and that religion therefore is to be accorded attitudes on a continuum between bemusement and hostility.

The other way to view socially constructed religious symbols is as the means to engage their objects. Instead of displacing the religious objects, or making it seem as if religious objects exist when they do not, this pragmatic vision of religious semiotics sees symbols as connectives, allowing their interpreters to discriminate what they otherwise would miss. It is the view for which I shall argue, and let me begin with a fable.

Human beings are natural creatures in a large environment that bombards them with stimuli of many sorts. Simpler creatures such as amoebae have only those responses constituted by elementary chemical reactions. But complicated human beings, with discriminating nervous systems, construe such elementary chemical reactions taking place in the olfactory, auditory, optical and other groups of brain cells to be signs of distant and far more significant things than the presence of the chemicals. Included in the complicated human nervous apparatus in fact are systems of signs that in their most elementary physical components might be little more than chemical "feels," but in their interrelationships have the characters of symbolic codes. Indeed, without evolving symbolic codes, the complicated nervous system itself would not have evolved. Moreover, because the codes are learned socially, the individual nervous system evolved with evolving social patterns.

The result, however, is that a human being can engage the environment with far greater depth and discrimination than an amoeba, can have purposes based on semiotically constructed future hopes, and can even learn to discriminate and perceive general habits or tendencies in things, moods in social groups, general connections such as causal relations, spatio-temporal fields, and general virtues such as kindness, wisdom, and honesty. Reflecting on life's opportunities and goods, pitfalls and tragedies, we can ask what large purposes are worth having and what characters to cultivate in civilizations.

These general or habitual elements are never fully real at a particular moment, and illustrate the fact that human beings can discriminate and perceive by means of hypotheses, that is, hypothetical signs that are taken to be well-founded or ill-founded as they are used to engage reality. Even simple visual perception has the form of an hypothesis, Charles Peirce argued, because we regularly fill in by means of inference the part of the visual field left vacant by the entrance point of the optic nerve into the eye's battery of rods and cones. I follow Peirce, in ways to be explained at length in chapters 6 and 7, in claiming that all experience involves the interpretation of reality by means of signs and that the interpretations treat the interpretive signs as hypotheses.[6]

The end result of the evolutionary process, according to my fable, is that you can speed down a mountain road in your BMW, taking in all the visual cues you need to stay on the road, using your kinetic sense to slow the car on turns, feeling the lean of the car in accelerating and breaking, judging the intentions of other drivers, all the while concentrating on Hegel's doctrine of the "labor of the notion." You have a finely tuned system of automobile-driving symbols, learned with awkward consciousness when you were a teenager, but long since so associated with your skeletal-muscular nervous system that driving is second nature to you. It is all interpretation, of course, though rarely conscious now unless there is an emergency; even in emergencies you wake up to the fact only when your foot has already slammed the brake and your heart begun to race. The automobile-driving symbol system allows us late-moderns to engage our world in a travel form that would be wholly inaccessible to a native of the Amazon jungle who had never seen a road or car; similarly, we would not have a clue about what not to step on in the jungle, though that would be second nature to its people.

Therefore, far from taking symbols to be distancing substitutes for realities, my pragmatism takes them to be means of engagement. Without the signs for them, we simply cannot discriminate and register things. Because we have evolved with signs, symbolic systems, and interpretive behavior, we discriminate and shape our environment with forms of the world, with future and past, moral identity, and the community forms that themselves enhance the richness of human life. Because of interpretation, we transform brute stimuli into the means for shaping intelligent, discriminating, and imaginative life.

For this view of signs, that symbols are projections and that the large traits of the human world are social constructions are positive values. The more inventive we are with the self-conscious construction of signs, the more likely we are to be able to discriminate some hitherto unnoticed aspect of reality. The use of mathematics in modern science is an obvious example of the enhanced powers of discovery in the development of signs and the testing of them through engaging the world. But so are the imaginative creations of poets, artists, and musicians. And so is the genius of religious symbolism. Of course the invented signs might be mistaken, which is to say that reality might not be what the signs take it to be. But there is no question on the interpretive-engagement view that reality is there and that some interpretation is being made: the crucial question is of the truth of the engagement.

Feuerbach should not be read to say that there is no object referred to by the projected ideas of God, that they are illusions; rather he said that our interpretation of those ideas as referring to divinity rather than humankind is mistaken: properly interpreted, he thought, theological ideas are true of ideal humanity. Karl Barth fully appreciated Feuerbach's argument that religion is a social construction, to use the more recent phrase.[7] But he held to the first, non-pragmatic view of religious symbols, and took Feuerbach's argument to support his own position that Christianity and other religions have nothing to do with the gospel because they are social constructions. Barth's argument against Feuerbach's conclusion about theology, however, was empirical: Barth claimed that the essence of humanity is not at all ideal or Godlike but in fact is sinful to the core. Therefore, however we understand God, as we must do in acknowledging grace, it cannot be through human analogies. He takes the occasion of his discussion of Feuerbach to criticize Schleiermacher and Luther in favor of Calvin, blaming them for turning theology to anthropology; but Barth forgets that the very first page of Calvin's *Institutes* says theology can begin with either God or humanity because each topic immediately leads to the other.[8]

With the pragmatic view of symbols as instruments of engagement, allowing us to discern realities otherwise opaque, theological anthropology takes on new and positive meaning. For, the assessment of the truth of theological doctrines and symbols requires that we understand the causal processes by which reality, including divine reality, affects interpreters and is discerned by them in religious engagement (I take "religion" here to mean the engagement with divine matters). Truth may be defined in a way congruent with the pragmatic theory of interpretation as follows: truth is the carryover of value or importance from the object interpreted into the interpreter, in the respect the signs or symbols are taken to represent the object, as qualified by the biological, cultural, semiotic, and purposive conditions of the interpreter.[9] A brief gloss on this definition of truth will reveal it to rest in a naturalism deeply satisfying to Feuerbach's stomach but also to provide access to realities as divine as Barth's source of grace and object of faith.

Like Aristotle's, this characterization of knowledge is causal. But whereas Aristotle claimed that what is carried over from the object to the mind is form, leaving the object's matter behind and informing mental matter, my pragmatic claim is that value is carried across, transforming itself through whatever forms the causal process dictates so that the interpreter gets what is important in the object in the respect it is interpreted. Aristotle's form-carryover has led to the problems of mirror theories which fail because there is no third standpoint from which to compare forms. The pragmatic theory says that if the interpreter does not get what is valuable, there will be discernable pragmatic consequences. In the evolutionary short run, the interpreter picks up on the value of the object insofar as that has immediate importance for the interpreter: is the object good to eat, or is it about to eat the interpreter? In the longer run, especially when human beings enjoy complex and discerning semiotic systems, values more obviously intrinsic to the objects and less merely instrumental to the interpreters are interpreted: so, a proper mix of sun and rain is good for crops, loyalty is good for families, laws of attraction and repulsion acting in very small particles explain large motions, the cosmos is made so as to send both rain and sun on both the just and the unjust. Under ideal circumstances, to engage the world guided by interpretations such as these is to make them vulnerable to being corrected if they are mistaken.

Although this is a realistic correspondence theory of truth, it does acknowledge that interpretation of objects is always in respects determined by the interpreters. The classical pragmatists wrote eloquently about the roles of human purpose in determining the respects in which interpretations are made. Their almost exclusive attention to this made it seem as if interpretation is always instrumental, that we treat objects only as objects of use, picking out how they are helpful or harmful for purposes; the evolutionary understanding of intelligence reinforces this. But the theory I advance says that prior to carryover into forms that serve purposes, the realities of things are carried over into forms that register in human biology, culture, and semiotic systems, and it is these to which theological anthropology should be alert. In fact, human purposes themselves depend on what can be troped by human biology, on what is a possible cultural practice, and on what can be imagined within the semiotic system at hand.

With regard to biological qualifications of trajectories from things to interpretations of them, we are barely beginning to have much steady understanding. Sensory perception is probably the best understood, and much work is being done on how an interpreter can grasp the meaning of a sentence. The perception of subtle beauty and sublimity is less well understood, and religious experiences have been studied mainly indirectly through simulacra in epileptic episodes. The lines between neurophysiology, cultural practices, and specific semiotic systems are not sharp. A kind of bio-psychic dance integrates activities from digestion to ritual meals to metaphysics. To understand how a real thing can be carried over into an interpreter, however, requires knowing how its forms are transformed and limited so as to register in the interpreter's biology, culture, and semiotic systems. There is no such thing as truth save insofar as what is valuable is registered through interpreters' biology, cultures, semiotic systems, and purposes, according to my hypothesis.

Therefore, the first order of contextualization in religious truth is to realize that divine matters can be interpreted only in ways filtered through, or embodied through, the interpreters' biology, culture, symbol systems, and purposes. We have long been sensitive to cultural, symbolic, and purposive embodiment. William James went so far as to suggest that the difference between first-born and second-born religious personalities is a function of the physiology of optimism and melancholy, though our biological understanding lags far behind understanding of culture, symbols, and purposes.[10] What we have often failed to realize, however, is that there is no truth at all without some particular historical biology, culture, semiosis, and purpose. We have tended to assume that reality is there to be mirrored in some ideal form which would be the real and pure truth. Such an ideal mirror would only be relativized and distorted by the biases of purpose, the idiosyncrasies of language, the historical particularities of cultures, and the limitations of what can be registered through the nervous system. My pragmatic theory says there is no such thing as truth, or even candidates for truth, except insofar as objects interpreted are carried over into particular contexts of biology, culture, symbol systems, and purposive life. Rather than these qualifiers being distancing and distorting screens, they are what make possible cognitive engagement in the first place. Therefore the first order of theological contextualization is to be alert to the anthropological character of particular historical biology, culture, symbol systems, and purpose.

RELIGIOUS SYMBOLS: INTERPRETATION

The second order of contextualization derives from the structure of interpretation itself. In his theory of signs, Charles Peirce distinguished three problem areas: issues of meaning, of interpretation, and of reference, which will be discussed at length later.

Theology, Christian and otherwise, usually has focused on the first, issues of meaning. These are difficult enough by themselves. Religious symbols range from concrete to abstract, personifying to metaphysical, idiosyncratic to systematic, connected to fragmentary. Unlike scientific symbols, for instance, religious symbols are difficult to fit into a univocal scheme without losing their force. But Christian theologians from Justin Martyr on have attempted to interpret the symbols in terms of one another so as to provide consistent symbol systems. At any time, these religious symbol systems are set within wider semiotic systems with which a society deals with domestic life, politics, economics and a host of other symbolically shaped activities. Moreover, a religious symbol system develops through time with changing circumstances, acquiring new symbols in the system, trivializing others, and changing their inter-definitions. We are accustomed to acknowledge the diverse contextualization of Christian symbol systems in the West, noting the separating histories of Orthodoxy, Roman Catholicism, Protestant, Anglican, and free-church symbolic systems. The Nestorian Christians who went to China had other ways of symbolically shaping their practice and thought. The Copts in Africa had their own trajectory, and so did the early Christians in India. Recognizing the historical differences between theological and other religious symbols set in specific systems, we can become conscious of the historical contextualization of any such symbol.

As Kant said about concepts, symbols are "rules for unifying a manifold." Within a semiotic system, the manifold unified by a given symbol is a group of other symbols, and the determinate character of the symbol as rule lets it be defined over against other symbols that might unify the same manifold differently or that connect it with other manifolds through inter-definition. The semantic and syntactic structures of semiotic codes describe how symbols are such rules for unifying manifolds. From the pragmatic perspective, a symbol can be viewed as an hypothesis for unifying its manifold according to its determinate structure or rule. Part of the justification of a symbol as an hypothesis consists in determining whether in fact it unifies its manifold, a formal question; another part asks whether the manifold at hand is worth unifying, or whether it includes symbols that themselves are bad hypotheses. Yet another part of justification is to ask whether the symbol connects clearly to other symbols with respect to which it is defined, or is confused. Most theological discourse consists of pursuing these lines of justification, asking questions of conceptual clarity, symbolic resonance, inclusiveness, and the ability to render whatever is taken to be religiously important. All that this kind of analysis would prove, however, is that the theologians have a set of well-formed hypotheses, not that any are true.

To ask whether the hypotheses are true requires dealing with how they are used by interpreters to engage their objects, determining whether they in fact carry over what is important in the respects in which the hypotheses are taken to interpret the objects. It is tempting to short-circuit the issues of interpretation and reference, however, and attach truth to the symbol systems or hypotheses themselves. One popular way to do this is to attach the symbol system to some authority, for instance the Bible. Another is to cite faith to assign truth by an act of will. But neither of these devices would even recognize that the very meaning of truth claimed for the symbols is that they actually and habitually carry over what is important in the religious objects into interpreters.

The issues of interpretation and interpretive context are well-known if not always at the center of attention. It would be foolish to attempt any list of standard contexts for the interpretation of religious symbols, but for purposes of illustration, consider the contexts of theological inquiry, of communal practice and life, and of personal devotion, all relative to the symbol of the cross. In a theological context, the cross would be interpreted by further symbols connecting Jesus' historical death and resurrection with a vast array of other symbols made precise as doctrines and concepts, clearly defined, usable across as wide a field of different communities of practice as possible, and framed so as to facilitate communication across difficult semiotic and cultural gaps. Theologians usually try to develop interpretations of their symbols that do not require qualifications regarding context, symbols that apply across contexts.

In the practical context of a community's life, however, the virtues of universality are likely not to be important unless the community's neighbor has a competing symbolic system. Rather, the community would put crosses on its church roof, on its altar, perhaps in its floor plan; it would teach reverence to the cross, perhaps gestures of genuflecting. And it would be concerned to array its symbols concerning the cross so as to connect Jesus' death with resurrection and to teach the faithful-suffering/new-life juxtaposition to be an epitome of life before God. The interpretation of the cross in the community would consist in how people's lives and practices are transformed by the deployment of crucifixion and related symbols. Theological explanation might play a part in that, especially for 13-year olds in confirmation class, but the real interpretation is the effect on people's lives.

The context of devotion in which one meditates upon the cross differs from the theological and communal. The theological context shapes up symbols for clarity and universality of communication; the communal context shapes them up for effectiveness in people's lives. Both pay close attention to errors of exaggeration that can lead to conceptual mistakes or immoral community life, taking "moral" in a broad sense. Devotional meditations on the cross can be wild, exaggerated, fanciful, and wholly false if interpreted descriptively. It did not happen to Jesus the way crucifixion is often imagined devotionally, and a community would not want symbols of blood and gore to unbalance the practical crucifixion/resurrection juxtaposition. But in devotional life, concentration on "the fountains of blood flowing from Emmanuel's veins" might be just the work to move the soul to receive grace more realistically.

The interpretive context with its biological, cultural, semiotic, and purposive characteristics determines in what respect a symbol is taken to interpret its object. A given symbol might interpret quite different objects in different contexts, as for instance the historical Jesus is part of the object of the symbol of the cross in a theological context but might be wholly irrelevant in a devotional one. The same object might be interpreted by different and contrary symbols in different contexts, as when God is said to be the Ground of Being or the Act of Esse in a theological context and the Lover of my soul in a devotional one. Also, the same object might be interpreted by the same symbol in different contexts with quite different truth values as when God is said to be "for us" in a theological context but (therefore) "against our neighbors with whom we are at war" in a political context.

When asking the truth question, whether the symbol carries over the real value in the object into the interpreter in the respect interpreted, the question must be specified as to interpretive context. In a theological context, God might well be truly understood as Act of Esse. But that would carry over little or nothing in a devotional context unless the devotee were a theologian who could use abstract theological hypotheses to engage the divine.

Interpretation takes symbols to refer to objects and it is because of this that symbols shape our engagement with objects. Charles Peirce pointed out that reference is of three kinds, and I believe that most religious symbols in most interpretive contexts refer in all three ways. According to Peirce, as will be explained later, reference is iconic, indexical, and conventional. Iconic reference is by some kind of similarity between symbol and object or one-to-one mapping of the object by the symbol. The cross on the altar is somewhat iconic of the cross on which Jesus died because of its shape. Our visual perception of the shapes of physical objects is iconic even though the object's contours are, for instance, wood whereas our perceptive images are made of pixels of light. Any descriptive symbols, for instance in propositions or theories, are intended to refer iconically, which is to say they claim reality is like what they say. In religion this includes not only theologies but also myths and basic imaginative structures: a myth is a symbolic structure that we take the world in some respect to be like, often not distinguishing between the symbol and the world. Most theologians want a heavy dose of iconicity in their theology, especially those whom Lindbeck labels propositional in their approach to doctrine.

Indexical reference is just as important in religion, however, and in fact more important when the soteriological intent of religious symbols is acknowledged. An index is a symbol that is in causal connection with its object and points to it. Or better yet, when truly interpreted, an index causally reorients the interpreter so as to embody what is important in the object; the notion of "performative linguistic acts" in analytic philosophy gets at this sense of reference. Indexical reference is involved in all interpretations in which the interpreter realizes something, actualizes a better relation to the divine, or is transformed in the engagement. With iconic reference, an interpreter has a map for engaging, but without at least minimal indexical reference does not actually engage in the interpretation. Indexical reference makes a causal carryover connection. This is obvious in cases where a symbol, or more likely a symbol system, is both iconic and indexical: complicated interactions engage realities in ways that make the interpreters more alert to and indeed filled with the objects. Sometimes, however, a symbol that does not refer iconically does refer indexically. This is to say, a symbol that is plainly false in a descriptive, iconic sense, might in fact function so as to carry over what is genuinely valuable and transforming. Many devotional symbols are iconically distorted if not downright false, and yet indexically potent and valid.

Perhaps the deepest theological conflicts of our time come from the failure to distinguish iconic from indexical reference. I take Jesus to have been referring indexically when he said to think of God as our Father; when he was pressed by the scribes and Pharisees iconically to explain gender relations in heaven, however, he said there aren't any. Through Christian history, with parallels in other religions, there have been many contexts in which it has seemed appropriate to refer indexically to the divine with personifying images. Something important in the divine is carried over into the interpreting community or devotee by personifications of God. Yet when theologians attempt to give iconic theories of the divine, God so far transcends any personifications referred iconically as to render them worthless, or idolatrous. God as the One, the Act of Esse, Being, the Ground of Being, the Creator of everything—that cannot be a person with subjective consciousness waiting for our prayers in any descriptive sense. But not to pray to God for life with all our hearts is to miss what might be the most important part of divinity. The indexical character of reference is nonobvious where iconic reference is expected.

Conventional reference has been assumed all along in talking about icons and indices, for we cannot talk about any of these things except through the conventions of language. Moreover, conventional reference connects the object and symbol at hand with the vast system of other symbols within the particular semiotic code. Religion could have no bearing on the rest of life if it were not for the conventional references contained in its interpretations. By means of conventional reference, people engage reality together in communities, employing iconic and indexical reference to carry across the value of things into their communal interpretive experience.

Reference has another dimension (not noticed by Peirce) besides iconic, indexical, and conventional reference to what I call its primary objects. Because reference engages interpreters with their objects, it makes sense to ask whether it is possible for given symbols actually to refer to those primary objects for the interpreters at hand. For instance, while the Christian symbol system says it is true to engage God through the symbol of Father, to do so is not likely to be possible for someone who in childhood was traumatized by an abusive father. Although the accepted symbol system and the interpretive context at hand legitimate that reference, it simply cannot actually take place for that person so as to engage him or her with God. I say, therefore, that the secondary object of reference is the proper state of soul of the interpreter. Similarly, just as some symbols can actually refer for adults that are not engaging for children, secondary reference is also to the stage of cultural and semiotic development. So we should specify that symbols refer iconically, indexically, and conventionally to certain primary objects for interpreters of the right state and stage of soul who are the secondary objects of reference.

I argued earlier that the first order of contextualization is to locate a truth claim in the various qualifications that our biology, culture, semiotic systems, and purposes put on our engagements with the world. The second order of contextualization derives from the structure of interpretation itself, and may be summarized from the above sketch as follows:

- To understand whether a particular interpretation is true it is necessary to locate the historical and social context of the symbols and symbol systems it employs, remembering the subtle differences among apparently similar symbol systems within Christianity.
- To understand the truth question in a particular case, it is also necessary to identify the context of the interpreters, for it is into that context that the

value of the object interpreted might be carried. What is carried across in one context as true might be false in another.
- To understand the truth question, it is necessary to sort out the kinds of reference involved, especially as between iconic and indexical, and to ascertain whether the interpreter is of the right state and stage of soul to engage the objects through those references. A symbol might refer as an index truly in the sense of carrying over the important point even though it is descriptively, that is iconically, false; the meaning of truth here is whether the interpreter is reoriented so as to connect in the appropriate respect with the object, embodying its value in that respect.

ALL TRUTH IS CONTEXTUAL

My argument here, sketchy and anecdotal as it is, has presented a theory of truth which rests on a theory of interpretation as engagement. Rejecting the view that symbols distance us from reality, I have shown how symbols allow us to engage reality more discerningly and pick up on what is valuable in it insofar as that is qualified by our biology, culture, symbol systems, and purposes. Moreover, I have argued that the very meaning of truth is the contextualization of interpretation so that real objects are carried over into real interpreters with respect to what the symbols say is important and valuable in the objects. Symbols themselves are hypotheses, and their use in interpretive engagements tests them. In order to tell what the tests prove, it is necessary to specify the various contextualizations so as to identify the causal process of value carryover. There is no such thing as uncontextualized truth. Every truth claim is particular to what we might call its contextualization-complex.

Reflect for a moment on how complex the truth question is. In order to tell whether a truth claim is true, its entire contextualization-complex in principle ought to be identified and worked into the assessment of whether the relevant value is carried from the object into the interpreter. Perhaps we can assume that biological qualifications on carryover are "standard conditions" and do not vary so as to make a difference; but we need to remember that God is still being filtered into what can be registered in the human nervous system, and this might be different for depressives from what it is for those whom William James called the "healthy minded." For the cultural, semiotic, and purposive qualifications of interpretation, particular historical definitions of context need to be identified in order to tell what is happening in the alleged carryover. Similarly, for the second order contextualizations of particular symbols as hypotheses, practical contexts for interpretation into which the value is carried need to be identified as well as the different forms of reference, primary and secondary.

All of this seems bafflingly complex, and I believe that facing the truth question in theology requires taking on a set of vast research programs to allow for the understanding of the various contextualizations. Clearly, this program is aligned with Tillich's legacy as sketched in chapter 1. Perhaps there was a time when male theologians could ignore contextualizations because they all shared the same contexts: same biology, culture, language, purposes, symbol systems, communal contexts, and confusions of reference. If there ever was such a time, the women knew better. And now we all know that different contextualizations make a difference and need to be sorted.

The great advantage to our recent awareness of important pluralism in these contexts is that it undermines the sad attempts to treat truth as a function of symbol systems alone, affirming validity by authority or will. Those are simply irrelevant to truth which would be actual carryover of value in the relevant respect. Rather, communal practices regarding authoritative texts or persons, and regarding faith as a commitment of will, are among the contextual elements to be identified and analyzed in assessing important religious truth claims. Lindbeck was exactly right to say that doctrines, and by extension other symbols claimed or assumed to be true, need to be understood in their concrete contextual functioning. He was exactly right to say that there is no pure and context-transcendent form of truth. And he need not be interpreted as meaning that the contextualization of doctrine entails that any doctrine is true in its context, because we can still ask whether it carries over what is of importance in its objects. Lindbeck may observe that a set of doctrines does in fact function as the grammar of a cultural/linguistic community without having to say that all the doctrines in the set are true: he can identify the misguided, mis-descriptive, disorienting or demonic as well as anyone without having to abandon his functional analysis of doctrines.

The negative side of the theory I have been advocating is that the more concrete and particular the contextualization-complex of a truth claim, the more problematic the public for theology. Lindbeck's own personal context for the development of his theory of doctrine was extensive participation in ecumenical dialogue. That brought to his attention the concrete contextual differences between Lutherans and Roman Catholics, or between Christians and Buddhists. He rightly noted that there is no neutral concrete contextualized Christian theology indifferent to Lutherans and Catholics, and that an ecumenical discussion would have to create a new concrete context through negotiation. The same is true with regard to dialogue among world religions. Lindbeck's acknowledgment of different concrete contextualization-complexes has led some to interpret him as saying that they are all true in their own way, and each is entirely true.

He need not say this, however. In the first place, the fact that truth is to be found only in concrete contexts does not mean that every truth claim in such a context is true. In the second place, a theologian, or theological community, need not confine itself to analyzing the truth claims of its own context but can enter into public scrutiny of other concrete communities, albeit with due attention to the importance of participation for accessing what is going on, a point stressed by any engagement theory of interpretation. In the third place, part of the vitality of contemporary intellectual life is the creation of new concrete contexts through dialogue and other forms of mutual practice. This requires the development of fair comparative categories so that different contextualization-complexes can be brought into connection and comparative truth claims assessed, a point to be developed in the next section. Comparative categories need to be initially vague enough so as to register the different things compared without bias; they need to be capable of being specified by the differences so that they provide a common language; and they need to be made concrete by embodying all the things compared, so as to be a new context for truth. We are barely beginning such comparative work.[11] This comparative task is not inimical to Lindbeck's project; indeed, it is supported by his interest in interfaith dialogue.

The intent of my argument has been to affirm Lindbeck's point that doctrines and other theological claims and symbols need not be taken to be descriptive in the iconic sense but might very well be indexical and conventional in their engagement of people with the divine and with each other in communal response. As non-iconic, but indexical and conventional, the doctrines still might be true. Those who interpret Lindbeck as having to deny this are wrong. If Lindbeck were to embrace a pragmatic theory of interpretation and truth such as promoted by Peirce and developed here, he would still be able to claim that doctrines functioning as the grammar of a cultural-linguistic community might be true or false. To determine whether they are true or false would require examining them in context, as he insists. But the context is not just that of a community; it is at least as complex as all the kinds of contextualizations cited here. Whereas some draw a fideistic lesson from Lindbeck, namely, that you pick your community and you've got your truth, I draw the lesson that theology has a complicated set of research programs to develop if it is to make fair assessments of truth, stretching from neurophysiology to comparative religions. He is right, I believe, to see theology as an interdisciplinary adventure, moving far beyond our old models of confessional hermeneutics. His program can be dragged from the legacy of Barth to that of Tillich.

THE COMPARATIVE CONTEXT FOR RELIGIOUS TRUTH

Postliberal theologians such as George Lindbeck and Hans Frei rightly have brought renewed attention to the fact that religion is lived in what they call "cultural-linguistic systems." Liberation theologians have made a similar point when they call for contextualizing theologies to register the voices of the marginalized. Christianity in non-Western cultures is being indigenized to cultural forms that might be radically different from Western cultural forms and that reflect instead the heritage of African tribal religions, Native American religions, Confucianism, shamanism, or other historical cultures.

I have argued above that there is no such thing as truth in Christianity that is not concretely contextualized with actual interpreters engaging the religious realities with the symbolically rich cultural artifacts and natural conditions of their situation. If universal Christian truths apply across all the cultural embodiments of Christianity without qualification, that can only be because there is something concrete about the universal context such that cultural differences do not make a difference. So far, we do not have language to express such a possible concrete cultural universal that is not biased to one culture or another.

Recognizing the contextual character of all Christian truth claims, however, we can note that the vitality of Christianity and its theology lies in translation from one cultural context to another. St. Paul's Christianity lay in the translation of the meaning of the life of a small-town Galilean, Jesus of Nazareth, to a largely urban Hellenistic world. We now understand the Gospels to be the interpretation of Jesus to specific communities. The Christian evangel then spread throughout the Roman world and beyond that to the Western and Northern reaches of Europe. According to legend, Thomas took the gospel to India, Philip to Africa. The Nestorians took it to China before the Tang Dynasty. In more recent times, the vital questions of Christian truth have been raised in Europe and America through encounters with secular culture and political idolatries. Challenges to inherited claims come from liberationists who point out that those claims marginalize people who should be registered at the center. The process of indigenization itself requires facing the question of what is true or false about the representations in our symbols and practices. The questions of truth arise when Christianity needs to be translated from one cultural context to another.

If some postliberal theologians are right, then Christianity identified with one of its concrete embodiments might limit the question of truth to matters of consistency and thoroughness for the particular context. Questions that would ask whether there is any external reference beyond the context would not be asked. Rather, truth within the context would be a matter of sociological, anthropological, or historical analysis of what that kind of culturally embodied Christians believe. Thus Hans Frei said that theology is description, and as such is closer to cultural anthropology than to philosophy which asks whether Christian claims correspond to reality.[12]

I have argued above against this analysis of contextualized Christianity and believe that in every context Christians are engaged with reality, reinforcing or correcting their cultural system in light of the experience with that engagement. Christian theology is not only or mainly intra-textual, as Lindbeck said against his better instincts,[13] but is the reflective correction of the texts and their systems of practice through engagement with a larger reality.

The question of truth is always whether interpretations made within a concrete context rightly engage their real objects, not merely how to think consistently within the symbolic structure of a context. Nevertheless, once a context is set and a Christian symbolic-cultural system is deployed, it is easy to forget the question of truth and concentrate instead on authentic living within the system.

The moments of truth in Christian history have come when the gospel has been translated from one culture to another, or when a culture undergoes a process of fairly radical change. The best way to understand Christian doctrine, therefore, is not to see it primarily as the intellectual grammar of a culture but rather as the outcome of translation from one culture to another or from one cultural situation through a significant change in that culture. What is it that survives the translation? How are modifications made? What tests were made for the translations?

All this suggests a different reading of Christian history from what has often been the rule in Western Christianity. Since the Protestant Reformation, many have taken a putative cultural embodiment of biblical Christianity as the norm, as expressed in the Bible. But biblical criticism has shown the Bible to record many different cultural settings for the new faith, and we are likely to learn more by following out the interactions of the settings and the development of the faith through those interactions than from any one of them alone. Others have taken the creeds of the patristic period to be the normative expressions of Christian doctrine, if not of practice. Yet we now see that conversation to be a cultural embodiment of Christianity in a Greek metaphysical world we no longer share. Indeed, the Nestorians who were rejected from patristic orthodoxy vastly expanded Christianity into Tang Dynasty China while European Christianity slipped into the Dark Ages.[14] Moreover, the Nestorian concern for the person of Jesus is far closer to more recent preoccupations with the biblical and historical Jesus than patristic orthodoxy's notions of the distinction between the generated and the ungenerated persons of the Trinity. So we should look at the patristic period and its creeds as the translation of the Gospel into the metaphysical culture of late antiquity, whence it was retranslated in many other directions, again and again. Although we might be excused for hunting down the progression of translations from Jerusalem to our own city, we would learn far more, I believe, by tracking the translations in all directions, viewing the history of Christianity as the progressive re-embodiment of the faith from context to context. The changes are more revelatory than the resting places. And the resting places should be viewed as the outcomes of changes.

All this is to say that Christianity needs to be understood as a cross-cultural phenomenon if we are to be alert to the real questions of truth in the faith. The broader our grasp of cross-cultural diversity, and of the considerations that have gone into translation from one context to another, the better taste we have for discerning how to negotiate the questions of truth in our own changing context of late modernity, or postmodernity, or whatever the name is for where we are going.

This perspective of course reflects a theological agenda, one that stresses the work of the Holy Spirit to interpret Jesus Christ and the biblical witness to him in every new circumstance. God the Creator works by the Spirit through all histories, in every culture, to provide ways in which the remembered and interpreted Jesus Christ can function salvifically. This fairly standard trinitarianism stands in some contrast with the Christocentrism of many Neo-orthodox theologians who privilege the historical past over the present and yet cannot reach it convincingly, depending on the Bible for knowledge it cannot give.[15]

Permit me now to change the cross-cultural context entirely and ask about Christian truth relative to other world religions. Suppose that contemporary Christian theologians were to have in hand a comprehensive cross-cultural historical understanding of the development of Christianity, with a sensitivity to the ways by which truth claims were forged and changed in the translations of the gospel. That still would be only part of the truth question for Christianity. What is Christianity as seen from the outside? What Jew could think of Christianity as a religion that seriously represents God as love and its faith as obedience to the command to love God and neighbor? For Jews, such representations could only be surface hypocrisy; the operational Christian beliefs that gave rise to centuries of Christian persecution of Jews have to be something else. In the last half-century, many Christians have come to see their own tradition from this part of the Jewish perspective and have rejected traditional supercessionist theology regarding Judaism with its attendant anti-Semitism.

The scandalous history of European and American Christianity relative to Jews dramatizes the need for a Christian theology of other religions but does not reveal its depth or breadth. The problem is not only that Christians need still to attend to how Christianity is viewed by other religions. The problem is that those other religions also have theologians and saints who have grappled profoundly with the nature of what is ultimate, with the human condition and its predicaments, with the fundamental obligations of human life, with the means to overcome existential predicaments, and with how to live toward spiritual perfection. The other great religions also have evolved through cross-cultural translations, just as has Christianity. Their intellectual beliefs have been honed through debate over time, and their practices have been shaped critically through historical trials. Moreover, those religions are translating themselves into exactly the same social contexts as contemporary Christianity, in Africa, Asia, Europe, and the Americas. Even in the small towns of the Midwest in the United States, there are Korean Buddhist greengrocers, Hindu policemen, Muslim physicians and dentists, Confucian business people, and Daoist martial arts teachers. The religions engage one another on school boards and in political elections. Christian priests and ministers make decisions about inter-religious marriages. There is no end to the practical need for Christians to understand themselves in relation to the different religions of their neighbors.

What does it mean for Christians to understand other religions? Obviously, one step is to enter into the historical culture of the other religions. But like Christianity, each of those other religions has more than one culture, and each is at present attempting to translate itself into the situation of late modernity. All the religions are struggling to come to terms with ecological matters, with the possibility of global distributive justice, with electronic media that vastly alter the boundaries between cultures, and with the very fact of engaging other religions and secular culture in a pluralistic world. Therefore to understand another religious tradition is to track its changes, its translations from context to context. Perhaps the most efficient way to do this is by studying the ancient core texts and motifs of the tradition and inquiring into how these have been reinterpreted in each age, with each change-point. Moreover, it is possible to see how the religions have interpreted one another's traditions at the points where they have intersected. Although gaining an historical developmental grasp of each of the world's major religions is a vast expansion of the curriculum for both universities and religious educational institutions, such an understanding is possible and can be institutionalized with varying degrees of sophistication.

Even that is not enough for an understanding of Christian truth relative to other religious traditions, however. The religions still need to be *compared* with Christianity and one another. Although many schemes of comparative categories have been proposed, mostly from the perspective of Christianity, none has won much scholarly acceptance as subtle and fair. All likely have some validity, but also bias. The scholarly world has much work to do if it is to identify the respects in which religions can be compared and begin to ask the relevant questions: in what do the religions agree? Disagree? Are they even about the same things? Is there a universal reality to the Ultimate? The human condition? Salvation? We are only beginning to ask these questions in ways that do not bias the answers toward one religion or another.

The reason for the difficulty of this task is not only that scholars exhibit the biases of their own culture. The reason lies in the very logic of interpretation. To interpret an object is to construe some ideas to represent it in certain respects. The respects in which those ideas can interpret the object depend on the semiotic systems within which the ideas lie as well as on the interpretive context and purposes of the interpreters. Each religious tradition has not only a semiotic system and a set of purposive practices, but also a long cross-cultural history developing that perspective. The perspective itself is alive and in process of translation to new situations. The historically developed perspective of Christianity, as contextually diverse and dynamic as it is, interprets reality in the specific respects that are lifted up by its symbols and practices. Christianity does not register those aspects of reality that cannot be represented in its symbols or admitted to its practices, except insofar as Christianity corrects itself to register reality in a new respect. The same thing is true for the other religions. Each is a complex cultural perspective on reality that registers some things and not others, as we have learned from the fact that we learn new things not previously registered.[16]

The logical problem is this. Diverse as it might be, a religious tradition is likely to be unaware of the respects in which its perspective engages reality because all of its thinking is within that perspective. Only by comparison with other traditions, with other perspectives, which seem to pick up other aspects of reality, by means of different semiotic systems, and with the interests of different practices, is it possible to identify the respects of interpretation and engagement that define a given religion's claims to truth. Without the awareness of other great religious traditions with alternative complicated developmental histories of engagement, a religion can hardly escape the assumption that the respects in which it interprets reality are the only ones there are. Therefore it is unaware of some of the most important qualifications of its own claims to truth.

The result of this innocence, in Christianity at least, has been deep confusion over what is meant literally and what metaphorically. In what sense is Christianity in a particular context committed to the claim that God is personal, or the creator of all finite things including personality, or a metaphysical ultimate such as the Act of Esse? To sort these questions, we must determine in what respects the historically evolved Christian symbols and claims interpret their real objects. Perhaps those different "names" for God interpret God in different respects. Or perhaps they contradict one another. Or supplement one another. To grasp the respects in which the collective and internally diverse truth claims of Christianity interpret reality, it is necessary to understand them in comparison with the other religions and the specific selectivity in their own perspectives.

Beyond any one religion, beyond the disjunctive participation in several of them, only a cross-cultural comparative perspective can lift up the diverse respects in which the historical traditions, context by context, interpret their objects. Only then can we begin to ask whether there is one ultimate reality and many paths leading to it or whether the religions are merely about different things, or some combination of the two. The process of cross-cultural comparison itself is what provides an improved language, a partly new semiotic system, that allows the articulation of the different respects in which the different religions might claim to be true of reality. Without a subtle cross-cultural comparative perspective, developed through steady scholarship, interfaith dialogue, and cooperative tussling with the translation of all the religions into forms that address current issues, we cannot identify and analyze the different respects in which the historically different semiotic systems and cultures of practice interpret reality. And if that cannot be done by comparison among the great traditions, then such consciousness cannot be brought to qualify the truth claims of even one tradition such as Christianity.

My argument therefore is that the very meaning of the central truth claims of Christianity requires that Christianity be understood in a cross-cultural context that compares it with other religions. The encounter with those other religions requires that Christianity check its truth claims with what those other religions claim to know and this in turn requires the specification of the various respects in which the different, historically evolved traditions interpret reality. To put the point another way, in a pluralistic situation, Christianity needs to make the case for its truth claims to every perspective that has an interest in the outcome of the inquiry. Precisely because religious inquiry is imbedded in the concrete histories of belief and practice, evolving through cross-cultural translations, no religion on its own provides the terms for making its case to the other religions. Rather, a new language translating the religions to one another needs to be cultivated.

Thinkers such as Karl Jaspers argued that the Axial Age religions were sharply innovative by virtue of conceiving the cosmos as a whole, its ground as one, and individuals as defined relative to that ground rather than exclusively in terms of local conditions. So, Jesus could say that only God is his father and that all people are his sisters and brothers. Perhaps we are entering another axis in history in which we recognize that even those universal ideas are themselves interpretations that have historically conditioned respects in which they represent reality. The plurality of trajectories of religious belief and practice is not a scandal relative to an alleged neutral truth but rather a blessing of different interpretive approaches, each of which lifts up aspects of reality obscured by others. This is not a challenge to the truth of Christianity, but a clarification of it. The challenge to Christianity would come if its particular place in cross-cultural perspective were ignored.

FOUR

How to Read Scriptures for Religious Truth

THE QUESTION OF how to read scriptures for religious truth is a subset of the larger issue of finding truth about the real world of ultimate things in theology.[1] Because of the authority of scriptures, however, it is perhaps the most important subset. Buddhism, Hinduism, Confucianism, Daoism, Judaism, Christianity, and Islam all have scriptures from which they have derived religious truth claims over the centuries. Their scriptural texts are mostly different from one another, although there is some sharing. They have different kinds of authority and the kinds of authority are disputed and altered within each tradition's own history. Judaism, Christianity, and Islam share some scriptures, but each takes a different line of interpretation and understanding of authority; the same is true of Confucianism and Daoism. Hinduisms affirm the Vedic scriptures that the Buddhists define themselves as rejecting. Confucianism, Daoism, and Chinese Buddhism learn from one another's scriptures although Buddhism was viewed by the others as a foreign religion in China and therefore not authoritative. Despite this diversity, I shall argue that there are common issues in reading scriptures for religious truth.

Recent historical criticism (of the last three centuries, "recent" in the time-scale of the great religions) has obscured the question of how to read scriptures for religious truth. That criticism attempts to get behind the ways subsequent generations interpreted the scripture to the analysis of the historical composition of the scriptures and of what they meant in their original context. Then historical criticism studies how successive generations interpreted the scriptures in their contexts, historically understood. From this we get a story about how scriptures have been read in various contexts that comes down to the modern era in which the scriptures are read as historical documents. Many of our contemporaries continue to read scripture in "believing" ways, not as history but as true in some sense.

What most modern historical criticism fails to understand is how anyone ever could have found religious truth in their tradition's scriptures. Historical criticism can say why social or cultural conditions, or perhaps psychological ones, explain why people prefer this or that reading of scripture. This argument too often is reductive and circular: the reading derives from the conditions. Why not say that people adapt their reading to their conditions? That is the way the practice of reading scripture for religious truth seems to the readers, particularly in novel or threatening conditions.

My argument here has three main parts. First I will give an interpretation of what goes on in reading scripture for religious truth: scriptures are a means of engaging religious realities. Second I will make some observations on why scriptures are so hard to read for truth at an historical distance. Finally I will make some suggestion concerning what to do about that for those who are interested in scriptural truth.

SCRIPTURES FOR ENGAGEMENT

No matter what theologians, historians, sages, commentators, religious virtuosi and adepts, or the texts themselves say about the origin and authority of the scriptures of their religious group, scriptures shape the way religious people engage ultimate matters. In theistic religions, scriptures shape the way the people engage God, the religious dimensions of the human condition, and matters of piety. Other things besides scripture also shape engagement of the ultimate, including commentarial traditions, legal traditions, teaching authorities, religious leaders in various capacities, and important historical events taking place after the scriptures' composition and reception. Religions differ in the weight given to these and other factors that shape engagement. Yet scriptures have a kind of primacy in that most of the other factors include a reading of the scriptures to give themselves authority, even when two commentarial traditions or two religious leaders are in direct contradiction with each other. This is as true for the anti-authoritarian and anti-revelational Confucian tradition (whose primary genre of religious thought is commentary) as it is for the classical Vedic or the revelational Jewish, Christian, and Islamic traditions. Scriptures shape not only engagement with ultimate matters but also most of the other factors that also shape engagement with ultimate matters.

What does "engagement" mean? The two previous chapters sketched a pragmatic theory of engagement that will be elaborated further in subsequent chapters. The theory of engagement has two "moments." One is to determine whether and how the religious symbols, scriptures in this case, do engage interpreters with ultimate reality. The other is whether they do so truly.

"Ultimate reality" is particularly difficult to engage. What most religions take to be "ultimate" came to human attention during the Axial Age, as

Jaspers argued.[2] During that time cultural traditions in East Asia, South Asia, and West Asia, as well as Northern Africa, acquired conceptions of the cosmos as a whole, of some ultimate creator, ground, or Dao of the cosmos, and of human individuality that is defined by relations to that ultimate in addition to relations to kin, place, and nation. Confucianism, Daoism, Buddhism, Hinduism, Zoroastrianism, Judaism, and Greek philosophic religions all developed such conceptions; Christianity and Islam built upon them later. Among themselves and within themselves, those religions have different conceptions of the cosmos, its ultimate ground, and human individuality as defined by ultimate relations. Yet the important vague universal truth is that they all have conceptions defining ultimacy relative to the world and individuals, and these conceptions are embodied in their scriptures.

What does it mean to engage ultimate matters? Like engaging the road with a shifting complex of interpretations with driving signs, engaging ultimate matters is the ways by which people live before the ultimate as their religious symbols conceive the matter. Religious traditions are organized ways of life embodying, as habits, the religions' signs for ultimate matters. For instance, in ancient Israel life was understood to be lived "under obligation" given by God, creator of the cosmos. How one responds to such "ultimate" obligation defines one's worth as an individual, and one's group's worth before God. For the Israelites and their Jewish successors, the ultimate obligation was mainly laid out in the Torah, along with the story that gave it meaning. Much of the pattern of living so as to be engaged with God consisted in following the commandments and ritual life described in Leviticus and elsewhere. The commentarial tradition in Judaism spelled out the obligations in new circumstances, and this was doubly mediated because much of the commentary about ultimate matters was in terms of life in the Temple after the Temple had been destroyed and most observant Jews lived in the Diaspora. Christianity kept the sense of obligation but gave it new interpretations; Jesus was taken to be a new supplementary revelation regarding its content, and some of the old obligations were set aside. The rituals, such as that of the atonement, were given a new cosmic interpretation with Jesus symbolized as both high priest and sacrificial lamb. Islam was born of Judaism and Christianity, strengthening the sense that people are created to live under obligation, as spelled out in the Qur'an, and sharpened by an intense prohibition of idolatry.[3]

The patterns of daily and annual ritual life in all three religions are a curious mixture of moral and conventional obligations, truly puzzling to the Enlightenment mind. All three Abrahamic religions strongly emphasize the moral virtues of love, justice and mercy, virtues believed to be divine as well as well as binding on human beings. At the same time some of the ritual *patterns* are taken to be binding on a special religious community and not to be expected of those in other communities who have different patterns of reverencing God and behaving with love, justice, and mercy. Contrary to Enlightenment sensibilities, the point of the obligations is not to sift the moral from the conventional but to constitute communal and individual ways or patterns of life for living so as to be rightly engaged with the ultimate. The Confucian sense of ritual, especially as developed by Xunzi, is an excellent way of understanding this point about patterned ways of life that engage the ultimate.[4]

What is the religious truth in scriptures, over and above the bare fact of engagement? It is the capacity of scriptures to engage people in ways that carry over what is important in the ultimate realities. Of course religions differ theologically about what the ultimate matters are, about the nature of God, and so forth. Also, the question is very complex of how to tell when an existential interpretation of ultimate matters by means of particular symbols is true, a point elaborated in the previous chapter and to which I shall return. The contextual aspects of being able to tell what is true or false are extraordinarily complex.

Truth itself obtains when what is important in the object interpreted is carried over into the interpreting subjects in the respects in which the signs or symbols stand for the objects, as argued in earlier chapters. Truth is an interpretive carryover of value, as qualified by the biology, culture, semiotics, and purposes of the interpreters. Religious truth is the carryover of what is important in ultimate matters—God, salvation, faithfulness, etc. in the monotheistic traditions—into patterns and decisions of life that engage the ultimate. Patterns of life can engage ultimate matters but not be true, as the feminists remind us of traditional patriarchy, or history reminds us of the religious elements of Nazism. Paul Tillich called false religious engagements demonic.

If the claim be accepted, that the religious truth of scripture is a matter of symbolic engagement, we can dismiss a number of false leads about that in which the religious truth of scripture consists. For instance, in many scriptures, particularly in the biblical traditions, much purports to be history. Is its religious truth refuted if the history is shown to be false? Not necessarily, because living with that history, identifying with it (even though it is false as history), might engage one truly with ultimate matters. Consider the early Christians. The first Jewish Christians took Jesus' life and teachings to be a purification of their own Second Temple Judaism. The first Gentile Christians (the majority of Christians, apparently, within twenty years) adopted the history of Israel as described in the Septuagint as their own. But they knew full well that their own history was a pagan one, and they used their adopted history to come to terms with that, not caring to purify Judaism. If that historical appropriation helped make them into good Christians following the pattern of love in communities as advocated by Jesus (say, according to the Farewell Discourse in John's Gospel), then it was in that respect true even if the history was not really theirs and if it was historically false. Or consider the laws attributed to Moses that presuppose a temple versus those that suppose the Israelites are still in the wilderness. If the rabbis can work out a plan to live with both formulations before God, does it matter which Moses really handed down, or whether he was in historical fact the source of any? Jewish life takes the laws attributed to Moses to be symbols for how to engage God faithfully as Jews.

The point about accurate history not being the heart of the religious truth of scripture can be applied to the scriptural passages that seem like science. The texts that present God as creator of the cosmos, with the proper engagement that follows from that, do not depend on the details in Genesis of the creation. That religious truth is a matter of symbolic engagement also means that the legendary stories, say in the Vedas, do not have to be descriptively true, true in a mapping sense, for them to be existentially true, pointing people in the right direction so that what is important about ultimate matters is carried across into their way of living before the ultimate. Even the didactic elements of scriptures, as predominate in some Buddhist scriptures, and in Daoism and Confucianism, need not be descriptively true to be existentially true.

The semiotic point in play here is the distinction Peirce drew between the two elements of reference, which he called the iconic and the indexical, discussed in the previous chapter. Iconic reference works by saying that the object referred to is *like* what the interpretive symbols say it is, a kind of mapping, a carryover of form. A description or a theory is mainly a complicated icon. Indexical reference works like a pointing finger to get the interpreter to look in a different direction; it effects a change in the interpreter to establish something like a causal connection to put the interpreter in a better position to grasp what is important in the object to which reference is made. Most religious symbols have a heavy weight of indexical reference. Many of them require years of being meditated upon for them to effect the change and maturation in interpreters so that they can appreciate their deeper meanings, i.e., receive the value the symbols would carry across from the ultimate realities they interpret. Symbols in prayer are particularly like this, functioning indexically to transform the pray-er rather than to communicate to God a wish list. My point is that reading scriptures for religious truth needs to be particularly sensitive to the indexical dimension of scriptures, not merely the iconic.

IMAGINATIVE DIFFERENCES

The above defense of an interpretive theology of symbolic engagement has not yet faced the hardest issue for reading scriptures for religious truth, namely, the vast difference between the imaginative world of the centuries in which the classic scriptures were written and the imaginative world of our own time. By "imaginative world" I mean the operative interpretive assumptions that form the cultural background within which conscious interpretations and decisions are made and within which intentional life is lived. Immanuel Kant pointed out that imagination is the causal synthesis that allows experience to have its shape. Without imagination, the human organism is conditioned by its environment, bombarded with pushes and pulls, and stimulated according to the physics and chemistry of its nervous system. Imagination is the synthesizing of those otherwise merely biological actions and reactions into the stuff of experience.[5] Imagination has extraordinarily complex layers of development, beginning with the bio-psychic dance of physiological reactions we take to have significance, for instance, hunger pangs. Semiotics in the largest sense is the logical and causal structure of imagination, and of the assertions, theorizing, and practical intentional behavior that constitute experience. The physiological basis of elementary imagination is probably common to all people, who alike get hungry, and see in a bifocal way (not like cattle who look in two different directions or flies who see with multiple facets). Cultures differentially shape what we notice in perception, however, and what different peoples take to be responses to hunger. Semiotic differences among cultures give different senses of space and time, of human friendliness or threat, and of what constitutes the furniture of the world. The religious dimensions of imagination have to do with the boundary conditions of what makes up a culture's sense of the world, the "worldliness of the world" as some philosophers call it after Heidegger. Peter Berger's notion of the "sacred canopy" nicely articulates many aspects of these religious world-defining imaginative conditions.[6] The "imaginative world" of a culture includes much more than the strictly religious elements, being shaped by the arts, by the understanding of history, by world events, and by the variations in world-perspective that a culture tolerates among its various social classes.

The scriptures of antiquity were written against the backgrounds of the ancient imaginative worlds. Their inbuilt assumptions about what things there are and how they work assume one of those imaginative worlds. Of course, the scriptures themselves were mightily powerful in shaping the imaginative world of the culture in which they arose, and also subsequent cultures in which they played some of the roles mentioned above. Nevertheless, the imaginative world of our time is different. Our world has been shaped by modern science, by an encounter of world cultures more complete and complex than anything in history, by global communications such as the internet, and by appreciation of global problems relative to the environment and world economy that could not have been imagined in antiquity. Perhaps modern science is the most pervasive novel influence on our imaginative world because it gives us the sense of how things work, and why. We know scientifically, and have built in to our imaginative backgrounds, that things do not work the way the ancients of any culture thought they did. Nature *is* uniform, and the supernatural cannot be explained as a visitation from another plane with a different nature.

Contemporary religious people have to interpret as symbolic, that is, not literally true, what the ancients did not conceive that way. The more our historical critical methods allow us to understand just what the ancients did assume and believe, the wider the ditch between their imaginative world and ours. The familiar story of the development of hermeneutics in our time addresses these complex disconnections, and connects them with the arts of the hermeneutical circle.

There is a special aspect of the hermeneutical circle to which I want to draw attention, however. On the one hand, Christianity in Western late-modern societies continues its decline in plausibility occasioned by the increasing tension and distance between the imaginative world of modernity and that of antiquity. On the other hand, Christianity outside those societies is growing at a rate that exceeds that of any prior period of Christian expansion. In the several societies of Africa and Asia, and among the nonelites of Latin America, Christianity is proliferating in numbers and in new, non-European, forms of worship, polity, and theology. In those societies, the contemporary imaginative structures are not very distant from that of Christian antiquity. The ancient biblical imagery that late-moderns construe to be supernatural, and therefore problematic, resonates with contemporary supernaturalism, so-called, even when the spirits, divine beings, sacrifices, and other "magical" manipulations are specifically different. Although the Bible with its contemporary witnesses presents a challenging new gospel in these non-modern societies, it does not have the additional plausibility problems in imagination for them that it does for Western late-modern societies.

Nevertheless, the contemporary conditions for global economic, political, and internet communications structures will not leave the now non-modern societies untouched, any more than Western late-modern societies are unchanging. They surely will be drawn into the late-modern imaginative world of science, inter-culturalism, and global ecological alertness. They will not become *Western* late-modern societies because the past cultures from which they grow are not Western, and we must be wary about predicting their coming imaginative structures. We can be reasonably sure, however, that they will have tensions with the imaginative structures of the ancient biblical world at many points analogous to the experience of Western modernity, especially as regards the nature of the physical cosmos, physical and social causation, inter-culturalism, and ecological sensitivities. Christian theology in those emerging Christian cultures will have its analogues to the mediating theologies of Western modernity.

Therefore a central theological task for our time, not only for Western late-modern Christianity but for the plural forms of global Christianity, is to think through the commitments lodged in basic Christian symbols as these are embedded on the one hand in the imaginative world of late antiquity and on the other hand in the emerging imaginative worlds of various forms of late-modernity. (The theologies in other religions have similar problems, and the collective theologies of the world's religions are merely different localities for a common public conversation.)

To understand what the scripture-writers assumed and believed is not to understand the religious meanings of their scriptures, meanings that are religiously significant for us. So it has become the custom of the contemporary religious people among us to interpret the texts symbolically. The tragedy of this is that too often we simply project into the scriptures the symbolic meaning we want to find. Antebellum Christians found in the Hebrew Bible a justification for slavery; black liberationists find in it a song of freedom from slavery and oppression; that same song persuades Zionists of their right to take a land by force to which others seem to have a prior claim. Is there no better way to read scripture for its religious meaning?

STRATEGIES OF SYMBOLIC INTERPRETATION

I suggest three strategies for improved reading of scriptures for religious truth, a comparative strategy, a metaphysical strategy, and a strategy of pragmatic test. If these can be employed together, they can both enhance the depth of our meditative reading of scriptures controlled by the genius of the texts and allow the scriptures to illumine our own religious lives.

The comparative strategy looks a lot like Bultmann's hermeneutics, namely to distinguish the ancient and late-modern cultures and find a common fundamental human issue that the ancient texts addressed in ways no longer possible for us; then we find out how to express the scriptural truth in ways that are possible to us. Actually, it was Spinoza who first suggested the germ of this strategy in his *Tractatus Theologico-Politicus*. The comparative strategy should not be taken too much in Bultmann's mode, however. First, whereas Bultmann thought of the ancient world as primitive and ours as modern, with an historical assumption of progress relating them, I think the comparison of the two cultures with their different cultural imaginations should be simply comparative. Like comparing Islam and Buddhism, the ancient and late-modern cultures in a single tradition ought to be allowed their separate integrities and well as causal connections. Second, the work of finding the common fundamental human issue is harder than Bultmann recognized. For him, the existential philosophy of his time was revelatory to him, and so he hunted for the elements in the Bible that resonated with the existential emphasis on faith, a strategy that was not far from projection from our time to find a symbolic scriptural meaning to our liking.

I propose rather that we search out the common fundamental human issue as we would find a respect in which two religions might be compared. We always have to begin with an hypothesis about some respect in which particular religions are comparable; that "respect of comparison" functions as our working comparative category. And of course that initial hypothesis usually is prejudicial, coming from our favorite religion, as Bultmann's existential categories came from his favorite philosophy. But the work of making comparisons is vulnerable to correction, and the understanding of the respect in which comparisons are being made grows in sophistication along with the understanding of the ways the different religions say or do something in that respect. Although all comparisons, if made responsibly, are hypotheses subject to further correction, the process of making comparisons in the presence of critical colleagues holding different forms of expertise steadies the hypotheses. In collaborative conversation, foolish comparisons are quickly rejected and more subtle formulations are developed to take into account new evidence and to avoid newly discovered bias. In this comparative process, we come to discover precisely what is being compared only as we discover what the comparisons are in that respect. In religions, "just what is being compared" are how the religions address the common fundamental human issues.

In this regard, I propose as a summary hypothesis that the common fundamental human issues fall into four classes and their combinations.

One class has to do with how to embrace our existential situation, our historical moment, our social position, and our personal and interpersonal environment. This was Bultmann's favorite, and we can honor him by calling this the class of issues of *faith*. Instead of denying or attempting to escape our existential situation, Bultmann, Tillich, and others emphasized the courage of will to embrace that situation and deal with it, an act or habit of will that constitutes our existential self.[7] The Confucian decision to become a sage and the Buddhist vow to become a bodhisattva are other rhetorical expressions of this human issue that Bultmann might have taken to heart if he were trained in comparative theology.

The second class of fundamental human issues has to do with finding the right pattern of life, or *justice*. The existentialists were surprisingly silent about problematic issues of justice, both for society and for the organization of individual and interpersonal life, except to say that justice is good; perhaps they thought Kant had solved the basic moral issues. Nevertheless, as we now realize, the issues of justice in an age of global economics and nearly unlimited access to information are baffling. Old tensions between the right to keep what one owns or earns and the obligations of equality of opportunity have extraordinary new manifestations. With religious wars currently in all nations whose name begins with "I," and others, wars based on claims of religiously sanctioned justice, the issues of justice are deep. And they have been addressed in the scriptures of the ancients.

The third class of fundamental human problems is far less obvious than those of faith and justice. I have in mind here a kind of natural *piety* toward the components that make up human society. As components they are organized in higher patterns, the issues of which are justice. Yet they also have an integrity of their own that is often choked by being forced into larger patterns of justice. Some of these are elements of nature—the fields, forests, and beasts that are domesticated and destroyed in their wildness for the sake of human civilization. Others are components of human organization itself—the proud clans whom just civilization prevents from avenging themselves on hereditary enemies, families forced to suffer a diminished domesticity because of the call of clan or nation; individuals prevented from flourishing because of roles they must fulfill in families. Piety is recognizing and deferring to the integrities of things bent into larger patterns of justice. Justice and piety are not easily reconciled. Justice usually sets the terms of the argument, with the result that some issues, for instance many of those in ecology, are represented as justice issues in disguise when really they are matters of piety. Religions generally have moments that transcend and relativize the human perspective that defines justice. The Dao treats all people as straw dogs.[8] In the monotheistic traditions, the creator is equally close to all things, viewing them with a kind of aesthetic disinterest or love for all; piety involves approximating a God's eye view, or the Buddha-mind, or the "Tat tvam asi" principle of the Vedas.

The fourth class of fundamental issues has to do with the religious quest, with finding meaning or value in the cosmos, with finding ways of thinking of oneself and one's group as standing in ultimate perspective. All the other classes of issues have to do with achieving the values of faith, justice, and piety relative to one's conditions. People are also concerned with how these things add up absolutely, ultimate, nonrelatively. Of course our lives are contextual and relative, but does that mean they do not also have some absolute meaning? The religious quest is to find a way of bringing the relativities of life to some kind of nonrelative consummation or judgment. All religions have images of "final judgment," of putting out the flame of samsara. These issues have to do with matters of immanence and transcendence, of effing the ineffable, of finding God. These are the issues of transcendent *hope* for finding finite selves in ultimate perspective.

My comparative hypothesis is that the way to compare religions, and to compare the ancient scriptural culture with late-modern culture within a religion, is to track how they address the issues of faith, justice, piety, and transcendent hope. I have expressed these as if they were separate from one another and, to be sure, they are not. They are intimately bound up with one another, and yet they are often in tension. A further hypothesis worth pursuing is whether the emphasis on *love*, compassion, humaneness or benevolence so common and yet so elusive in religions is not the issue of harmonizing or balancing these obligations in tension.

The comparative strategy is to read our scriptures (whichever they be) and the thinking of our own time to see how both of them, comparatively, address these fundamental human issues of faith, justice, piety, hope, and love. We can learn from scriptures how to think deeply about these things.

The metaphysical strategy should already be apparent. To be responsible for what we assume about ourselves and others we need to develop metaphysical systems that express them, and integrate as best as possible what we know, so that those systems with their assumptions can be made vulnerable to correction. Is existentialism right? At best it is partial. Metaphysics is unpopular these days with people who want to have certainty in their metaphysical principles. Certainty, however, is not worth much. Far better it is simply to engage with the most knowledgeable people from all fields, including metaphysics, and have the best "system" in the room. Tomorrow someone will improve on that, or, alas, forget something important. A metaphysical system makes assumptions vulnerable and allows for taking responsibility for what we know and do not know. Moreover, a metaphysical system makes it possible to understand the differences in metaphysical assumptions between the imaginative world of scripture and our own time.

Metaphysical systems, of course, are hypotheses, vulnerable to correction. Part of my own metaphysical hypothesis is that things are harmonies with existential location, form, components, and achieved value. Although I cannot defend this here, the hypothesis is important with regard to human beings because we can have some control over what we are and become. With regard to existential location, we can embrace it actively or try to flee and deny it; with regard to form we can have the best form in justice, or less than the best; with regard to how we relate to the components of life, we can have proper piety or not; with regard to summary achieved value, we can pursue a perspective on that or not. The four classes of comparative fundamental human issues derive from this part of my metaphysical hypothesis. So they can be criticized by criticizing the metaphysics, and thus made doubly vulnerable. And should the criticism steady down to reinforcing the metaphysical hypothesis, this would lend extraordinary weight to the comparative classification. The point here is not that my metaphysics is right, although of course I think it is the best in the room. The point is that metaphysics allows us to take responsibility for assumptions that control even the way we comparatively relate ourselves to others and to our scriptures. Without metaphysics, we do not notice the large elephant of assumptions in the room.

The strategy of pragmatic test pulls the other strategies together. In reading scriptures for religious meaning we *first* have to be aware of the differences between the scriptures' own imaginative world and that of our own time. We live in our own time—a truism—and need to be faithful to the integrity of the imaginative world insofar as that arises from the best in our knowledge. Of course, our own imaginative world is faulty, behind the times, and filled with prejudices that we should efface as soon as we identify them. Moreover, our imaginative world makes assumptions about what we think we know when we do not. The critical examination of our own imaginative world requires a responsible metaphysics that integrates what we know and elucidates what we do not. Serious metaphysicians have an important role to play in reading scriptures aright for religious truth, namely, to tell us about the truth and limits of the imaginative world that defines our own integrity. Some theologians have argued that we should abandon our own imaginative world and read the events of our lives solely through the terms of the Bible. But this is naïve escapism unless we carefully discriminate the terms of the Bible from the ancient imaginative background that gave them their original significance. If that discrimination can be made, and the terms transferred to our own imaginative world, then it is possible that the Bible's terms can speak to our own authentic existence.

Second, in order to tell whether scriptural terms can be transplanted into the contemporary imagination without escapism, it is necessary to identify the respects in which the scriptural claims, stories, symbols, etc., represented the ultimate in the scriptural imaginative world. Then we can ask whether they can represent the same respects of interpretation in our own imaginative world. Or perhaps they can show us that we need different ways of getting at those respects of interpretation of the ultimate in our lives. Only by tracking comparatively the religious significance of the scriptural texts in their imaginative world relative to the respects of interpreting the ultimate that need to be addressed in ours, can we address the question of the religious relevance of scripture for our time.

CRITERIA FOR READING SCRIPTURES FOR TRUTH

With those two strategic layers as background, it then is possible to ask two questions about the religious meaning of scriptural texts: do they engage people today and, if so, do they carry across what is important in their objects to the interpreters whose lives are patterned by them?

Whether the scriptural texts engage (surely within any large scripture some texts engage far better than others) is an empirical question with at least four parts. The first is determining whether the conditions of contemporary life for our group or an individual include the purposes and contextual values that would make the respects in which the texts interpret the ultimate important. The second is to determine whether the network of symbols in the ancient text can be connected with the symbols that are significant for current life, or improve on those symbols in ways revelatory to us. The third is to understand just how the texts are referring, in what respects their reference is iconic so that we have to believe reality is like what they say, and in what respects their reference is indexical so that it transforms us better to address the reality of their objects. The fourth is to determine the conditions that make some among us ready to engage ultimate matters through the texts. Sometimes people are too young, or are in the wrong state of soul, for texts to be meaningful that should be meaningful in principle according to objective criteria. Sometimes individuals can know perfectly well what a textual passage or symbol is supposed to mean but are alienated from it. All of these are empirical questions that need to be answered contextually for particular people. Whether symbols engage is a function of the people that interpret by means of them as well as a function of the symbolic structures themselves.

The second question is whether the symbols, if they engage, do so truly. If they engage but are not true, they can be demonic. We have so many religions of peace whose scriptures have been read as giving ultimate sanction to rape and pillage against neighbors, oppression of women and minorities, and prejudice and violence against people who are "other," that we should be suspicious in principle of any alleged religious reading of truth. The only way to tell whether the scriptures carry across what in fact is important or valuable in their objects is to see whether those who live by the scriptures embody that in their own lives. Does the way they think and behave express what is important in the objects interpreted by the scriptures they read?

To answer this question, of course, involves partly standing outside the particular interpretive context in question. We have to have some independent source for what is important in the ultimate matters addressed in the scripture. If scriptures were extremely spare, this would be a very difficult matter; but scriptures are complex, and all have been set in very rich interpretive contexts. Readings of Christian scriptures that do not foster communities of love for God and friendship for one another are likely to be false, given the predominance of the theme of divine and human love in the whole of Christian scriptures.

Just as important as getting some independent purchase on what is important in the ultimate objects of reference is getting some independent judgment on the theoretical and practical meaning those scriptures have in the lives of their contemporary interpreters. I have written here of "us" as the contemporary readers of scripture. What we also need is a contemporary expert perspective of discernment on "them," our contemporaries who are reading scriptures. And our contemporaries ought to advise us discerningly. Spiritual discernment is an intimate process, but in the long run an empirical one. On the one hand, reading scriptures is often a deep, inward, soul transforming activity, very difficult to objectify to others. On the other hand, reading scriptures is a community affair with roles for discerners who can be skeptical and critical. In principle, it should be possible for anyone, from any religious tradition, to enter into the reading of the scripture of another tradition by persons from that tradition, judging with discernment whether their reading is true. After all, it is an empirical matter whether the value in the religious object is carried over by the interpreted scripture into the interpreter in the respects in which the scripture interprets its object.

From these considerations several morals can be drawn.

First, uninterpreted scriptures are neither true nor false; only interpretations or "readings" of scriptures are true or false. This has implications for debates about the authority of scriptures.

Second, readings of scriptures are always contextual in the sense that the question of truth is whether what is important in the scriptures' objects is carried across into particular actual interpreters. So the verbal statement of a "reading" that is true in one context might be false in another, or meaningless as nonengaging. A real "reading" is fully contextual.

Third, readings of scripture for religious truth are ineluctably communal or collaborative, because it often takes an outsider to judge whether what seems so compelling in the reading is really the right thing to be carried across into the interpretation. "Collaborative" is better than "communal" because communities can be collectively deceived. "Collaboration" means that readers submit to judgment from people who are more devoted to discerning the truth than to enhancing a communal purpose.

Fourth, reading scriptures for religious truth is a form of religious practice, not merely epistemological pizzazz. On one side religious communities count on and, in varying ways, shape themselves around reading scriptures for religious truth. On the other side, even disinterested scholars reading scriptures become religious in learning to read them, because to read scriptures means engaging the ultimate things to which they refer. The historical critical method of scripture study is wonderful, but not a full reading of the scriptures. Comparative theology requires entering into engagement with ultimate things on all sides of the comparison. Given the contextuality of religious reading, this means entering into various religious contexts, not conducive to innocence.

Fifth, part of the collaborative character of reading the scriptures for religious truth is roles for experts. Not everyone in a community can be expert in the hermeneutics of antiquity, in the critical imagination of the contemporary world, in metaphysics, or in spiritual discernment. Most religious traditions have versions of the extreme view of some sixteenth century Christian Protestants that scriptures can be perfectly well understood by anyone who can read them. If what I have argued here is somewhere near the mark, that is a mistaken view, one set up to foster the worst forms of projection and intolerant otherworldliness. Most religious traditions also have versions of the opposite extreme, that only the elite few, the Brahmins born to the right class, gender, and educational opportunity, understand religious truth while the masses are consigned to controlling myths. In between these extremes lies the truth about reading scriptures. Scriptures are irrelevant if they do not have something for everyone, because they purport to say what is ultimately important, a topic universally relevant. Therefore the extreme elite view is wrong. Scriptures are violently disastrous tools for harnessing ultimate passions to proximate, finite, and biased programs if the discriminations of different imaginative worlds, metaphysical responsibility, and pragmatic tests for carryover are not carried out.

FIVE

Systematic Theology in a Global Public

"RELIGIOUS APOLOGETICS and philosophical argument" names a cluster of intellectual interests that have been pursued together within the Christian tradition at least since Justin Martyr and that has claimed the attention of such great thinkers as Augustine, Thomas Aquinas, and Paul Tillich.[1] Philo in the Jewish tradition predates Justin Martyr, and Maimonides and Hermann Cohen were giants among Jewish apologists. Averroes, Alfarabi, Alghazali, and Avicenna dominated Muslim apologetics in ways that affected the entire Western ecumene. Although these figures are associated with great living religious traditions, religious apologetics and philosophical argument began earlier with the Greeks, for instance Xenophanes, Plato, and Aristotle, who critically examined religious beliefs known to them from several traditions, purifying and defending some by means of philosophic argument.

Religious apologetics and philosophical argument is a helpful characterization of the response of Vedic thinkers to the rise of Buddhism in the 6th century BCE. Buddhism had made a sustained attack on the authority of the Vedas and the conceptual and social organization of Upanisadic learning. "Hinduism" as we know it arose in response with the formation of the "six orthodox schools," Vedanta, Nyaya, Vaisheshika, Samkhya, Yoga, and Purva Mimamsa, the first five of which are paradigmatically philosophical. Hinduism also developed more bhakti forms, for instance relating to the Bhagavad Gita and devoted to the worship of Krishna, Siva, or other deities, all of which had apologetic traditions that debated with the others. In the first millennium of the common era, extraordinarily detailed philosophical apologetic debates took place between various Hindu schools and Buddhists, sometimes presided over by the king.

The Chinese philosophic traditions defined themselves in ancient times in part by explicitly rejecting the anthropomorphic language of popular religions, alleging them to be superstitious or counter-productive to the development of philosophic virtue. In practice, however, both Confucianism and Daoism developed popular forms that sustained continuity with a shamanist primal Chinese religious culture. After the advent of Buddhism in China at the beginning of the first millennium, Daoism developed institutional religious structures with priestly hierarchies, temples, and monasteries. The great Confucian philosopher Xunzi counts as an apologist who used philosophic arguments, as does the Daoist commentator Wangbi. Religious apologetics with philosophical argument reached its high point in China with the Song and Ming dynasty Neo-Confucian projects that reconstituted a Confucian tradition borrowing heavily from Buddhism and Daoism but explicitly rejecting both in special ways.

In the nineteenth and twentieth centuries the religions of South Asia and East Asia engaged in remarkable projects of recovering their traditions and defending them against intellectual, religious, and political domination by West Asian and North American culture. Part of the recovery required internalizing Western thinking. Many Indian intellectuals were educated at the best universities in Great Britain. East Asian intellectuals perhaps had closer ties to German and American universities. The nineteenth century philological projects of Western learning not only introduced the West to the "great books of the East" but stimulated a reappropriation in the Eastern societies of their own heritages, now understood in terms of, and in comparison with, Western philosophy and religion. The defenders of these Eastern religious traditions now are not only apologists with Western philosophic arguments, but also use the reconstituted tools of their own inherited philosophic traditions.

In this chapter I develop a program for religious apologetics and philosophical argument that I claim is worthy to be pursued today in a global context. From the beginning, that cluster of intellectual interests has had two foci. One is to understand a faith on its own terms, to articulate it to its own curious adherents, and to transform the community's own theological self-understanding with the resources of philosophy. The other is to explain the faith to those outside, to defend it as viable and true, and to show how it relates to the others. Sometimes apologetics has been identified more with the second than the first, but in point of fact its primary audience has been those seeking to understand their own faith in a larger context of other religions or, more recently, secular society.

Religious apologetics with philosophical argument ("with" is more pointed than "and") has come to be called "systematic theology" in the Christian tradition. Sometimes "systematic theology" is limited to tidying up a religion's doctrines without dealing with the basic issues that philosophy raises.[2] But more commonly since Hegel, systematic theology has included the full reach of philosophy within it, as in the work of Karl Rahner, John Zizioulis, and Paul Tillich. Therefore, in order to put forward my positive program that does for our time what earlier apologetic movements did for theirs,

I am going to call the enterprise "systematic theology." This program in fact does what apologetics with philosophic argument should do: it promotes the articulation and defense of concrete singular faith within internal and external religious and cultural environments, without alienating or distorting opposing beliefs, and with potential maps for understanding how differing truth claims compare with regard to meaning and veracity.

SYSTEM AND ITS PUBLIC: THREE VALUES

"Systematic theology in a global public" names a program for theology that I advocate and according to which my own theological work proceeds. Systematic thinking itself is not popular these days, and so this program is not for everyone; still, I shall give some reasons shortly for why systematic thinking is desirable. Global thinking is also controversial, associated with globalization that puts local cultures in jeopardy. Many theologians now are lovers of the local and contextual, and so this program might not be for them. I shall give some reasons why contextualized theological truth cannot be maintained with minimal arbitrariness unless set within a more global public, however. Theology itself is not a growth industry among intellectuals. But here is a case for this program.

Three controversial values prompt the program for systematic theology in a global public. First is the value of truth. Although few theologians would say that the truth of their theology is not important, a great many today would say that conformity to a religious community's commitments is more important than truth in any sense that transcends the community. To value truth in theology requires a theory of reference that shows how theological claims either do or do not represent their real objects in the respects in which they interpret them. Chapters 2 and 3 above elaborated the problematic of truth, and no more will be said about that here, though the second and third values depend upon the contested value of truth in theology.

The second value is the minimization of arbitrariness. The historical location of all thinking means that a base-line arbitrariness will always exist. But much theology is more arbitrary that it has to be. A previous generation distinguished general from special revelation. General revelation was thought to be what could be known about theological topics by anyone, based on reason and inquiry in which anyone could participate. Special revelation, by contrast, was thought to depend on specific relations to particular circumstances. The Israelites, for instance, thought their exodus from Egypt was revelatory of God's favor and protection; the Egyptians and Canaanites thought differently. Many Christians have believed that Jesus is revelatory of God to those who embrace him in faith, though not revelatory to those who have a different faith or none at all. Believers in special revelation claim that their revelation is true, but arbitrary. Scholars standing back a step point out that all religions claiming special revelation claim that theirs is the true, albeit arbitrary, revelation.[3] The Enlightenment response to this is to dismiss all theological claims to special revelation as special pleading. A better response is to develop a theory showing how at least some theology is context dependent, that is, true in one context, false or meaningless in another, as argued in chapter 3. With such a theory it would be possible to see how the Exodus would be revelatory to Israelites but a political pain to Egyptians and Canaanites. It would be possible to see how Christians engaging God in faith with the symbols of Jesus would find Jesus revelatory for salvation whereas those who do not engage God with those symbols would find Jesus merely interesting, if that. The values of truth and the minimizing of arbitrariness call for a semiotic theory of theologically important symbols explaining both the dyadic quality of truth—right or wrong—and the contextualized condition for truth—true here but not there. These contextualizing issues were explored in chapter 3 above.

The third value shaping the program of systematic theology in a global public is to make theology vulnerable to correction. Vulnerability seems to be a perverse value to those who want their theology well-grounded, well-entrenched. Theological foundationalism, or fundamentalism, is popular these days, particularly when it is integrated with a theological program that focuses on religious identity first: to be a Jew *means* taking Torah to be the foundation, to be a Christian *means* taking the biblical witness to Jesus Christ to be clear and certain. Foundationalism, however, is under attack now by those who say the foundations need to be interpreted and that interpretation is always vulnerable to correction.[4] Often the foundationalist response is to repeat the appeal to identity, saying that any theology that makes itself vulnerable to correction by further interpretation puts Jewish, Christian, Muslim, Hindu, or Buddhist identity at risk. That response is valid: ongoing vulnerable theological inquiry does indeed put religious identity at risk, as evidenced by the great theological revolutions that have occurred in all religions. The intellectual or theological side of religions is not the only thing that puts their fixed identity at risk, however. The value of making theology vulnerable to correction is what leads systematic theology to seek out a broader public, hunting for those in other religions, in the sciences and the intellectual arts that can correct it. It is also the value that demands system, the best defense against dogmatism.

With these three values sketched, the argument of this chapter becomes clear. Whatever else it does, theology should seek the truth about religious matters. An adequate understanding of truth-seeking in theology acknowledges that theology is hypothetical and historically contextual, and therefore inevitably arbitrary. So theology needs structures that minimize arbitrariness, and these structures involve setting theology in wider and wider contexts. Indeed, the contexts are precisely those that make a theology's mistakes or biases vulnerable to correction. There is no limit to the contexts from which theology might learn. Therefore, theology's public needs to be global, involving all religions, their secular alternatives, and all disciplines that bear upon ultimate matters.

TRUTH AND REALISM

The pragmatic theory of truth and inquiry for theology presented in earlier chapters, and to be discussed in its historical origins in subsequent chapters, is realistic in a philosophical sense, which is to say, anti-idealistic and anti-nominalistic. Three dimensions of realism need to be elucidated: the independence of reality, the generality or habit-character of reality, and the peculiar character of religious reality as ultimate and boundary-marking.

The most efficient pragmatic definition of reality is that it is anything about which one might be mistaken. Another way of putting the point is to say that the real is independent of what anyone thinks of it. It is what it is, regardless of what we think about it. Of course, ideas themselves are real, our thoughts and arguments. But the fact that they are mere thoughts does not mean that we cannot be mistaken when interpreting them. We are often mistaken in memory and in understanding the implications of ideas.

The opposition to the independence dimension of realism is the view that the object of interpretation is always another interpretation. Thus, idealists long have argued that the objects of our ideas are other ideas and that we cannot refer to external things. David Hume was the ultimate idealist when he claimed that we have no "impression" of external reality, so that the very idea of a real world independent of thought is merely a confused or bad idea. The contemporary form of this idealism is the deconstructionist claim that everything is a text, that we interpret interpretations and then further interpret those interpretations of interpretations. In theology this takes the form of the Yale School's suggestion that the object of theological analysis is the grammar of a community, not the objects that seem to be addressed in the community's speech.

A distinction can set aside this alternative rather neatly. Interpretations can be understood extensionally and intentionally. The extensional analysis of an interpretation is to place it within a semiotic system and see how it refers to other elements, for instance, interpretations, within that system. Also, the explication of an interpretation is always in terms of other interpretations within the semiotic system. So long as we are using language, when we say what the "real" objects of an interpretation are, we are using language for that, and the objects seem to be the words used to express them. The intentional analysis of an interpretation, however, treats the whole semiotic system that defines its terms and grammar as a mediating sign that engages the interpreter with the world interpreted. Intentionally, in the real lived experience of an interpreter, the world is engaged by the whole semiotic culture supposed in a given interpretation, like the driving habits that allow us to speed down the highway. To be sure, the interpretation, however understood as intentional, might be mistaken. So, Feuerbach might be right that the reality we think is God is really our ideals for humankind; the realistic question of truth, then, is whether those God-shaped ideas articulate what we really hold as ideal. This illustrates the point made several times now, that the question of engagement and the question of the truth of the engagement should not be conflated. The very idea of truth as contextual, versus truth as merely relative to one's location in a language game, supposes an intentional sense of interpretation. The theology of symbolic engagement is realistic and anti-idealistic, because engagement employs the whole of semiotic extension to mediate the real to interpreters. The causal character of engagement has already been discussed in terms of indexical reference, a topic to which I shall return.

Realism is also anti-nominalistic. Nominalism is the view that the only elements of language that refer are particular names, and that only individuals exist in reality. General traits, or universals, are abstract constructions of the mind, according to nominalism. The pragmatic alternative to nominalism is that general traits or habits are real, and therefore the universals describing them have real reference. In classical pragmatism, realism seemed to follow from scientific discoveries that laws of nature exist. What is real is not merely instances of law-like change, but also the habit or tendency of things to behave in law-like ways. No habit is ever exhausted in actual singular things. Reality contains habits just as much as singular things that illustrate them. Precisely because actual things are singular, they cannot exhaust the whole of reality. Therefore, reality cannot ever be fully encompassed in a "present" actual state. Perhaps the best way to express this is with the language of the medieval realist Duns Scotus. Every present actual thing is a singular "this." But every this has a character consisting of natures that can be had in common with other things, "common natures." Thus, every human being has the dignity and worth of humanity, even those each person is a singular exemplification of humanity. Sometimes the common natures of things are far more important than the singularities that make each thing a "this." Pragmatic inquiry is often less interested in static universals ingredient in reality than in the developing habits of habits taking on new habits, or growth and decay.

The contemporary theological defense of nominalism is not the strict metaphysical claim that only singulars or particular exist and that general traits are mere mental figments. Rather, it is that things can be reduced to their roles within singular narratives. In a narrative, the whole meaning of a thing, or person, is the role it plays in the story. All the other elements of a thing are irrelevant. Hegel was the supreme nominalist in this regard when he claimed that the real is the rational and the rational is the real. For him, reason had a dialectical narrative form, and things were "real" in the sense that they played roles in the unfolding of reason in history. He acknowledged that there were individuals and people who happen to exist who are irrelevant to any stage or episode in the unfolding of the world-history of reason. But because they are irrelevant, they are accidental and they just as well could have not existed. For this reason he called them unreal. This kind of metaphysical narrative, with its atrocious marginalizing of so many people and cultures, inspires the deconstructionists who rail against "master narratives." As I argued earlier, Karl Barth's theology is a master narrative of creation and redemption in Christ. The Buddhists, Hindus, and all the rest not in that story, including women in any but subordinate roles, I fear, are "unreal." Of course the master narrative has to be rejected on behalf of the marginalized and oppressed.

The question is whether that rejection needs to take the form of affirming other narratives. We might say, for instance, that the master narrative of Israel's exodus from Egypt and entrance into the Promised Land should be supplanted by an Egyptian narrative of Israelite ingratitude and theft, or by a Canaanite narrative of a barbarian invasion. Narratives by their very form are attractive simplifications, and much theology thinks it makes progress by telling multiple stories. Nevertheless, narratives, even a multiplicity of narratives are always lies because of what each excludes. Things are grasped by interpretations, and interpretations always address things in the respects in which their signs or symbols refer to those things. Any thing can be interpreted in an indefinite number of respects. What are the important respects in which to interpret them? That is the question. If we always answer by taking importance from some story line, then we systematically build in the bias of that story and systematically obscure those matters that might be very important but that do not fit any clear story. The singularity of people, events, and communities consists of an indefinitely rich array of common natures, not all of which are significant for stories. The God's-eye view of things takes all these into account, not only those that fit some story, or set of stories. Narratives impose meaning and value from the structure of the story-line, distorting the meanings and values things have in themselves as situated in infinitely dense contexts.

The anti-nominalist realism of theology thus should take the form of something like Tillich's sense of system, following out connections wherever they appear, and rejecting any attempt to reduce theological truth to a narrative form, or even a set of narratives. In our own time, of course, we have seen the devastatingly evil consequences of stories that pit the "righteous" against the "unrighteous," with Christians and Muslims differing only in who gets to claim the righteous role.

In a special respect, theological realism needs to deal with the fact that ultimate realities are not ordinary things in the world, but are what I earlier called "finite/infinite contrasts." A finite/infinite contrast is some basic trait of the world, as recognized by a religion, by means of which some world-defining element is established. As a trait, it is finite, that is, determinate. But its religious significance consists in the contrast with what would fail to be if the trait did not exist. If the trait did not exist, the world would be nonfinite or infinite. In West Asian religions, the existence of the world itself is such a basic trait, as reflected in doctrines of divine creation. The contingency of the world is a finite/infinite contrast. That the world has value, that human life has meaning, that myths of origin define a people, that the character of things has a rationality that can be comprehended, that the world has both diversity and unity—many different traits from the general to the highly specific are invested with religious meaning because they are world-defining for people in some religion or other. In this sense of world-defining, finite/infinite contrasts are ultimate or have some dimension of ultimacy.

Realism with respect to religious dimensions of ultimacy in finite/infinite contrasts requires a rather common dialectical stance in theology, a peculiar combination of kataphatic and apophatic affirmation. One the one hand, the finite side of the contrast is kataphatically asserted. On the other hand, its religious significance must call to mind what would be the case were that trait to be nonexistent, the infinite side; the apophatic moment in all references to finite/infinite contrasts is a kind of "what if it were not so?" The apophatic glance out of the corner of the eye bespeaks the *mysterium tremendum et fascinans* of ultimacy in things. A stronger sense of apophatic theology exists, to be sure, namely, the positive denial that the finite side expresses the infinite, an attempt to transcend any finite characterization of the divine. As Duns Scotus pointed out, however, any fundamental denial or negation rests on some positive affirmation, and the mystical theologies that attempt to transcend all finite expressions do so because of the peculiar dialectic of kataphasis and apophasis in finite/infinite contrasts.

MINIMIZING ARBITRARINESS

The value of minimizing arbitrariness is usually pursued by standing back to take a larger look, setting the arbitrary theological claim in a context in which it not so arbitrary. Some theological symbols are extremely metaphorical, fantastical, and plain false from a purely iconic standpoint, yet might be true from an indexical standpoint in the right context for the right secondary-referent interpreters. Other theological symbols are those used to make just that point—to explain how the metaphors might be true when literally false, how some people are ready to use them and others not, how some get what is true through them and others get what is false. In fact, theology has many levels of discourse beginning with those involved in religious practice and moving to the abstractions of metaphysics. A standard strategy to minimize arbitrariness is to treat the allegedly arbitrary theology from a meta-level. I want briefly here to indicate four levels of intentionality in theological discourse. This is a rough schematic list, and anyone could break it down into a much more refined set of distinctions.

The first level of theological intentionality is pre-reflective and pre-critical, consisting of the select, historically developed primary sets of tradition-shaping symbols, such as those in different religions' ancient canons of scripture. Buddhist symbols, for instance, are largely different from Muslim ones. Jewish, Christian, and Muslim traditions share some symbols, but these have somewhat different meanings in each of the traditions by virtue of meaning-connections with other symbols that are not shared. Cross-cultural comparative theology begins by sorting similarities and differences at this first level of theological intentionality; history of religions works at explaining how each got to be the way it is. To call this level pre-reflective does not suggest that the events and persons who generated and developed the symbols were not reflective; indeed, those founding symbolizations often took form in classic self-reflective texts. It is only to suggest that, once founded, communities operate within the assumptions carried by the symbols, often without reflecting on the symbols as such. So, Buddhists think in Buddhist symbols mainly, and Muslims think in Muslim symbols mainly; they become self-conscious about the differences between the symbol systems only when a comparative moment arises. The somewhat pre-reflective level of theological claims serves as an imaginative reservoir or environment within which higher-level claims are made. Claims on this first level are in the form of assumptions about reality carried in the symbol systems that people use, often without consciously asserting the claims.

The second level of theological intentionality consists of explicit claims about religious realities that use those first-level symbols, and perhaps others, to make specific points. The six orthodox schools of Hinduism, to take an example, all agree on the revelatory validity of the Vedas, but sometime disagree quite pointedly about what the Vedas reveal, as disputed, for instance, in the case of the dualism of Yoga versus the non-dualism of Advaita Vedanta. Claims at this second level involve a denial of some counter claim. Disagreements at the secondary level might be framed relative to the same first-level context, as competing Hinduisms all claim the Vedas. Where awareness exists of different possible primary contexts—a Yogin who knows about Islam, for instance—the secondary claim means to be true without limitation to its primary context of origin. It aims to be true of a reality, and if some other symbol system seems to be registering that reality, the truth of the claim needs to be negotiated through comparative study. Theological claims at the second level are intended to be true of their objects, not merely what people say within a given community shaped by a set of pre-reflective symbols.

The third level of theological intentionality consists in the rules within an interpretive tradition that set the limits as to what counts as a valid claim within the tradition. George Lindbeck has argued that formulated doctrines are not so much about the realities they purport to be about but rather are rules for determining what can be said about those realities. For instance, the patristic Christian doctrine of the "two natures of Christ" is not so much about Christ (in fact it is a flat contradiction) as it is a rule that says that no theological claim should deny the divinity of Christ nor should any theological claim deny the humanity of Christ. From this Lindbeck and others liken theology more to cultural anthropology than to philosophy, as mentioned earlier. Theology is mainly the study of the rules of intellectual and practical behavior that are observed by a particular community and that constitute its "orthodoxy." Christian theology is really Christian self-description of the community's deep structure of intellectual commitment in theological matters, and of the practice that flows from this. Buddhist theology would be self-description of the Buddhist community, and so forth. The question of theological truth at this level of intentionality can be raised only internally with each community, and it consists in whether a particular claim is within the rules that define orthodoxy for that community, never a matter of apparently conflicting claims between communities. This third level of theological intentionality is the main thrust of confessional theologians, those who speak for specific communities, perhaps witnessing to their first level selection of pre-reflective symbols, articulating second level claims, and then justifying them as being authentic to the rules of the community. Nearly all religious traditions have "confessional theologians" in this sense.

The third level of theological intentionality is inherently unstable, however. It assumes that communities are fairly tight cultural-linguistic systems, to use Lindbeck's term, with clear boundaries. In point of historical fact, religious communities have permeable boundaries. They often borrow from one another. In our situation many individuals have multiple religious identities in the sense of belonging to several communities. And very often, serious inquiry into claims at the second level of theological intentionality lead individuals to distance themselves intellectually from the communities to which they are committed in practice, thence to urge the communities to change their deep structure rules for what counts as acceptable. When communities do not change in the face of strong evidence, people leave to start new communities with the underlying grammatical rules modified so as to include some second level claims previously ruled out by the third level rules. The question of truth is thus pushed back up to the third level, asking how a community's rules for orthodoxy should be affirmed or modified in order to get at the truth for theology and practice. The constant shifting of communal identity, and of individuals' intellectual participation in that community, are far more common in our situation than the state of affairs where communal boundaries and grammar are fixed, constantly recognized, and people know just where they belong. In light of this, the third-level concern for fixing the doctrines as rules for orthodoxy, when disconnected from second-level inquiry into the truth of religious claims, should be interpreted as the politics of factions, the efforts of some group to draw lines to exclude others.

The fourth level of theological intentionality operates in the real historical context that includes not only the other levels but also the movement among them, letting concerns for the truth of claims raise questions about the adequacy of the primary pre-reflective symbol base as well as about the probity of the third-level doctrinal authorities. The fourth level is where the case is made for theological positions *all things considered*. Encounters among different cultural systems often raise new questions at the secondary level of theological claims and further questions for the self-descriptions of the religious communities. Theological inquiry at this fourth level includes consideration of the philosophy, sciences, arts, comparative studies, history of religions, and methodological and theoretical concerns about the nature of religion itself that allow for the understanding and assessment of claims at the other levels. Systematic theology is in this fourth context. The global public for theology is not free-floating but is itself a particular context whose shape comes from where the discussion stands on all the elements in the fourth context. Following Plato, this fourth level can be called a *dialectical* theological intentionality.

VULNERABILITY IN A GLOBAL PUBLIC

The value of making theology vulnerable to correction is best pursued in two ways. The first is to engage as large a public as possible, indeed a global public. The second is to present theology as systematically as possible so that all angles of criticism might be exposed.

Concerning the public for theology, the main principle is to be able to make a case for a theological position to any who might be interested or have something critical from which theology might learn. A theological position ought to be able to engage theologies from other relevant religious traditions. If theology were to remain internal to a confessional community, it would be hard to claim that it is more than sociology or cultural anthropology, as Lindbeck would say: Christian theology is what Christians believe, Buddhist theology what Buddhists believe, and so forth. The creation of a global interfaith theological discourse requires at least three steps. First is a theological paideia in which theologians learn the core texts and motifs of thought of all the religious traditions involved. Theological education justifiably should be more complicated than it is.[5] Second, serious comparative work remains to be done relating the theological concepts of the various religious traditions. Comparative categories need to be developed and tested within the scholarly community that reveal what is important in the traditions and how the basic symbols in each deal with that, detailing similarities and differences. Moreover, the comparative work needs to be at all the levels of theological intentionality: basic symbol systems used pre-reflectively, specific theological assertions, normative rules for community orthodoxy, and dialectical intentionality. Third, actual dialogue needs to take place among theological representatives of the religious traditions to establish new language for making the connections. This process inevitably will augment the theological languages spoken within the separate religious communities.[6]

In addition to comparative theology, a global public for theology needs to embrace the dialogues between religions and their secular cultures. These dialogues have been underway for three centuries in the West, manifest recently in the brilliant work of Paul Tillich. Each of the world's traditions exists within an ambient secular context, however, shaped by different cultural ways of responding to European modernity. Global secularism is more plural than North Atlantic secularism, and needs to be engaged theologically.

A global public for theology needs also to include the sciences. Interactions between Western religions and science marked the heyday of modern European philosophy from Descartes through Whitehead. Physical conceptions of the universe have changed greatly in the last few years, however, and the scientific challenges to religious conceptions need to be related to non-Western religious traditions. Developments in biology and ecology have brought new challenges to theological thinking. Instead of seeing science as presenting threats to theological convictions, in a global public they first should be seen as resources for improving theology.

Theology has learned from and informed the arts at many times in the histories of religious traditions, and continues to do so today in some quarters. Nevertheless, with the professionalizing of theology in the last few centuries to make it a self-contained discipline, and with the defensiveness of Christian communities against a growing secular culture that claims the artistic community, theology and the world of art have often lost touch. Art deals with deliberate imagination, the base of religious symbolism. Criticism of the imaginative arts is a second-order reflection. Both need to be enlisted in a theological public so that theology might be vulnerable to learn from them.

The creation of a genuinely global public so that theology is a discourse that makes its cases with regard to all religions, secular learning, the sciences, and the arts is an historically contingent process marked by particular successes and failures. As historical, the development of the public is always arbitrary. Nevertheless, within a genuinely global public, no noticed arbitrariness needs to go unchallenged.

Concerning system in theology, the point is not to present a textbook of complete answers to theological questions. Rather, the point is to guard against arbitrariness and to be vulnerable to correction from all possible angles. Hence, systematic theology is the development of theological views from as many angles as possible. The constructive part of system building is the creation of perspectives for questioning that themselves can be questioned. The standard criteria for system—consistency, coherence, adequacy, and applicability—help shape systematic structure.[7] Another shaping element is that theological ideas need to be articulated, interpreted, and justified on all four levels of theological intentionality. That is, they need to be analyzed in terms of how they shape the imaginative assumptions of pre-reflective thought and religious practice in the relevant communities; they need to be analyzed and criticized as truth claims themselves; they need to be analyzed as they provide identity for religious communities, life within which internalizes the theological notions into true subjectivity; and they need to be carefully formulated as summary hypotheses that dialectically integrate all the levels of intentionality. Moreover, the theologically relevant sciences and arts have analogues to the intentionality levels of basic assumptions, explicit claims, communal definitions of orthodoxy, and dialectical integration, all of which should be made explicit in the theology that draws upon them.

The form of a theological system needs to be properly determinate so as to be vulnerable to correction. Perhaps many forms would accomplish this. Nevertheless, at least these four elements should be in it: dialectical argument and theory, evidentiary illustrations, discussion of historical counter-claims, and explicit summary truth assessments. All four should be hypothetical in mode, well-tested but still fallible for further correction.

Dialectical argument and theory. At the head of a systematic theology, and at the head of each major topic or question, should be the statement of a summary hypothesis, a theory. The theory needs to be clear about what the alternative hypotheses are, in which respects the theory interprets the subject, and why those respects are the fundamental ones for the topic. In order to do this, the statement of the theory needs to be dialectical in the sense of laying out the alternatives and justifying the interpretations of meaning, reference, and context involved.

Evidentiary illustrations. The next kind of hypothesis in a systematic theology in a global context is the illustration of the main features of the theory from the various domains of reference and from at least the four levels of theological intentionality. The theory and the subcategories making it up should be treated as vague categories to be specified by evidence.

When the evidence comes from religion, the global theological public dictates that the categories be vague comparative ones, with careful attention paid to how the religions differently specify them, or fail to specify them. Evidence from the sciences needs to be sorted as to how it confirms or contradicts, or fails to engage, what the formal theory says about the ultimate. Similarly the deliverances of the arts and normative discourses need to be related as potential specifications to the terms of the formal theory.

Historical counter-claims. The two kinds of hypothesis just discussed, the theoretical and the evidentiary, constitute a continuous project. Although the two kinds of hypotheses are generated to correct one another, the aim is for them to work together and to attain stability through being made vulnerable and subjected to criticism in the global public. Any such continuous project has alternatives, and the alternative hypotheses might have dialectical arguments of their own concerning different ways of taking all the evidence as illustrative. Although the alternatives might well have been considered in the project's dialectic, they also need to be set alongside the project as competitors that have their own way of representing the hypothesis being defended.

Summary truth assessment. Because theology at all levels is interpretive and hypothetical, its systematic presentation calls for a summary assessment of its truth-value. The assessments summarized would include judgments such as that the formal hypotheses are too influenced by Western modes of thought despite efforts to gain balance and authority, that the evidence treated comes in more nuanced form from Buddhism than from other religions, that the issues raised by physics are well treated but those raised by biology are given short shrift, that the discussion is enriched by the visual arts more than the musical arts, and so forth. Because of the historical location of any theology, it will have strengths and weaknesses, and is stronger for being explicit about its weaknesses. The summary truth assessment tries to put the strengths and weaknesses in balance compared with the same for other alternative hypotheses. The point of a summary truth assessment is to stimulate further theological work.

The pragmatic vision of systematic theology in a global public that I have urged is daunting, and will not be attractive to many. Perhaps its least attractive feature is that, despite its systematic character, a theological system is never finished. But its most attractive feature is that it is the best bet we have for getting at the truth in theological matters. If a theology developed according to this project is mistaken in any particular, or even its main thrusts, this can be found out and corrected. Being corrected when mistaken is the greatest blessing that can befall a theology.

PART II

Realism in Pragmatism

SIX

A Peircean Theory of Religious Interpretation

ENGAGEMENT AND REFERENCE

THE PRINCIPAL DISTINGUISHING characteristic of Charles S. Peirce's semiotics or theory of interpretation is its claim that interpretation is the way by which people engage the world.[1] The more usual approach to semiotics is to say that it is the way by which people engage texts. This has been the claim from Spinoza and Schleiermacher through Saussure and Derrida. The connection of semiotics, hermeneutics, or interpretation-theory with religion comes historically from the fact that the main text to be interpreted is often the Bible. Peirce's paradigm of interpretation, by contrast, is experimental science, epitomized in the laboratory but generalized to mean an engagement with nature (Americans, the frontier, and all that) and indeed the long natural-historical engagement of the evolutionary process.

Roughly put, for Peirce the form of an interpretation is an hypothesis about the real relative to the interest of the interpreter that is disconfirmed, reinforced, or corrected somewhat when the interpretation is put into play. Or to put the point from the opposite point of view, all human interactions with nature involving any kind of human response are shaped by interpretations, from the most passive perceptions to the most aggressive actions. In his famous early papers on "The Fixation of Belief" and "How to Make Our Ideas Clear," Peirce argued that the best if not only way to improve our ideas about things is to put them in the way of being corrected if they are wrong, as a scientist does.[2]

Peirce was a speculative metaphysician of very great originality and power, and extended his semiotics beyond the usual scale of interpretation-theory. For instance, he argued that the human self is not an entity that uses signs or makes interpretations but is itself a living sign whose reality consists in interpreting.[3]

Moreover, he argued that all physical and other causal processes can be analyzed according to the developmental structure of interpretation. Material causation he regarded as "frozen mind" and the line between that and "psychical" or "mental" causation is not sharp.[4] He generalized the main categories of his theory of interpretation into phenomenological categories with which he constructed an entire evolutionary cosmology. These are his famous categories of firstness, secondness, and thirdness, related so as to give rise to synechism (continuity), tychism (chance), and agapism (evolutionary love or development).[5] These fascinating parts of Peirce's philosophy are not to our direct interest here except to note that they go a long way toward making good on his claim that interpretation is engagement with the world; bodily processes metabolizing the world are as much interpretations as are flights of fantasy and directed intellectual inquiries. Peirce's general claim that interpretation is engagement was taken up in many diverse and fruitful ways by Dewey who called it "transaction" in his early writing and "interaction" in the later.[6]

The most pertinent point of Peirce's semiotics for the claim about engagement is his theory of reference. Peirce argued that semiotics has three main topics: meanings and meaning systems (which he called signs), reference or how the signs stand for their objects in interpretation, and the interpretation itself in which signs are actually taken to stand for objects in the concrete context of the interpreters.[7] Engagement has first to do with how the interpreters' signs relate to their real objects.

Reference has three main kinds, according to Peirce. The simplest reference is iconicity in which a sign or set of signs is taken as an icon of the world.[8] Or rather, in an interpretation, the world is taken to be like the iconic sign. In an icon there is some kind of mirroring or iconic mapping of the object. This was the only kind of reference admitted by Wittgenstein in the *Tractatus*, and everything else which he believed to be real was mystical and should be treated with non-reference (silence).[9] In religious symbols, an icon might be a crucifix referring to Jesus' crucifixion, Peirce's example. But his idea has much greater generalizability. A religious mythic world is taken to be iconic of reality. In mythopoeic times, no distinction between the myth and the reality is recognized. In Axial Age religions, however, such a distinction is recognized and problematized. This is not the place to dissect the many levels of myth in human culture. But at very deep levels it structures elementary imagination about the size, shape, age, and contents of the cosmos, as well as basic causal patterns. The distinction between biblical and late-modern imaginations made earlier can now be called a distinction between basic myths, and the religious conflict between those two imaginations can be recognized to be a clash of mythologies. It does not matter that we late-modern sophisticates know our scientific worldview is a myth: we have no other myth congruent with the rest of our knowledge with which to image or mirror the world. Though we know our scientific myth is fallible, indeed doubtless inadequate in ways to be proved sooner rather than later, we have no practical choice save to take the world to be like the late-modern myth says, at least in certain crucial respects.

The positivist conception of science took scientific theories to be iconic of their objects. So too do positivist theologies which believe the function of theology is to describe religious realities. This is plainly true of conservative theologians who defend propositions about religious realities. But it is also true of many theologians who talk in narratives, metaphors, and paradoxes. In a sense, the entire modern era as influenced by Descartes has supposed that mental representations are supposed to be iconic of extra-mental realities, and the problem from the beginning has been how to compare them.

The second kind of reference Peirce called indexical.[10] An index is a sign that refers by some kind of causal connection with its object. A pointing finger (Peirce's example) employs the perceived physical geometry of the scene to indicate its object. More generally, indexically referring signs connect the interpreter causally with the realities interpreted. Indexical reference, if valid, should align the interpreters with the causal processes of their reality insofar as the referring signs interpret those realities in respect to those processes. For religions indexical reference is very important indeed because it is crucial for any kind of attunement to ultimate realities that might be attained. When religions speak of people realizing religious truth, that is not so much having true icons of religious states of affairs but rather the people becoming true to those realities. To become a saint, to be more holy, to actualize religious truth, is to interpret reality with those indices that align people to what is objectively and causally real in their objects. Indexical reference is necessary for engagements with reality that allow interpreters to learn from their experience. Many religious themes put soteriological interests ahead of theological ones, claiming that interpretations which are a bit silly when interpreted as having iconic reference are true and valuable when interpreted as having indexical reference. A person indexically related to Jesus such that love of God and neighbor animate the person's life has a true reference, even though the person might be hopelessly naïve and false in matters of ascertaining who the historical Jesus really was and whether he really gave the Great Commandment.

The third kind of reference Peirce called "symbolic," and I call it "conventional."[11] Conventional signs refer by virtue of the structure of a semiotic system. The semantics and syntax of a language system is a good example of the complexities of conventional reference. The semiotic system is structured so as to spell out the meanings of signs in codes, to indicate possible versus impossible references to other signs within the systems, and to shape possible interpretations where an interpretation is a complex sign taking another sign to stand for yet a third sign.

Any sign we can think about and mention must be in the semiotic system of some language or gestural matrix. Therefore the iconic and indexical reference mentioned above really are abstractions from a richer kind of reference that includes the conventions by which we *speak* of crucifixes, myths, fingers, and religious practice. In point of fact, any religious reference we might discuss is at least conventional and is likely also to involve indexical and iconic elements. What the conventional reference adds is to connect simple mirroring or brute causal interaction with other signs, other meaning systems, other mirrorings and other interactions. Thus religions have very complex symbols. The crucifix is an icon of Jesus' crucifixion, but the meaning of that is connected with his life and teaching, the culture of the Messiah, the significance for disciples and others, and nearly the whole of Christian thought and practice. Moreover, the conventionality of religious symbols is what allows religion to be connected with the rest of life, with morality and politics, with art, and with domestic living. Conventional reference is what can imbed religion in larger practice.

Peirce's point that interpretation is engagement with the realities interpreted requires all three kinds of reference. Conventional reference is required because all interpretations take place within the ongoing contexts of living, with a physical and social situatedness, with inherited practices and habits, with expectations and purposes. Conventional systems of meaning make the integration of these possible. Moreover, conventions are publicly learned. Whether or not Wittgenstein was right in saying there is no such thing as private language, there certainly is not a lot of private language. The evolution of human society depends on communication through shared semiotic systems.

Our interpretations are not solely functions of internal mentalistic fantasy, however. Because of indexical reference those conventional signs can be oriented to connect interpreters causally with the reality around them. Indeed, the elaborate conventional systems of civilized life evolved precisely because the signs that can refer conventionally within the system can be used indexically to engage reality. If the conventions did not have some crucial indexical reference, they would be pragmatically and evolutionarily useless. Not all religious interpretations need to be iconic in explicit ways, though a great many are. Nevertheless, religious interpretation supposes that its fundamental system of images, its basic imagination, picks up on what is important in reality and mirrors it. For practical purposes, with one important qualification, it assumes that what its imagination can register is what is important to register really. The qualification is that nearly every religion, especially the biblical ones, have an element of apophatic theology. They say that no image or idea is adequate to ultimate religious realities. But at a higher level of reflection they are saying that the inapplicability of any finite images or ideas is just the way the religious things are, which is meta-iconicity if you will.

If iconicity is the paradigmatic reference for positivists and indexicality for thinkers of praxis, religious and otherwise, conventionality is the paradigm for postmodern deconstructionists. Peirce himself worried about the view that reduced iconicity and indexicality to convention. He called that "degenerate" firstness and secondness, and suspected Hegel of the fault.[12] In our time deconstructionists have argued that, because any iconic and indexical reference can itself be represented within a conventional semiotic system, and because any speaking about iconic and indexical reference is done within the signs of a semiotic system, there is no reality outside the system of signs. Everything is a text and nothing is signified but more signifiers. If everything is internal to the semiotic system, then there is no reality to engage, and human life is only discourse, conversation.

But both indexical and iconic reference involve a dualism of the interpreting sign-system and the objective reality to which the signs refer; this is so even when the objective reality is something in the semiotic system itself. Peirce's theory of reference shows how semiotic systems themselves arise through human evolution as they provide ever more sophisticated ways of interacting with the environment so as to survive, multiply, and flourish. It also explains why semiotic systems have structures that appear to refer to real things outside the systems. Peirce's theory not only saves the appearance but provides a ground for engaging reality with more deliberation and the desire to make our interpretations vulnerable to correction.

REFERENCE AND APOPHATIC THEOLOGY

A deep problem has lurked beneath the surface of this discussion of reference in engagement, showing itself so far only in the brief allusion to apophatic theology. Most of the traditions of biblical religion have a point at which they say that God is not an object or thing, and transcends all that. Moreover, all the finite manifestations of God in burning bushes, the leadership of Israel, still small voices, or even in Jesus, are not religiously interesting in their finitude alone. The finite elements can be referred to without difficulty, or with only the difficulty of historical and other kinds of inquiry. What makes them religiously interesting is their connection to a divine ground that in some sense is not finite, that is infinite, otherwise indeterminate. Reference to the finite elements has to be made into an analogy to refer to the infinite elements, as in the theory of finite/infinite contrasts defended above.

Theological traditions affirm the apophatic character of the religious object in different ways, depending on their affinities for reference. The Aristotelian tradition that fed Aquinas assumed that something like the syntax of language is iconic of reality, so that reality is made up of substances with properties whose icons are propositions with predicates. So Thomas Aquinas affirmed the apophatic character of the religious object by saying that God is not a substance, nor in a genus of substances, nor even a genus itself. Theologians with an affinity for indexical reference begin with stories about

God's participation in their story, usually put the other way around; but they end the dialectic of anti-idolatry by embracing mysticism, the practical plunge of the soul into the Abyss drawn by the index of love. Theologians with an affinity for conventions, such as in the rabbinic tradition, talk as if the talk itself defines God but move to the margins if not the center of the Kabbala, a language that so intensifies finite reference as to become incommensurate with finite things of life.

If the religious object, God, the Ultimate, the Ground of Being, is beyond any kind of reference to finite things, is God beyond reference? If the answer is yes, then God cannot be engaged, and Peirce's theory of interpretation is of no help here. If the answer is no, then we have to speak to the issue of nonfinite reference. Peirce's semiotics suggests two responses.

First, there is a distinction between a logical object and the kind of reality that object might have. A logical object is simply something that is or can be referred to. What that object is, for instance finite, infinite, or a finite/infinite contrast, makes a difference only to the signs that are used to interpret it. If the sign is complex enough, as is the case with a fancy apophatic theology, it can refer to a logical object that is not a finite thing, or at least is more than a finite thing. The question then becomes one of meaning, of getting the right signs and theories.

Second, Peirce severely criticized nominalism, which he called the great error of all modern philosophy (where it is in error).[13] Only a nominalist would expect that the objects of reference be objects in the sense of finite things, especially particular finite things. On the contrary, said Peirce, most of the important things in life are quite general. What is the tendency of the universe? In what does the ideal of the good life consist? What is the spirit of an age? On a more prosaic level, we can enter a room full of people and pick up its mood, its tensions, frustrations, or glee. None of these "objects" are finite particulars, and yet we refer to them in discussion and assume them in life. The reference to them is very complex, because we identify them through a great many details integrated together. Most of us could not even say what particular things we notice when we pick up on tension in a group. The signs by which we refer to such things are extraordinarily complex, referring in mediating ways to a great many other things, but integrating all those other references by means of what Peirce would call an hypothesis or theory. On the intellectual side of religion, it takes a whole theology to refer to God; that's why theologians are so verbose—the fragment of a theology likely fails of its ultimate reference. On the practical side of religion, it takes a vast nest of symbolic networks, supplementing and balancing one another.

With these two observations about why reference to a transcendent God might not be impossible, we move from a Peircean study of reference to one of meaning or the symbol systems themselves.

MEANING AND TRUTH

Signs, including religious symbols, have content, and the question of truth is whether that content applies to the reality referred to in the respect in which the symbol is taken to represent the reality. Peirce had an extraordinarily original and creative theory of signs, dividing them into trichotomies of trichotomies and into ten different classes. His theory of the internal structure of sign systems is not to the particular point here, however.[14] More important is to develop Peirce's theory to characterize the structure of systems of religious signs or symbols.[15]

Signs (or meanings or symbols) are defined within semiotic systems. What does the *definition* of signs mean in this context? In a classical development of Peircean semiotics, flawed though it is, Charles W. Morris says that the definition of signs has three senses: syntactics, semantics, and pragmatics.[16] Syntactics he defines as the structure of the semiotic system of signs itself, semantics as the relation of signs to their objects, which Peirce called reference, and pragmatics as the relation of signs to their interpreter, which Peirce called simply interpretation. But for Morris, the semantic objects of signs are objects as referred to by other signs, and so are within the semiotic system. For him, the interpreter is not a real interpreter but an interpretive interest and summary interpretation, also within the semiotic system. Thus in Morris's sense, syntactics, semantics, and pragmatics are all parts of what I call the *extension* of a semiotic system. Their study is study of the nature of the system itself, not of its referential relation to realities nor of the system's roles in the actual lives of interpreters. In contrast to the *extension* of signs within a semiotic system we should note the *intention* of signs in actual interpretation, wherein the signs with their defining system shape actual interpretive engagements of people with reality. Interpretive engagement with reality is the use of signs intentionally. Intention involves real reference and real interpretation. But that is not my concern for the moment. For the moment we should look at the extension of signs and its role in truth.

Roughly put, the syntax of a semiotic system is its grammar, its underlying structure defining possible relations among kinds of signs. Since the work of Morris in the 1930s much has been done with transformational grammar and theories of deep structures. This is not important now for what I want to say about religious symbols, however. Semantics has to do with the way signs are defined in terms of one another. Dictionary definitions are very great abstractions of semantics. Semantic definitions are often not univocal but equivocal, with the polysemy playing one meaning off over against another, in metaphorical and other semantic tropes. Semantic meanings also include the shades and resonances of historic or customary use: the metaphor of "rosey fingered dawn," so often cited in discussions like these, carries resonances of Homer epic. Pragmatics has to do with how signs are defined within their semiotic system by interpreters' interests, purposes, and various interpretive contexts. Put more formally, interpretive intent defines the fact that a sign refers to its object in a certain respect; this is a formal property of any interpretation—a sign represents its object to an interpreter in a certain respect. So, the sign "red" in our semiotic system represents the barn to the viewer in respect to color; it represents the movie actor to Senator McCarthy in respect of political affiliation; it represents the bottom line to the auditor in respect of financial trouble. Students of semiotic systems, whether they be verbal languages or the visual symbols in European churches—notice I am avoiding a definition of the boundaries of semiotic systems—can and should study the syntactics, semantics, and pragmatics of the system's extension. I suspect the distinction between syntactics, semantics, and pragmatics is not as clear-cut as Morris imagined when he took his cue from Peirce's quite clear distinction between signs as meanings, reference, and interpretation. Surely fundamental levels of imagination, such as distinguish the biblical from the late-modern worlds, lie at the juncture of syntactics, semantics, and pragmatics.

For the case of religious symbols, let us look more closely at the semantics or systems of meanings. Most important religious symbols are semantically defined through networks and nests of symbol systems. By *symbol system* here I mean a relatively tight and unique association of interdefining symbols. For instance, the symbol of Jesus as the Lamb of God is defined within the system that likens him to the first Passover, when the Jews in Egypt slew a lamb or goat and painted its blood over their doors so that the Angel sent to kill all first-borns would pass over the Jewish homes. In this symbols system, Jesus is our Passover lamb. But there is another symbol system defining Jesus as the lamb of God, namely, the one that associates him with the scapegoat or lamb sent into the wilderness every year in ancient Israel on the day of the Day of Atonement to carry off the sins of the priest and the people. This is the symbol system that says Jesus bears our sins, something not connected at all with the Passover lamb which is about divine wrath. Those two symbol systems have been employed within Christianity to symbolize the atonement work of Jesus as redeemer. Two other symbol systems have been important for that too. In one, God is symbolized as in conflict with Satan over the future of humanity, and Jesus is given to Satan who has deserved possession of human souls in order to ransom those souls so that they can return to God; but Satan cannot keep Jesus in death, and so is cheated while humankind is redeemed. The fourth symbol system for atonement, made popular by Anselm, represents God as having such justice and dignity that human beings should be damned for their sins despite God's love of them; Jesus, God's own dearest son, is sacrificed to balance out the evil of humankind so that God's justice and dignity can be kept while humankind can be restored by God's love.

How do these symbol systems of atonement fit together? Classical theology has attempted to fit them into a network of symbol systems, showing how they all play roles in a larger univocal picture. A theological network is a system of conceptual signs that integrates various components coherently and consistently. Calvin, for instance, developed a theory of Jesus' work under the rubrics of king, priest, and prophet, according to which he was able to integrate a great deal that various biblical symbols say about Jesus. But in respect of the systems of atonement symbols, they just do not seem to fit together. In the face of this, theologians have three main options. They can adopt one symbol system as the true or dominant one and dismissed the others as false or merely supplementary metaphors. They can back away from the whole problem, attempting to explain what Jesus does to save in ways other than through the problematics of atonement. Or they can say that the several symbol systems, though not consistent in a theological network, in fact function truthfully as a nest of symbol systems. The nest itself is functional in the lives of Christians, with application of all the symbol systems in the liturgies of the Church, for instance, or in devotional literature.

In actual religious practice, symbol systems are most often if not nearly always nested rather than networked. Even where a religious community has a large and sophisticated theology that networks the main symbol systems for the theologians, most people in the community are not theologians. They do not apprehend the symbol systems as networked, only as nested in various practices. Consider the symbol systems that are exercised in the Christian Eucharist or Lord's Supper: death and resurrection as the emblem of authentic human existence, the elements as nourishing food for the soul, the celebration of a common meal by Christians, Jesus' inclusive table fellowship embracing the unembracible, the sacrament as an exercise of solidarity with Christians all over the world and through time, the reference to the historical Jesus by whom contemporary participants define their historical identity, the reference to Jesus as God or the Son of God, the fact that participants both as individuals and as members of a voluntary community are presented to God, the fact that the host is the just king who is imposing his own order, and the cannibal rite of eating Jesus' flesh and blood. These are only some of the symbol systems in the Eucharistic rite, and do not include those over which Orthodox, Roman Catholics, and Protestants dispute. The symbol systems here are not congruent, but lived with through the liturgical practice of the Eucharist, they come to resonate together, to reinforce, and sometimes to correct one another. The cannibal rite, for instance, is properly tamed by the system that introduces the participant to Christ the just king and Lord of the table.

Religious symbols range from the concrete and particular to the universal, abstract and theoretical. Stories, for instance those of the Exodus and Jesus' ministry, are particular, whereas the symbol of God as creator has a kind of universal application and is assumed more than discussed throughout the

Bible. The distinction between particular and universal does not cash out to a distinction between vividly gripping and blandly theoretical, however. The story of the Exodus is gripping if your and your group can identify with it, as many African-Americans do; but if you identify more with the dispossessed Canaanites or do not identify at all with who gets to own a land, then the story has no vividness or gripping quality for you. A symbol such as God as creator which is present and presupposed in most other biblical religious symbols is not vivid, perhaps, but certainly gripping in the sense of being operative and having effect. For persons of an intellectual bent, even a symbol such as an abstract theory, a comprehensive theology, might be gripping in the sense that it provides the main symbols by which the theologian engages the divine. Just as most of us can perceive when there is tension in a gathering through signs that integrate the intricacies of a thousand unnoticed sub-interpretations, some theologians can find God in the vast hypothetical network-symbols of a complex theology.

The difference between gripping and indifferent religious symbols has to do with whether they have indexical reference. Gripping symbols put the interpreters into a causal nexus with the religious objects, in the respects in which the symbols represent those objects. If an interpreter can identify with the Exodus story, that story serves to connect the interpreter with the divine in respect of liberation and divine care, making the interpreter part of the people of God. Without the identification, the person can know the story but still be indifferent. Similarly a nest of symbol systems that cannot be integrated into a network, or that is not known to be so, can function in a gripping way. The symbol systems about the atonement are such a nest and for some people they can function so as apparently to effect the work of salvation or justification. Those people can identify with the symbol systems, nested together, in such a way that they are indexically connected with the redeeming history. Other people, of course, do not connect indexically with those symbols at all, especially in this enlightened age. Modern people do not have much to do with blood sacrifice of pigeons or bulls for the purification of sin, let alone blood sacrifice of humans. Most moderns think it childish and unworthy of God to need horrendous punishment to set the scales of justice in balance, and think of God's sacrifice of his son as child abuse. Most moderns indeed are embarrassed on an explicit conscious level by the bloody atonement imagery in all its symbol systems. And yet the liturgies using these symbol systems are powerful even today to many who would disown their apparent content. Perhaps this is because there is some depth of evil in the human soul, felt but not acknowledged, which can be addressed only by a blood sacrifice, recognized only in a cannibal rite. Perhaps there is a profound human grasp of sinfulness such that in the face of the Ultimate, with no excuses or extenuating circumstances or second chances, God must be personified as a judge whose only way to acknowledge humanity is to condemn it. The profound religious symbols can grip people by engaging them indexically with the Ultimate even when the iconic reference of the content of the symbols is rejected. In the terms of our Peircean semiotics, I suspect that we moderns reject the bloody atonement imagery as having any true iconic reference, while embracing it as having indexical reference. Iconically, we do not believe that reality is such that killing somebody else justifies our sins, or that God would enjoy that. Indexically, those same stories and symbol systems have a healing power and are true for some people who disbelieve their iconic reference.

Notice how carefully the argument has sidled up at last to the question of truth, claiming that certain symbols can be true when interpreted with indexical reference at the same time that iconically things are not like what those symbols say.[17]

Now as to truth, I propose the pragmatic hypothesis that truth is the carryover of value or importance from the objects into the interpreters in the respects in which the signs interpret the objects, as qualified by the biology, culture, semiotic systems, and purposes of the interpreters. This formula goes beyond anything Peirce said but it is a clear extension of his pragmatic correspondence theory. Like Aristotle's this is a causal theory of truth. For Aristotle, the senses, ultimately touch, causally carry over the forms of things without their matter into the interpreters mind, which then takes on the forms of things. The purest, most divine, knowing for Aristotle is of those truths that are eternal and have no matter, so that nothing is left behind and the carryover of form carries over the whole reality; Descartes' theory of the light of reason is an echo of this. The theory that truth is the carryover of value or importance differs from Aristotle's in respect to what is carried over. If form is what is carried over, then all reference would be iconic only, and we have seen that there are other kinds. Also, it is hard to see how there could be a carryover of form into the mind or brain without supposing a very crude sense of microcosmic duplication of macrocosmic form.

From an evolutionary point of view, organisms need to know what is important in their surroundings for their own security, growth, and flourishing. They evolve sensors and neural responders that register these things. As soon as the capacities for the causal operation of the brain in terms of semiotic systems are evolved, people are able to question what is really important and valuable in their surroundings at a great distance from their immediate survival and flourishing needs. Or rather, given the extraordinary beauty and value of the cosmos, people define their flourishing by being able to ingest the deepest and most important things, becoming transformed in the process into creatures capable of bearing those profoundly wonderful things. Religion, of course, deals with precisely this level of engagement with what is ultimately important and glorious, and with the human flaws that stand out so starkly in contrast.

That truthful carryover is qualified by human biology simply makes the point that the causal processes for mediating what is important have to pass into human biological life. This point fosters inquiry into the scientific understanding of actual logic. That truthful carryover is qualified by culture and semiotic systems means that the symbolic forms that embody the valuable and important will be different in different cultures, and people cannot use symbols effectively when they do not have the culture and semiotic systems that define them. That carryover is qualified by the purposes of the interpreters has reference to understanding the act and contexts of interpretation, to which we shall return shortly.

The content of a religious symbol is true if, for appropriate interpreters (with the right culture, maturity, state of soul, etc.), it carries over what is important in its object to which reference is made into the interpreter in the respect in which the symbol is interpreted as representing the object. For those who are not appropriate interpreters, the symbol cannot be true. For those interpreters who are not capable of referring with the symbol in the appropriate respect, the symbol cannot be true. Those issues of appropriateness being put in place, the question of truth comes down to the question of content: does the content of the symbol, appropriately used to interpret its object, carry over what is really important and valuable in the object, or not? It is false if it introduces into the interpreter a value not in the object, or if it fails to introduce the value that is there in the respect in which it interprets the object.

Carryover *defines* truth, I argue, and this is different from determining *whether* an allegedly true interpretation in fact is true. The latter issue involves criteria of assessing what is carried over. To address this properly, we must turn to interpretation as such, the third of Peirce's topics for semiotics.

INTERPRETATION

Peirce is famous for his extensive development of the thesis that interpretation is a triadic relation. Whereas much early modern philosophy supposed a dyadic relation of mental picture to real object, and much late-modern Continental semiotics contents itself with the signifier/signified dyad, Peirce argued that a sign relates interpretively to its object only because an interpreter takes it to do so. The interpreter takes the sign to stand for an object in a certain respect, and that "taking" is the interpretation. The expression of the interpretation Peirce called an "interpretant," so that the triad of interpretation consists of sign, object, and interpretant.[18]

I have stressed first the issues of reference and meaning for a Peircean account of religious interpretation because they have usually be subordinated in pragmatic discussions. William James especially, but also John Dewey and George Herbert Mead, have focused the concerns for the interpreters and their contexts as the genius of pragmatism. John E. Smith, probably the most astute interpreter of pragmatism in relation to other forms of empiricism and rationalism, named his principal book on pragmatism, *Purpose and Thought*, both features of interpreters. Smith's principal topic throughout nearly all his writings is *experience* which he always develops in terms close to what I have called *engagement*, with direct though mediated connections of interpreters with real objects; yet *experience* names the interpreter's side of the engagement. He is surely right that pragmatism's lever for changing the tradition's approach to "correspondence" is its attention to the interpreter's purposes, contexts, and community.[19]

The general pragmatic point, begun with Peirce and echoed throughout our tradition, is that the interpreter's purpose determines what there is about the object the interpreter is interested to know. Crudely put, that is *instrumentalism*, the view that people recognize only what there is in reality that serves their purposes. Peirce, like Dewey, was far subtler than most views of pragmatism in that he argued that what is most important for us to recognize in things are the considerations that help determine what purposes are most worth having. A formal way of stating the point about purpose is that objects are interpreted in terms of the respects in which they are of potential interest to the interpreter's purpose. The purpose selects the respect of interpretation.

That is a very abstract point, however. Only in rare moments do people consciously look for what in reality is relevant to their purposes. But in every moment people engage reality with selective interpretations arranged in archeologically deep layers, starting with the most basic imaginative levels. Individuals have particular purposes, say, enjoying a song, but this itself rests on larger purposes of leisure, and the enjoyment of beauty, which in turn rest on one's subculture's determinations of what music is beautiful, and the cultural determination of what music is, and how life focuses on beauty in sound, and how that fits together with the economic and security purposes of life, and indeed on what fundamental human imagination determines as the sorting of sensations into sounds and other sorts and the ordering of them through temporal experience. Purpose in some sense lies at each of these levels, for there has been some evolutionary reason, if not deliberate choice or the encounter with genius, that shapes the individual's semiotic system to consider that reality needs to be interpreted in the respects in which the signs of the cultural system pick up. Indeed, one cannot say that the world's great civilizations have different conventions for picking up on the *same* things. Perhaps their different semiotic systems pick up on reality in somewhat different respects. If so, there are subtle differences among the purposes of different civilizations.

At any rate, the purposes of interpreters are defined within interpretive contexts, and these contexts are nested from Earth-boundedness to the particular concerns of the moment in one's neighborhood. Moreover, interpretation is an ongoing affair, with many processes of personal, social, and natural life going on together. The forms of integration of these many processes might well be called a *bio-psychic dance*. The integration of organic bodily processes with metabolism is not exclusively an organic matter, because a spirited conversation after dinner can speed digestion and result in a friendship that has powerful social significance for the community. Some parts of the integration take the forms of semiotic systems. While the pragmatists were always careful to keep natural, nonconscious processes at the center of analytical attention, they also drew attention to the fact that the contexts of interpretation are permeated by meaning, shaped by semiotic systems. All human purposes, at whatever level, reflect the shaping of the deep context by semiotic systems.

Therefore, the carryover of what is important in the object into the interpreter requires the transformation of the object into what fits into the interpreter's semiotic context. This is the reason for saying that the carryover is qualified by the biology, culture, semiotic systems, and purposes of the interpreter. The deep structure of the semiotic context includes the basic level of imagination.

Because of the function of purpose, either cultural in many layers or communal or personal, it is necessary to clarify what is meant in saying that truth is the carryover of what is valuable or important in the object into the interpreter in the respects interpreted. So long as the epistemological supposition is that form is what is carried over from the object into the mind, it is easy to assume that the subjective purposive side determines what is important exclusively, as when importance or value is reduced to what serves as a means to the purposive end. But precisely because reality is what it is irrespective of what we think about it, what serves or fails to serve a purpose is the character of the object. If one believes, as I do, that objects all have value, and that their forms are a function of the values they achieve and exhibit, then what is carried across is the value those objects have, insofar as that is relevant to the respects in which they are interpreted, that is, insofar as the objects' values are relevant to the contextualized purpose.[20]

When the primary paradigms of interpretation are propositions, it is easy to assume that what is carried across is information. This occurs when the reference is dominantly iconic, and the value involved is the value the interpreter achieves through the information of being able to respond to the interpreted realities in terms of purposes. When the dominant reference is indexical, however, the carryover involves a value that affects the interaction of the interpreter with the interpreted objects. If an interpreter sees something and thinks, "that would be good to eat," and the object truly is a good food, the interpretive reference is mainly iconic; it goes into the interpreter's repertoire of knowledge and might subsequently be the basis of action. But if the reference is mainly indexical, the interpretation will make a habit of reaching for the food and eating it, and the interpretation will be true if the food nourishes rather than poisons. The indexical causal reference so orients the interpreter in causal ways with the object that its value is carried over into the interpreter, in this instance, literally ingestively. To see a person iconically as "friendly" is informative, but different from seeing the person indexically as friendly by smiling—the smile is the interpretant that embodies the carried-over friendliness in the interpreter's contextualized behavior.

People of course interpret many different things on many levels in a vastly complicated intermixing of interpretive processes, and have to integrate all the values carried over into their own singular realities. Therefore, the values of interpreted realities are transformed as they are integrated in interpreters to form their personal lives and their interactions with communities and the rest of the world. The value of a person is the sum of the harmonies the person makes of interpretive responses to the world, including the ongoing self-reflexive processes of life in community. For the sake of simplicity I have spoken of interpreters in the singular here, but it should be clear that singular interpreters are interdefined in communities when their contextual and purpose realities are semiotic systems.

How does all this apply to religious symbols? In the case of biblical religions it means that a true interpretation of God carries across something of divine value into the interpreter in the respects in which the symbols interpret God. Remember the complexity of religious symbols, how their meanings themselves are networks and nests of symbolic systems. So, the Exodus interprets God's liberating identification of the people of Israel to those in which some divine liberation comes from it. Christians interpret the gospel of Jesus in such ways as God's redemptive action transforms their experience. The complexity of the interpreter's purposive context is even greater than the complexity of symbolic meanings, however.

Consider the context of theologians, for instance. For their purposes what is carried across needs to be received in terms that are highly communicable, that can be defined with precision within their theological community, that have metaphoric reach that can be contained and controlled for and with which it is possible to minimize apophatic cautions that they don't fully mean what they say. Much theological reference then is iconic, its meanings systematic and dull, and its interpretations intellectual in form and not easy to be acted upon. Sometimes, however, an abstract theological system can provide a kind of sudden enlightenment, a healing of alienation, and then it functions indexically to reorient the theologian to engagement with God and perhaps more authentic to participate in a community. I suspect most theologians would not stay in the profession for intellectual purposes alone, but only if also theology serves some more direct religious function.

Consider by contrast the context of nonintellectual believers who practice their lives as strongly informed by the symbols. Their interpretations of the symbols are less likely to be in what they say about their objects than in what we might call practical inferences. But they probably do not make conscious inferences either. Their shaping, transformation, or development in practice is simply the way they receive what is carried over. A Jew or African-American might have a richly developed solidarity with the community of Israel, or a surrogate of that, without any "true" verbal interpretation of the Exodus story. A Christian might be richly practiced in love of neighbor and God without much clarity of verbal interpretation. Yet in both kinds of case there is likely to be verbal interpretation accompanying the practice, words that do speak of the symbols at hand. What is said could not be defended as iconically true from a theological point of view, but bears some kind of causal connection with the affected practice which itself is the true carryover of divine liberation or love.

To claim pragmatically that truth is not the replication of form but the carryover of value in interpretive respects is to weaken formal criteria of truth in favor of pragmatic criteria. The pragmatic criteriological question is whether the value really in the object is carried across into appropriate forms for the interpreter in context. What then are some of the main pragmatic criteria for truth?

The criteria for truth all come from whatever would make a "good case" for the claim at hand within the public that cares about the issue.[21] Therefore criteria are contextualized to the topic at hand and to the particular communities that jointly make up the public. Perhaps the most important singular contribution a Peircean semiotic can make to assessing claims to religious truth is to diagram what the question is. Before testing a claim with appropriate criteria, at least the following needs to be identified and distinguished from elements easily confused: What exactly is the interpretive symbol, its symbolic systems, its networks and nests of symbols? (many hermeneuts stop here); What exactly is the kind of reference involved, iconic, indexical, conventional, all three in various ways? (failure to clarify this gives rise to extremely inappropriate inferences); What exactly is the respect in which the symbol interprets the object? (much confusion comes from the fact the same symbol can interpret a given object in several respects, depending on the interpretive context); What is the interpretive context, the semiotic system in terms of which the object needs to be interpreted, its purposes, inertial practices of interpretation, its assumptions? Only when all of these questions are sorted and clarified is it possible to ask whether the interpretation of the object by means of this symbol carry across what it really important into the interpreter in the respect interpreted. Only when these complex triadic questions have been answered is it possible clearly to ask the dyadic question of truth.

In religious matters, the emphasis on living in the truth, being true, practice, and authentic salvation, enlightenment, or harmony, gives great weight to the differences among the kinds of reference symbols might have. So there are, Peircean fashion, three main kinds of criteria, bearing in mind the complexity of prior questions that need to be answered.

Because religious symbols are interpreted with iconic reference there is a class of criteria that have to do with how an icon or theory or symbol system or religious way of life might be good and in correspondence with what it maps. Whitehead's famous discussion of speculative philosophical theory in the first chapter of *Process and Reality* is the most eloquent statement of this class. He noted that formally a theory should be consistent and coherent. Consistency means no contradictions, and coherence means that the parts hang together. Where religious symbols can be integrated in networks, these criteria can be applied fairly directly. Where they are nested instead, and resistant of networking, the formal criteria of consistency and coherence might have to be translated to aesthetic ones of harmony, resonance, dissonance within greater harmonies, and so forth. The other criteria Whitehead mentioned are applicability and adequacy, which together define iconic mapping. Applicability means that there is no part of the system that does not have some objective reference, and adequacy means that there is nothing in reality for which the system does not have a sign. Because there is no privileged perspective from which to compare reality with iconic theories or symbol systems, applicability and adequacy are very high-level criteria and need all sorts of other criteria to be applied themselves. Indeed, they need criteria that are functional with indexical and conventional reference.

The criteria for the truth of interpretations with indexical reference are what Jesus had in mind in saying (Luke 6), "by their fruits you shall know them." He likely had in mind specifically the hypocrites who profess godliness and act out its contrary. St. Paul generalized the point by listing such marks of the Holy Spirit as "love, joy, peace, patience, kindness, generosity, faithfulness, gentleness, and self-control" (Galatians 5:22). These and like virtues are precisely the kinds of criteria we use in judging saintliness, the realized or perfected state of godliness. Nevertheless, it is usually extremely difficult to make such pragmatic "fruits" be very differential in judging the comparative truth of particular symbols. In response to this, some people dismiss appeals to the fruits of godliness. Could we really expect Orthodox Christian who believe the Holy Spirit proceeds from the Father alone to be different in such virtues from Western European Christians who believe the Spirit proceeds from the Father and the Son together? Perhaps instead of saying that the criteria are inapplicable, however, we should say that both doctrines, verbally and iconically contradictory, are true in the different contexts of Orthodox and Catholic cultures. Similarly, given the unexplored differences in symbol systems among the world's great religions, and the different respects in which they might interpret ultimate reality, perhaps we should say that, to the extent that they all give rise to sages and saints, they can all be true in their own ways, with respect to indexical reference. That is, they all orient people in ways that lead to profound accomodation to the Ultimate. The great weakness of the appeal to practical fruits to assess claims about interpretations with mainly indexical reference is obviously that they are not easily tied to verbalizable expressions of interpretations. They compare the practices and ways of life resulting from interpretations with that which is interpreted, but can find no stable verbal way of describing those results as interpretants. Hence it is difficult to make intellectual cases for truths claimed with indexical reference.

Fortunately, the criteria for interpretations with conventional reference have to do with the breadth and depth of making and testing connections. To call these "coherence" criteria, which is tempting, is too rationalistic. Because of the conventional nature of our religious symbols and the rest of our semiotic systems, it is possible to see how religious symbols fit with one another and with the rest of life, with politics, morality, aesthetics, domestic economy, and the rest. It is possible to connect putative religious interpretations with the kinds of analysis and understanding that come from the natural and social sciences. It is possible to compare the symbolic interpretations of one religion with those of other religions. In all this conventional reference makes possible a critical dialectic in which ideally every point of view on a religious interpretation can be brought to bear in assessing it. Conventional reference means that there is no fixed limit to the ways by which we can triangulate in on signs, their objects, and their interpretations. This is the breadth of conventional criteria.

At the same time, there is depth to religious interpretation afforded by criteria for conventional reference in the following sense. Religious symbols, or rather the concrete habits of thought, feeling, and behavior shaped by religious symbols, stack up in a person in many layers and interweaving connections. By analogy they do the same thing in communities. Most of us are thoroughly confused in the ways we integrate all the symbol systems that let us engage reality. Superficially, we can line up our symbol systems and the myriad interpretations of reality they give us so as to be successful pragmatically. We get along in society and survive, even flourish. But to question beyond crude social levels of success, most people do not have a clear sense of what is important, of how to relate to what is Ultimate consistently, to "will one thing," as Kierkegaard put it. Spiritual formation, in the biblical religions as in the others, has to do with lining up the many systems and layers of interpretive life so that they resonate consistently and with mutual reinforcement. Or to switch from musical to visual metaphors, saints see through system after system with translucence so that their engagements with reality seem like spontaneous intuitions. Or to use emotional metaphors, spiritually advanced people can be sincere so that what they feel in one interpretive system is multiplied through the other systems of their lives. These considerations lie behind the quite valid claim that the understanding of religion requires considerable participation. Perhaps the faith-seeking-understanding principle begs too many questions at the beginning and seems to be too much about intellectual belief; but it surely describes the depth of religious critical understanding.

Putting together the breadth of a critical public with the depth of spiritual achievement in lining up the interpretive spheres of life, the criteria for interpretations with conventional reference provide maximum vulnerability to correction and maximum internal confirmation. Criteria for truth in conventional reference mark out disciplined ways of integrating various iconic and indexical references with long-range tests of ways of life. We test comprehensive "ways of life," that is, religions, by living with them, testing their flexibility in changing circumstances, their inspirational power when the Ultimate seems absent, and their long-run capacity to stimulate deeper and more subtle engagements with the whole of reality to which they open us.

Before we get giddy with the prospects of the Great Conversation guiding humankind to evolving ever-more-subtle civilized engagements with reality, including the Ultimate, we should remember the limitations already mentioned. In the first place, it is rare that much clarity is achieved regarding the meanings of symbol systems, the nature of their reference, the respects in which they interpret reality, and what the interpretation comes to in the interpreting community; hence it is rare even to raise the question of truth in a fair way. In the second place, the breadth of the critical public is never actualized enough for full dialectical engagement; too often the perspectives that might have critical corrections are neglected or deflected, and vulnerability is thwarted. In the third place, the depth of being attuned spiritually in ways that integrate the vast array of interpretations brought into play by the breadth of the critical public is extremely difficult to achieve, and if achieved, to measure; there is a tension, perhaps unresolvable, between the private intensity required to align the shaping images of one's soul and the engagement with enough different spheres of reality to have the right images there in the first place.

All these limitations notwithstanding, this Peircean vision of a community of investigators reveals an extraordinary long-run stability and sophistication for the assessment of the truth of religious interpretations. Politicians check with voters and physicists include a few other natural sciences and mathematics within their critical public; but the community of inquiry for religion needs to be open to every perspective within creation. Inquiry regarding religious truth defines its depth by being able to line up everything depending on the Ultimate with harmony, translucency, sincerity, and the capacity to will one thing. Put these together and religious inquiry need not be fooled by any limitations to its questioning, and is therefore in the long run more stable and subtle, because more vulnerable, than modes of inquiry that aim at only part of creation with antecedently defined methods.

SEVEN

The Contributions of Charles S. Peirce to Philosophy of Religion

CHARLES SANDERS PEIRCE was probably the United States' most important philosopher. If pragmatism is defined as an epistemological theory of meaning and truth, Peirce was the founder of that movement but himself far more than a pragmatist. If pragmatism is defined as the great imaginative and systematic vision initiated by Peirce and carried on by many others since then, as I would prefer, then pragmatism itself is an important world philosophy, like Platonism, Aristotelianism, Confucianism, Daoism, Samkhya, and Vedanta.

Pragmatism is often associated with science, not least because Peirce himself was a practicing scientist as was his colleague William James. John Dewey associated pragmatism with the hope that science is the instrument of social progress, and George Herbert Mead connected pragmatism closely to the social sciences. Pragmatism is essentially non-Kantian, even anti-Kantian. Therefore, most Europeans, who seem to be genetically hard-wired to be Kantians, cannot see anything in pragmatism except its similarities to technologies and usefulness to achieving preset goals (despite Peirce's claim that the question most interesting to pursue pragmatically is what goals are worth having). That Peirce's pragmatism has important contributions to make to philosophy of religion thus might seem something of a surprise.

I want to single out four connected topics in philosophy of religion for which Peirce has important insights, which conveniently can be labeled (1) the evolutionary weight of religion, (2) contributions to theology, (3) the importance of erudition, and (4) comparative theology. The discussion will make apparent how each of these topics opens out into many more fields of fruitful inquiry.

THE EVOLUTIONARY WEIGHT OF RELIGION

In 1898 Peirce delivered a series of lectures at Harvard that he called "Detached Ideas on Vitally Important Topics," the first of which was entitled "Philosophy and the Conduct of Life."[1] Peirce sharply distinguished (untypically for him) reason from instinct or belief. For reason he advocated utmost dispassion and objectivity, with as much imitation of mathematics as possible, and urged philosophy to be rational; most of that essay consists in classifying sections of philosophy as reason. For instinct or belief, however, he advocated the greatest trust in dealing with the vitally important topics of life. The truly important matters of life, on which human beings need to act, should not be trusted to reason, Peirce argued. Indeed, his argument took an extreme polemical turn. He criticized philosophers who sought to guide morals and the search for the good life by philosophical reasoning, reaching back to attack his ideal, Plato. On the one hand, such moralizing philosophy is likely to corrupt the dispassion of rational inquiry. But on the other hand, and even worse, philosophy is relatively superficial and is likely to introduce false distinctions and misleading ideals into the guidance of life, which is better left to instinct and commonly evolved belief.

Now this point was Peirce at play, not his typical position. In his more systematic moments he regarded logic as the ethics of thought and ethics as the aesthetic beauty of life. He emphasized continuities and mutual reinforcements rather than separations, in ways I'll mention later. But here his moral is that the deep things in life are those best formed and trusted to evolved belief and instinct.

In his celebrated "Neglected Argument for the Reality of God," he developed this point in an epistemological context directly relevant to religion.[2] There he argued that the evolution of the human mind/brain has been such that it has come to pick up on what needs to be known of vital importance for human life. Otherwise we would not have survived. In particular, he notes that just about everyone in every culture who has thought about how it is possible that there be a universe with radically different things in it that are still related to one another, has come up with some vague notion that the universe is created. This notion is extremely vague, he noted (and he did not bother to give historical evidence that every culture indeed thinks this way, though obviously many do); as soon as theologians or philosophers start to explain it in more detail, they introduce complications that are problematic. The philosophers are usually specifically wrong, he said, though the vague belief is very likely right and worth guiding life in fundamental respects.

From this point I believe contemporary philosophy of religion can learn three points. First, its inquiry should be guided by the image of religion as sets of elementary behaviors and practices, mostly unreflective, and shaped and guided by beliefs that are more like instincts than objects of consciousness. Or better yet, religion should be imagined as having a hierarchy of behaviors and practices, shaped by a hierarchy of symbolic forms that run from unreflective instincts through greater and greater responsible elaboration up to conceptual theologies. The warning contained in this image is that we should not identify religion first with its elaborated conceptual doctrines and then work down to their expressions in practice, but the other way around. This point puts philosophy of religion in much greater consonance with anthropological, sociological, and psychological studies of religion than is possible for the epistemological approaches to philosophy of religion deriving from Hume and popular in the United States today.

The second thing for philosophy of religion to learn from Peirce's emphasis on the evolutionary weight of religion is the importance of genetic studies of religion, studies of how it evolves through history, reaching back to prehistorical times. Religions need to be studied in terms of their biological bases and the adaptive pressures of human evolution. The warning that comes with this lesson is that structuralist accounts of religion have limited value unless set in the larger genetic context. This is an anti-Kantian point to which I shall return shortly.

The third lesson is that philosophy of religion should reject nominalism in favor of realism. Peirce recommended this rejection in all fields, and here is what that means for philosophy of religion. The most real and important elements of religion are those very vague adaptations that orient human wonder, gratitude, fear, and guilt. These are specified in many ways by different traditions, with different situations for adaptations. But what is real and important are the vague commonalities they all have developed in response to common elements in the human environment. I shall return to the notion of vagueness shortly.

CONTRIBUTIONS TO THEOLOGY

Having begun with what amounts to Peirce's insistence that religion deals with a depth of human reality more safely formed by evolution and expressed in instincts than in theology, permit me now to draw out a contribution his thought does make to theology. For Peirce, theology is the cognitive study of the meaning and truth of hypotheses about God and related matters as these have been symbolized in religion. He did not use the word "theology" often. Most of the time he spoke instead of metaphysics and the science of being and beings, as in the essay on "Philosophy and the Conduct of Life." He was also interested in how religious symbols such as the Eucharist might be meaningful and true. All of these are embraced under the contemporary meaning of theology. Peirce has three main contributions on this head.

First, his theory of interpretation shows that signs function to engage us with reality, not to substitute for reality. He understood semiotic systems to be themselves part of the adaptive developments of human life, serving to allow people to make ever more accurate and relevant discernments and responses to the important features of reality. Such systems have syntactic and semantic structures, or codes, as later semioticians would say. But the actuality of semiotic structures within personal and social life itself serves to mediate or interpret reality into meaningful units by means of which intelligent differential human responses can be made. Any interpretation of a reality by means of a sign and its defining semiotic system can itself be represented by a proposition within the semiotic system; I call this the extensional meaning of signs. This has led some thinkers to conclude that the object of any sign is another sign within the semiotic system, with the result that there is no reference to real things outside cultivated human semiosis. But this is a mistake, from Peirce's point of view. The intentional character of signs has to do with their actual use in engaging reality, employing the signs with their defining semiotic systems as the engaging media.

A result of this is that to say that a sign such as "God" might not have a real referent is unhelpful. Obviously something is engaged by religious people attending to God. The question is whether the real referent is what the sign says, or something else indeed. The sign of a personal God, for instance, might refer to something that is not personal, or not a being, or that is a dream and hope rather than an external agent (however real the dream is as projection). So the big question for philosophy of religion is not whether God or some ultimate exists or, put more subjectively, whether there is something to which theological ideas refer, but rather what those ideas say and whether they are true.

The second part of Peirce's contribution to theology within philosophy of religion thus deals with truth and derives from his well-known semiotic theory. Whereas many thinkers have believed that truth consists in a likeness or formal correspondence between ideas or propositions and their objects, Peirce pointed out that this assumes that all reference is iconic. To refer to an object iconically, as discussed in the previous chapter, is to affirm that it is like the sign in some way, isomorphic with it. This might be physical resemblance as when a crucifix in church resembles the cross on which Jesus died. Or it might be more formal kinds of isomorphic as in the old logical positivists' theory that propositions mirror or express the forms of facts. Indeed, any description, no matter how poetic or periphrastic, has an element of iconicity in that it says its object is "like this." But Peirce pointed out that some reference or dimension of reference is indexical, that is pointing. An indexical reference determines a causal relation between the object and the interpreter so that the interpreter gets the object. Pointing with the finger gets the interpreter to turn toward the object to see; an indexical shout wakes the interpreter up to what is happening. An index lifts an object into attention. Or more pointedly, an indexical reference changes the interpreter so that the object can be taken in. Religion, obviously, is deeply involved with indexical reference for symbols. Religious symbolization involves the practitioner in changing so as to be more open to religious realities. It brings to attention dimensions of life obscured by profane existence. It articulates in profound emotional ways depths in realities about which there is little customary consciousness but to which our instincts might be attuned. A very great many religious symbols are obviously false, in fact silly and stupid, if taken literally or iconically. No geologist would say that God is a rock, and no religious people would ever expect that when they point to God as the rock of salvation. The most common kind of reference in religion is indexical, not iconic, however much there might also be iconic elements. The third kind of reference for Peirce is symbolic, by which he meant that the sign's reference is determined within a semiotic system. All signs we can talk about are at least symbolic in their reference. Most are also iconic in some ways and indexical too.

Peirce's semiotic theory points out that truth is not a function of reference alone, however, even when made complicated by recognizing indexical reference. The act of referring to a religious reality by means of a sign is an interpretation, made by concrete interpreters in actual contexts. An interpretation can be represented by a proposition within a semiotic system. But the interpretation itself is a concrete reality. As such, it has contexts that determine what is important to interpret, what kinds of signs to use, what purposes are being served, and indeed the cultural meaningfulness of the semiotic system employed. The truth of an interpretation has to do with whether the object is accurately represented within the interpreter in context. A sign that renders a true interpretation in one context might be false in another. Moreover, signs always interpret objects in certain respects, and the interpretive contexts determine the respects in which it is relevant to interpret the objects. Although abstract theologians like to develop complex signs that are universal across many contexts, and might succeed in this, most signs employed in the practice of religions are rather specific with regard to context.

The third part of Peirce's semiotics is the analysis of the signs as meaning systems. Religious signs are unusually complex, often involving several different symbol systems playing off against one another, reinforcing one another or limiting their claims. What is striking about this point is that so much philosophy of religion is nothing more than worrying about meanings and how to distinguish and define them. The whole of several senses of phenomenology lies in this part of semiotic analysis.

Now my point about the contribution of Peirce's semiotics to theology is that it lays out in detail just how complicated a judgment about the truth of a theological hypothesis is. To assess whether an interpretation is true requires determining whether what is important in the object is carried over into the interpreter's interpretation in the respects in which the signs stand for the object. That is a fairly technical definition of truth that I have developed myself out of Peircean inspiration, namely, the carryover of what is in important in the object interpreted into the interpreter in the respects in which the signs stand for the object. To assess such claims for truth, it is not enough to determine whether there is some kind of likeness, correspondence, or isomorphism between the form of the object and the form of the signs. That kind of correspondence is not even relevant except insofar as the mode of reference is iconic. Rather, the modes of reference involved in the interpretation themselves need to be identified and interpreted; perhaps the question of truth requires that the interpreter be changed indexically so as to be able to pick up on what is relevant and important in the object. Moreover, whether the interpreter really gets what is important requires interpreting the context of interpretation, determining its theoretical and practical interests. Part of that is also determining in what respect the signs are supposed to interpret the objects. Much confusion comes when the same or similar signs are used to interpret objects but in different respects. Finally, the nuances of the signs and symbols themselves, their apophatic character and double entendre, need to be identified and specified. All this means that the very issue of identifying what is at stake in an interpretation in order to determine its truth requires a vastly more complicated hermeneutical apparatus than might be expected on positivist models. Peirce's semiotics shows just how complicated reference, interpretation, and meaning are in the logic of truth, and its application to religion needs to reshape the ways philosophy of religion asks the truth question.

The third part of Peirce's contribution to theology, beyond insisting on signs as instruments of engagement and the semiotic structure of interpretation, has to do with truth itself. My previous point had to do with laying out the complexity of identifying what has to be checked in assessing truth, namely reference, interpretive contexts, and meaning systems. Once that has been made clear, how can we tell when a theological claim is true?

Peirce's brilliant "Neglected Argument for the Reality of God" is really very little about God and mainly about testing hypotheses. Let me quickly sketch his theory about this, and then draw a moral for theology. Peirce said that explanation or understanding has three parts which he called retroduction, deduction, and induction. Retroduction is the move from something to be explained or understood, the object, to what might explain it, and thus has two parts. The first part of retroduction is the kind of instinctual guess at what might explain, like the common vague instinct that a complex universe is to be understood as depending on a creator. But then that guess needs to be transformed into an hypothesis, such as that the creator is a God with intentionality and infinite power. Neither part of retroduction is an argument that proceeds according to a logical form, but consists in giving rise to explanatory form. Deduction also has two parts, explication and demonstration. Explication is the translation of the hypothesis into logical form from which deductions might be made, and demonstration then is the inferences from the hypothesis to what should and should not be found in experience if the hypothesis is true. Demonstration results in empirical categories. Demonstration proceeds according to logical form, but explication is an "argument" (in Peirce's sense that it tends to produce a definite belief) without rules or premises. So far in his discussion of hypothesis Peirce was saying things that would be largely agreed to today in philosophy of science, albeit a century early. His greatest innovation has to do with the third stage of inquiry, induction, which in turn has three parts, classification and two steps of probationary induction. Peirce's point is that an examination has to be made as to whether the elements of experience fit the empirical categories. Classification is really the checking of the empirical categories derived from the hypothesis to see whether they cut reality at its natural joints, to use Plato's phrase, or whether they distort the phenomena, perhaps systematically so. This question is deeply important in religion where the abstractions of theoretical statements might be very far off from what is truly significant in the phenomena. I have developed this Peircean point to require a fairly elaborate phenomenological testing of the empirical categories. Only after the categories themselves are examined and approved is it helpful to use them to classify experience. Then probations can be made as to whether what appears in the empirical categories tends to confirm or disconfirm the theoretical hypothesis.

The effect of Peirce's theory of hypothesis formation and testing is to balance theoretical and phenomenological activities over against each other, each as a check for the other. Theorizing in any stage always has some empirical material, at least in the problems that give rise to questioning in the first place, and usually also in the convictions about what else is true that guide theorizing. Similarly, all empirical or phenomenological analysis has theoretical suppositions. With Peirce's scheme in mind, it is possible to check these against one another, correcting them as understanding proceeds. He would agree with Hegel that inquiry never begins at the beginning. There is no pure problem, but rather something problematic arising in a sea of relatively established convictions. Rather, inquiry is always in the middle, correcting previous assumptions and inferences, fine-tuning habits of thought by engaging reality with hypotheses under testing.

This point is particularly important in the study of religion because of the great danger of bias. Not only are there values and interests that bias researchers because of their social positions, as postmodern scholars love to remind us. Religious commitments themselves notoriously produce bias.

Most study of world religions so far has taken placed with categories assumed from European religions. To counter the bias of religious commitments with methodological (if not emotional) skepticism is only to create another kind of bias. Only a process of inquiry that continually objectifies and tests out biases, moving dialectically between theory and phenomenological engagement, can provide a way forward, not wholly unbiased of course, but not biased the way it used to be.

The upshot of Peirce's contribution to theology is to show how to make it vulnerable to correction so that it can learn from its engagements with reality. This is a clear alternative to theology by authority or by experiential self-expression. The nature of theology is a major topic for philosophy of religion.

COMPARATIVE THEOLOGY

Peirce's third main contribution to contemporary philosophy of religion has to do with establishing a public within which the theological assumptions and claims of the various world religions can engage one another. No excuse can be made these days for discussing religion in a context that does not include all the major world religions and such local religions as might be pertinent to the topic. Whereas Locke, Hume, and Kant might have identified religion with Christianity, usually of a deist sort, Hegel understood philosophy of religion to include the historical and conceptual relations among the world religions. The very politics of intellectual work these days takes place in a context of intercultural encounter and challenge.

But the plain fact is that the state of scholarship in comparative religions has not established a sufficiently well justified unbiased map of the interactions of the world's many religions to provide a background public for philosophic discussion. Comparison even at the elementary level is a work in process, an urgent scholarly need. This is true even for that limited portion of comparative religions in which different theologies or conceptual commitments are compared. To be sure, the separation of comparative theology from the larger subjects of comparative religion is not easy, precisely because of the first Peircean point made above, namely, that religions are deep and largely unreflective practices whose theologies articulate only the tip of the iceberg, if you will. Nevertheless, comparative theology would be possible, bearing in mind its abstract limitations, if there were a map of fundamental comparative categories that provide a background for discussion.

Peirce's conception of vagueness and specification is an extraordinary tool for comparative theology. Peirce defined vagueness as the character of a category to which the principle of noncontradiction does not apply.[3] So, for instance, the category "God" is vague with respect to whether specific candidates for falling under the category have to be intentional. Many biblical representations of God construe him to have a discursive mind that can argue with people, as with Abraham or Moses; Neo-Platonic and Thomistic conceptions of God deny the internal pluralism of discursive intentionality. That is, the popular biblical representations and Neo-Platonic-Thomistic representations contradict one another in respect of intentionality, and yet both fall under the vague category God. Comparison in theology has the logical form of finding a vague category under which all the candidates for comparison fall, and then specifying the category in their different ways, summarizing how they contradict, agree, supplement, overlap or show indifference to one another. Vagueness differs from generality, according to Peirce, in that whereas vagueness can contain contradictories, generality does not exhibit the principle of excluded middle and therefore admits of many different specifications, though perhaps not contradictories.

Another way of stating this point about comparison is to note that things always are compared in some respect or other. Comparison as such does not exist, only comparison in this respect or that. The "respect" in which things can be compared is a vague category, vague in that the things compared in this "respect" can specify it in contradictory ways. So, in respect of whether God is intentional, the biblical representations usually say yes and the Neo-Platonists and philosophical Thomists say no.

The scholarly process of comparison always starts with comparative categories that are assumed and then brought to attention; these categories have a history, usually one arising from their usefulness in one religion. As I've said, most studies of religion in the West, including comparative religions and comparative theologies, have arisen out of Christian interests. We can assume that such historically derived categories have a bias and are unable to be fair in allowing for radically different theologies to be compared. Many people used to define religion itself by reference to God, and stumbled over Buddhism which has no main God and altogether too many little ones without being animistic. If we now were to define religion by reference to something transcendent, it could not be God but something ultimate in a vaguer sense. Some forms of Buddhism cannot be encompassed even under the notion of the ultimate when that is given an ontological interpretation; ultimacy then needs to be redefined even more vaguely as the goal of the religious quest, for instance. The task of developing comparative categories thus is involved in a never-ending dialectic to criticize and purify the vague comparative categories to prevent them from building in bias.

At the same time, the comparative task of determining what the compared theologies have to say about the vague category is itself not obvious. Remembering Peirce's warning about testing empirical categories, the specification of vague categories according to each tradition compared has to include testing the applicability of the empirical categories. The inquiry needs to ask just how to represent the religion with regard to the respect in which it is being compared with others. Part of this representation is saying what the theology says in its own terms. But often theologies have not addressed the comparative question before and therefore do not have anything to say short of some creative extrapolation. Therefore, the work of specifying the comparative categories is an ongoing process requiring constant criticism. Both the elaboration of vague comparative categories and the specification of them for each position compared need to present hypotheses that are vulnerable to correction within the scholarly community, including the correction that comes from engaging those hypotheses in the living religions.

Comparison, as I mentioned, is not merely establishing vague comparative categories and filling them in with the specifications of the traditions compared. Comparison also requires saying just how the traditions compare. This requires translating the various specifications into the language of the vague category, for instance, translating the biblical language and Neo-Platonic language into the language of intentionality in God. Then it is possible to say that the former affirms intentionality and the latter does not, except perhaps in compromised forms. This translation and summing up process is yet another fallible undertaking, marked by hypotheses that are put forward for criticism and modified as the result of the testing. The summary part of this is triply vulnerable, depending on the vulnerable process of steadily redefining the vague category and the other vulnerable process of deciding how the compared positions specify the category, as well its own vulnerable process of tying these together.

Peirce's categories of vagueness and specificity thus lie at the heart of an urgent and massive research project for philosophy of religion, namely, the development of elementary categories by which the connections and differences among different religions and theological positions can be mapped. The research project calls for imaginative generalists to develop the vague categories through criticism, historically scrupulous specialists to represent the positions on the categories with vulnerable attention to amendment of representation, and cooperation between these two groups to bring the comparisons to explicit statement, again in a process subject to continual revision.

So far I have argued that Peirce has several brilliant and powerful ideas that make important contributions to contemporary philosophy of religion. His evolutionary approach to religion urges a careful discernment of the roles of instinct and responsible intellection in religion life, and deflects attention from defining religion by its cognitive beliefs, as earlier philosophy of religion had done. His semiotic theory lays out patterns of meaning and truth so that philosophy of religion does not have to be merely descriptive but can deal the questions of norms and truth that are so important to religions. His theory of logical vagueness and specificity shows the way to the urgent research project of comparative religions and comparative theology. Scholars of Peirce can investigate his own treatment of these topics in much more detail than I have given here in these brief allusive sketches. The fourth contribution I cite from him has a different character.

THE IMPORTANCE OF ERUDITION

Classical European and Anglo-American philosophy of religion in most of its schools defined itself so as to require little erudition in religious matters. The empiricist branch stemming from Hume assumed religion was either superstition in which it was not interested or a kind of natural-theology deism whose epistemological foundations it investigated. Contemporary American Calvinist philosophy of religion associated with Alvin Plantinga and Nicholas Wolterstorff has a different conception of religion, but not much different and surely not inclusive of the religions of East and South Asia or of traditional folk.

In contrast to the British empiricist approach to philosophy of religion is the Kantian transcendental tradition. I call this tradition "transcendental" because it believes that philosophy's special or professional contribution to the study of religion consists in pursuing some version of a transcendental reduction or theory of religion. Rudolf Otto's is probably the most famous example of this after Kant's own *Religion within the Limits of Reason Alone*. The enduring value in Otto's work is likely to be the phenomenological study of forms of mysticism. But its intent was to justify the transcendental conditions of the human mystical faculty responsive to the *mysterium tremendum et fascinans*. Neo-Kantian philosophers of religion such as Ernst Cassirer have done much to study religious symbols, but as constrained within quasi-apriori theories of categoreal schemes. The Kantians and Neo-Kantians have tended to see philosophy as an apriori discipline, setting the conditions for empirical studies that are to be done by the scientists. The major exception in philosophy of religion to this is Hegel and his tradition. Hegel thought he had to know everything, and in a way he was right.

The fourth contribution from Peirce is his conviction that philosophy of religion, like any philosophy, should be as empirical as possible and that apriori and transcendental arguments are to be distrusted. The reason they are to be distrusted is that they all require a certain, foundational starting point. Peirce's earliest articles, "Questions Concerning Certain Faculties Claimed for Man" and "Some Consequences of Four Incapacities," attacked what he called "intuition," any claim that represents itself as self-justifying. His target was Descartes, but his arrows also hit Kant's supposition that there is apriori synthetic knowledge in the sciences and hence all transcendental arguments. What Kant thought we need to affirm as the conditions for the possibility of knowledge Peirce showed could be affirmed as fallible and empirically vulnerable hypotheses about those conditions.

I have already mentioned three broad areas in which philosophy of religion needs to be empirical and thus requires great erudition. First, religion should be understood at least in terms of human evolution, which makes biological, anthropological, sociological, psychological, and historical inquiry relevant as well as the more reflective theological and philosophical. Put negatively, it is a mistake to identify religion by its intellectual beliefs without seeing how they rest on deeper and perhaps surer if vaguer evolved bases. Second, religious interpretation should be understood in terms of engaging reality in its religious dimension, which in turn can be understood through Peirce's semiotic distinctions between reference, interpretive context, and meaning systems. The truth of religious interpretation is to be ascertained by empirical studies that identify and analyze the modes of reference, the interpretive contexts, and the meaning systems in question; these empirical studies allow the question of truth to be formulated. Then the question of whether what is important in the object is in fact carried across to the interpreter can be pursued, again a matter of empirical learning. Third, the very context for the study of religion is a public within which all religions are recognized, which requires a background in history of and comparative religions, a background that even now is still in the making.

The result of all of this is that philosophy of religion, or any kind of philosophy, cannot define itself as a professional discipline with exclusive methods and boundaries. Rather, it blends in with the sciences and the arts of interpretation. More than any of these special sciences, philosophy of religion attempts to pull things together into as nearly whole an account as possible. Whereas special sciences tend to define themselves in terms of a few variables and constants, philosophy in principle cannot neglect anything.

Peirce had an arresting way of putting this. He said that an argument should not be conceived as a logical chain, which is only as strong as its weakest link. Rather it should be conceived as a rope consisting of many fibers, none very long perhaps, but each twisted with a few others, twisted against yet others, and spun cumulatively as a very strong cohering set of reinforcing forces. Peirce's essays tend to be frustrating bafflements to philosophers who like neat arguments. He appealed to various sciences, to historical examples, to anecdotes, to diagrams, all in apparently illogical ways. But the ways add up. Any number of them might turn out to be wrong. But if he can weave the justification for an hypothesis from many different strands at once, and not serially, they have a power that steadies itself under criticism rather than self-destruct.

I commend this conception of philosophy of religion as a comprehensive empirical study, requiring massive erudition and connection to experts with more erudition. Philosophic argument itself is absolutely crucial in philosophy of religion, and sometimes looks more like an appeal to logic, even mathematical logic, than to scientific studies. Peirce himself would be the first to characterize philosophy, at least metaphysics, in analogy with mathematical logic. But for Peirce, mathematics itself is the study of diagrams, and philosophical conclusions are always hypotheses vulnerable to correction by those who have perspectives beyond what have already been examined. Charles Peirce, who died almost a century ago, contributes powerful ropes of arguments for a new and vital approach to philosophy of religion.

EIGHT

Intuition

A *Platonizing of Pragmatism*

THE AIM OF THIS CHAPTER is to defend a complex doctrine of intellectual or aesthetic intuition.[1] The background for the defense arises from a more Platonic interpretation of intuition than was congenial to Peirce, especially as limned out in Plato's *Statesman*'s discussion of the art of normative measure. The general thesis is that judgment about or interpretation of any harmony involves intuition in a special sense, and that nevertheless such intuitive judgment is fallible.

INTUITION AND IMMEDIATE UNITY

Intuition is a general philosophical notion which is reconstructed and considered in nearly every philosophic age. The judgments of our own age are not unanimous. Many phenomenologists take intuition to be one of the chief elements of Cartesianism to be elaborated and defended. Other philosophers consider intuition to be the villain of the modern age. The criticism in the name of discursive thought which began with Kant reached its subtlest articulation in the early work of Charles Peirce.

Peirce attacked what he took to be Descartes' theory of intuition, defining an intuition as a cognition not determined by a previous cognition but rather directly by the transcendental object.[2] His strategy was to argue that even if we have such a faculty of intuition we cannot know that we have it. The difficulty with his attack as an attack on intuition in general (however appropriate it might be for Descartes) is that he took too narrow a view of the *subject matter* of intuition. This narrow view resulted from his beginning with a discussion of intuition as a faculty or method of knowing. If intuition can be defended, the defense must be to show that there are certain subject matters that can be known by intuition and by nothing else. The articulation of the faculty should come after acknowledgement that we must have something of the sort. To begin with the faculty is to make us too liable to take an abstract and misunderstood version of it for criticism. Consequently, although Peirce considered cases where he thought intuition might be required, and showed that they could be accounted for with a nonintuitive theory of knowledge, he never considered the crucial case where intuition seems to be required, the case of knowledge concerning harmony. My strategy here will be to consider first the nature of harmony as it is known in various connections and show that something like intuitive knowledge is involved. Next, I shall attempt a more detailed articulation of the nature of the intuitive knowing faculty. It will be argued that there is a general sense in which all judgments are "intuitive," and that there are several senses of intuition characterizing judgments about specific subject matters.

Peirce followed Kant in defining an intuition as a cognition in immediate relation to its object.[3] While this definition may in the long run be defensible, it is so only upon the supposition of the truth of a large-scale theory about the relation of cognitions to objects. When Peirce rejected intuition defined in the above way, what at heart he was attacking was not so much an alleged faculty of knowledge but an entire epistemological theory of the relation between cognitions and their objects. A definition of intuition more internal to the claims of the faculty would do it more justice. But since the latter kind of definition is dependent upon an articulation of the internal structure of intuitions, it is the very thing in question. As a result, the best to be done is to give an initial delimitation of the faculty of intuition by pointing out its subject matter.

Most of the philosophers who have defended intuition have meant by it a faculty for seeing that diverse things fit together, that they are compatible or, sometimes even stronger, that they necessarily entail each other. Intuitions concern whether one thing conforms to another, whether aesthetic elements hang together, and the like. In all these cases there is alleged a kind of immediacy in the fitness of the diverse elements for each other. The fitness is not to be explained or deduced from some higher principle but is something that must be just seen or appreciated. The "just seeing" is the justification of the word "intuition." The fitness of the diverse elements forms a whole or a new being that is not reducible to the diverse things as separate, if they could be separate. But the new being or whole is not based upon the mediation of some determinate third thing which makes the diverse elements fit. Rather the immediacy of their fitness is the whole. The form of the intuitive faculty is judgmental in the sense that to intuit the fitness of things is to judge that they fit together. Whether or not this characterization of the subject matter of intuition covers all that has been claimed in the name of the intuitive faculty, it is still a considerable portion, and it is what I shall defend as what is known intuitively.

In characterizing intuition as the faculty of apprehending or appreciating the immediate togetherness of things that so fit with each other, the question of whether there are such things is still open. It can be maintained, as it has been by those who attack intuition, that there are no things which fit together in such immediate fashion and that therefore we have no faculty of knowing them; or, conversely, it has been maintained that our faculties of knowledge all know by mediating the things they connect with determinate mediating principles and hence that we could not know an immediate togetherness even if there were such a thing. No one would deny, however, that we know *harmonies*, that we know certain things to be harmonious and certain things to be disharmonious, that we know harmonies of conformity and harmonies of intrinsic composition. My argument shall be, then, that harmony, which we all believe we know, involves the immediate fitness of things which characterizes the subject matter of intuition. Because we actually know harmonies, we actually use, and therefore have, the faculty of intuition in the sense characterized. Harmony, considered generally and abstractly, is the sort of thing that involves the apprehension or appreciation of the immediate togetherness of diverse elements.

A harmony is a unity of a plurality. Experience teaches that the kinds of things in a harmonized manifold can be diverse beyond our expectations. But the harmony of the manifold does bestow or constitute some kind of unity. In fact, any kind of unity can be called a harmony of sorts. The question here is, how does a harmony unify a manifold? What is it for a plurality to be harmonious? We may divide the possible answers to this question into two classes. On the one hand it could be said, and usually is, that the manifold is unified or harmonized by the mediation of some determinate third term; in this sense the mediating third term can be abstracted from the harmonized manifold and called *the* harmony or *the* unity. On the other hand it could be said, as I shall, that the harmony is non-mediated, not a third thing added to the manifold to unify it, but rather is an actual immediate togetherness of the distinct and diverse elements of the plurality. Let us consider the former alternative first.

To say that a plurality or complex thing is harmonized by the mediation of some thing distinct from the elements harmonized is usually to speak of the harmonizing thing as a principle, a rule, a law, a pattern, a formal structure, or the like. It is thought that this principle is imposed upon, embodied in the manifold—the manner of the actual conjunction is not important here—and that it thereby bestows unity on the plurality. The force of the claim that the unity or harmony is bestowed by something not itself just an element in the harmonized manifold is that the harmonizing principle is determinate in its own right; precisely because of the determinate nature of the principle is it enabled to unify or harmonize the manifold. If it were not determinate, the determinate unity of the harmonized manifold could not be derived from it nor could it be said to explain the harmony or unified plurality. Taking the word "principle" to be generic for all the varieties of such determinate harmonizing or unifying elements, the determinate natures of all principles must have at least two features for the principles to do their harmonizing or unifying job. They must be complex, and they must themselves be unified.

They must be *complex*, for there must be sufficient inner articulation in them to answer to the diversity in the manifold they are to harmonize. A unifying principle, if it is general, must have variables, as it were, for which the manifold supplies substitution instances. If the principle is not general but specific, it still must have individual characters which bring the plurality into the principle and give each item a place. If the principle is a political principle, a policy, it must be complex enough to take into account all the factors involved in bringing about the end in view. If it is a law, it must articulate the distinguishing features of cases and consequences. If it is a rule for a game, it must have the complexity of distinguishing the moves and their various significances. If it is a pattern as in a work of art, it must be complex enough to give each element in the work a place relative to the other elements. If it is a formal structure harmonizing the elements in an organization or in a growing organism, it must have an internal complexity which distinguishes and integrates the various functions and organs in the manifold. This is by no means a complete list of the kinds of harmonizing principles that there are, but it illustrates the point. The point can be summed up in abstract fashion: a determinate harmonizing principle must be determinate with respect to each of the members of the manifold it harmonizes and the plurality of these determinate respects makes the principle itself complex.

It might be argued against the above interpretation of the point about complexity that it distorts by speaking of the principle as separate from the manifold harmonized. Rather, it might be argued, as separate from the manifold the principle is an undifferentiated and indeterminate unity, not complex in itself, and it is only when schematized to the manifold that the principle takes on any complexity. The objection, however, does not vitiate the point. Assuming the "in-itself" versus "schematized" distinction, it is only as schematized that the principle in any way could be considered the harmonizing principle of a manifold; and as schematized it is determinate and complex. If the schematized complexity is absolutely nothing more than the complexity of the manifold, then it is misleading to call the principle a mediating third term. Rather it would fall in the class of interpretations of harmony that we called immediate: for, the determinations of the manifold would not be mediated by a further determination but would be immediately together just as they are.

Not only must the harmonizing principle be complex, it must also be *unified*. For if it merely had a complexity answering to the diversity in the manifold it could not add any harmony to what was already there; and by hypothesis the relevant harmony is lacking there. What is the unity of the principle, the rule, the law, the pattern, the structure, etc.? Philosophers have suggested three general answers to this question. (a) The unity might lie in some yet higher principle. (b) The unity might be constituted by the determinate nature of the complexity inside the principle. (c) Or the unity might be just the immediate togetherness of the complexity in the principle.

(a) Suppose that the unity lies in some higher principle. This higher principle would have to be either determinate or indeterminate. If it were determinate, it would have a complexity which in turn would need an account, and so forth. On this interpretation the question of what the unity is would not be answered. If it were indeterminate (something like the undifferentiated unity of which the principle in question is the schematization), then we must ask how it goes about unifying the schematization if it does not have a complexity answering to the complexity it unifies. No answer to this can be given except perhaps to suggest that there is either an infinity of levels of mediating schemata or that somewhere along the line a higher level would arbitrarily establish a lower level as harmonized. The former condition has all the difficulties of an actual infinite and still begs the question at the summation of the infinite in the last step. The latter condition fails to explain what the harmony established is; it really is a shift in the meaning of the question asking about the harmony. We shall return to this point below. Our conclusion here is that no way can be shown how the unity or harmony of a principle is to be found always in a higher principle.

(b) Suppose then that the unity is constituted by the determinate nature of the complex elements contained in the principle. This is the pluralistic answer to the problem of the one and the many. It claims that each of the manifold things is related to its fellows in determinate respects so that they all constitute a harmonious whole. But the question here is whether the principle which harmonizes has any contribution of its own to make, for if it does not then this answer reduces to the third. If the unified determinations just are what they are, then they are harmonized without the principle. But if the principle has determinations which it adds to those of the manifold, and if it is in virtue of this addition that the manifold is related harmoniously, then we might ask again for the unity of the whole. If the principle has a unity of its own when including the manifold, and if this unity is not in a yet higher principle, then it must be just the immediate togetherness of the complexity in the principle. But this amounts to the third alternative.

(c) Suppose finally that the unity of the principle is just the immediate togetherness of the complexity in the principle. On this supposition, however, the critical force is taken out of the claim that it is some *determinate* principle which harmonizes the manifold. For, it is the immediate togetherness of the determinations in the principle that constitutes the principle's harmony.

Our conclusion is that of the three interpretations of the unity of the harmonizing principle only the first, (a), provides a genuine alternative to the thesis that harmony is the immediate togetherness of the diverse elements. The second and third alternatives, (b) and (c), reduce to the thesis they are supposed to oppose, albeit on a higher level. If the determinate principle called upon to account for the harmony in an harmonious thing must appeal to an immediate togetherness to account for its own harmony, then why cannot the same appeal be made at a lower level? That there are principles embodied in things is by no means to be denied; but that the unity they bestow stems from some determinate mediating functions instead of from their own immediate togetherness is indeed to be denied. For the only interpretation which is a genuine alternative to that thesis, namely the first, is itself question begging. We should now consider whether the harmony can be accounted for as the immediate togetherness of the distinct and diverse elements of the plurality.

A THEORY OF HARMONY

How can the thesis that harmony is an immediate togetherness of a plurality be articulated and defended? Part of the very thesis is that harmony must just be seen to be this; it cannot be demonstrated to be so in any ordinary way, for ordinary demonstrations would mediated the very thing said to be un-mediable. My argument shall take its clue from Plato, who, when defending a similar view, staged his presentation on the four levels of the divided line.

On the first level, where we look for images and the testimony of others, there is abundant evidence. Many philosophers have cited examples of a knowing faculty which knows harmonious connections of the immediate sort. Aristotle pointed out that certain things, like the cogency of first principles and the validity of valid syllogisms, both kinds of harmonies, simply must be seen without argumentation. The faculty of doing this he called wit. Kant followed him and emphasized the role of good judgment in schematizing concepts to appearances. Many philosophers testify that rational argumentation is not at all the way to educate someone to grasp what must immediately be seen. Quoting Avicenna, Duns Scotus said, "Those who deny a first principle should be beaten or exposed to fire until they concede that to burn and not to burn, or to be beaten and not to be beaten, are not identical." Scotus added, "And so too, those who deny that some being is contingent should be exposed to torments until they concede that it is possible for them not to be tormented."[4] Hegel said that those who argue that their personal identity consists in phrenological and physiological characteristics should have their ears boxed and their heads cracked. The mediation of the fire, of the torments, and of the blows is not argumentative but merely serves to get the victim to see the immediacy of the truth. In fact, the brute presentness of the pain serves to show its immediate relation with its opposite, the ground of the immediate connections in each case; Peirce would call the relation between the pains and their opposites examples of secondness, or non-mediated connection.

Apart from philosophy, art critics have long argued that the beauty in something may be articulated but not explained. Poets say that the reduction of their work to explanatory principles loses the living harmony. Mathematicians are notorious with students for their capacity for impatience with those who just cannot see the point, regardless of explanation. Examples of interpreting knowledge or harmony as knowledge of immediate fitness or appropriateness of conjunction could be culled up indefinitely. Other thinkers would try to explain them away, however, and to defend the *prima facie* interpretation of them as we must, it is necessary to make a more direct appeal to experience.

The example of mathematics is one of common experience, an illustration from the second level of the divided line. When working out a long and complicated proof it may not be difficult to see how each step follows from its predecessor; but it often is very difficult to see how the whole proof holds together. The truth of this point is apparent when we have a theorem to prove but do not see how to do it although we are perfectly familiar with the operations connecting each of the possible steps separately. Our imagination suggests many possible approaches and when we hit upon the right one, the light flashes. We judge that it fits, that it works. Yet the right approach cannot be deduced from some determinate first principle: if it could we long ago would have done away with the hypothetical guess work and the flash of recognition that are so much a part of the experience of mathematicians.

Art is another experiential domain that involves knowing harmonies in the sense of grasping the immediate fitness or togetherness of diverse elements. The artist's experience is much akin to the mathematician's. The creative process is a continual interplay of speculative imagination making suggestions and aesthetic intuition criticizing the worth of the suggestions. Some changes in a painting are good, i.e., fit, and others are not; whether the change will be good or not cannot be deduced from some determinate higher critical principle in advance of trying it out, at least in imagination.

Although not many of us are artists, most of us have met this immediacy of aesthetic criticism in the course of defending the contested value of a work of art. Suppose we try to convince a friend that a certain work of art is good, that it has aesthetic integrity. (Integrity is an aesthetic version of harmony.) Our persuasion is limited mostly to two kinds of argumentation. On the one hand we use *ad hominem* arguments which criticize the friend for using standards that are inappropriate. It would be wrong to criticize a black and white drawing for its use of color, since it has none. Equally it would be wrong to criticize nonrepresentational art for the fact that it does not look like anything, since it makes no pretense to. If our friend were to say that those criteria *ought* to be relevant, that all drawings should be colored or all paintings representational, we would point out that his argument is either a moral one, and not aesthetic, or it is a suggestion for fruitful aesthetic projects; but in neither case is it relevant for the criticism of the given work at hand. Implicit in this side of the discussion is the point that aesthetic criticism must employ the standards that are intrinsic to the given work. Criticism of something on other grounds than aesthetic may be useful and important; but it would not be aesthetic criticism.

On the other hand we would use something like form criticism to persuade our friend. We would try to articulate the elements in the work that are important and that have a high degree of relevance. This may involve teaching a new vocabulary; but such is the job of art criticism every time a new movement of art produces styles that give importance to elements not much noticed before. We would point out things in the work that our friend might not have noticed. We might trace out abstractly the pattern of composition. If it is a painting we might indicate repetitions of color, rhythms of line, interplays of texture or unusual ways of rendering a subject matter. We might talk about the linear quality, the sense of space, the intensity of emotion, or whatever seems important in the painting.

If, after all this, our friend says that he or she still does not see what is of value in the painting, what more can we do? We might point out even more things, but we could not say what the harmony is that gives all the elements in the painting integrity or value. At some point we must rest our case and the friend either sees it or not. If not, either we begin to doubt our own judgment, or we suspect that the friend has some prejudice that we have failed to expose, or perhaps and lamentably he is "dull and a fool," an aesthetic clod. In the end, aesthetic value simply must be seen to be appreciated.

A third area of experience where the immediacy of certain judgments about harmony is evident is where we are concerned with principles. One kind of harmony that pervades human life is that which holds between principles (for instance, laws, moral rules, practical policies, etc.) and instances which fall under them; this is the harmony of conformity. As many philosophers have pointed out, whether a principle or category is to be applied to a case, or whether a case falls under a certain rule, is a matter of "judgment." "Judgment" in this sense means grasping the immediate fitness of the case for the principle or of the principle for the case.

Before making the judgment we may make guesses at various kinds of harmonious fitness. In law we appeal to the analogy of precedent and in nearly all instances of judgment of conformity some appeal to analogy is made. But at some point we must just see whether the analogy is appropriate. In the end, the judgment we see fit to make must be seen to be fit. After the judgment we can articulate rules or principles binding the special case at hand to the general principle and give these schematizing principles the same normative status as the general principle. But this is only *ex post facto*; and the only reason we can give them normative status is that we have already judged that the connection they articulate between the special instance and the general principle is fit and proper. As indicated above, the unity of such schematizing principles is not to be reduced to some higher determinate principle. Good judgment, a desirable faculty which experience cannot help but acknowledge, is the intuitive faculty of recognizing harmonies of conformity.

Mathematics, art and good judgment are but three of the many elements in experience that involve judgments of harmony which interpret harmony as an immediate fitting together of diverse things. The *prima facie* value of interpretations in experience, however, is sometimes not the real value: sometimes things are not as they seem. This discrepancy between appearance and reality is not likely in things as varied and pervasive as the interpretations cited here. But to defend the *prima facie* interpretation of judgments about harmony it is necessary to show theoretically what they entail, a process appropriate to the third level of the divided line.

The most general and abstract level upon which any real thing can be considered is that on which it is understood merely as a determination of being. The consideration of determinateness *per se* is at the heart of metaphysics. Now, harmony is present wherever determinateness is present; it is metaphysically transcendental. For, harmony is present wherever there is a unified plurality. In the first place it is or contains a plurality because it must be complex. To be determinate is to be determinate with respect to something, with respect to some other determination. This means that the determination must have at least one feature which grasps the other determination with respect to which it is determinate and which so grasps it in a characteristic way. Without such a grasping component a determination could never be sufficiently related to any other determination to be determinate with respect to it. But each determination also must have an essential or core component over against the way in which it grasps other determinations. If it lacked such a core component, then it would have no being of its own over against other determinations, no character in virtue of which its other feature could characteristically grasp the other determinations. Therefore, every determination is complex, for it must have at least these two features. If it has an identity of its own, however, in virtue of which it can be said to be a determination of being, then it is also unified; it is a unity of its component features. Therefore, every determination of being is a harmony of diverse components.

Since all of the component features of a determination are themselves determinate, they are in turn harmonies of pluralities, and so on down. Therefore, each determination is a harmony of other determinations which on a lower level are harmonies of other determinations, which on a lower level yet harmonize even lower level determinations *ad infinitum*.

From this general theory about the place of harmony in determinateness there follow three results which bear upon my present thesis.

First, according to this theory harmony is an immediate togetherness of the diverse elements harmonized. Each determination of being is a harmony of its diverse components or features. Each determination also, if it is really distinct from and determinate with respect to some other determination on its own level, is itself a component with that other determination of a third determination on a higher level. There are of course, many modes of harmony, some as tight as physical substances, some as loose as a mere context of inter-definable terms. At no point does a determination harmonize its components by mediating them with a determinate nature of its own; rather, its own determinate nature is exhausted in the characters of its components. The determination harmonizes its components only by being the togetherness of them which allows them to be determinate with respect to each other. If they were not together they could not be determinate with respect to each other. If they were not determinate with respect to each other, then their including determination could not be determinate with respect to others on its own level. Therefore, on every harmonious level, the determinateness of each determination presupposes the determinateness of the component determinations of each, which in turn presupposes the harmony of them components on the higher level. Each level is an immediate togetherness of the components whose individual harmonies are immediate togethernesses on a lower level, etc. Of course, not all determinations of being, if any, need be determinate in all respects. Most things are indeterminate in many respects, and therefore are not harmonized with many things. This theory of determinateness is not a commitment to a block universe by any means. But to the extent that any determination is determinate in any respect, it is both together with, which is to say harmonized with, the other determinations with respect to which it is determinate, and it is itself a harmony of its own components which are necessary for it to be determinate in its determinate respect.

The second result I want to draw from the theory should answer questions that are doubtless raised about the connection between harmony and mere togetherness. There is a crucial distinction to draw between two questions that might be asked about an harmonious thing. One question is *whether* it is harmonious and the other question is *why* it is harmonious. I have been arguing that the answer to the first question must involve intuition. Whether a thing is harmonious is something which, after all investigation and analysis is in, simply must be seen. The question *why* it is harmonious is of a very different ilk. To say it is harmonious because its elements hang together is not to answer the question; the question is why *those* elements hang together instead of some other elements. To abstract its pattern or structure and to say it is harmonious because it conforms to or embodies the pattern also fails to help; for the question in this case is why *that* pattern of togetherness is harmonious while some other pattern is not. We cannot say that the thing is harmonious because it stems from some determinate principle; for, as we have seen, the harmony it derives from the higher principle must be accounted for in that principle. If it is that higher principle, and we ask the question why, we are forced on to higher principles *ad infinitum*. If the answer is infinitely postponed, then either the question is meaningless or the answer is to be sought in some other kind of explanation than that of higher determinate principles.[5] In either case the nature of harmony is an utterly contingent matter. Why harmony is as it is, why certain things are harmonious and others not, is something not to be explained by any determinate principle. By intuition we tell whether something is harmonious; but why it is harmonious and certain other things are not is something we cannot deduce from any determinate principle.

Once the contingency of harmony is recognized, it is apparent that to speak of the immediate togetherness of diverse things and to speak of the harmony of diverse things are not altogether different. "Harmony" has the connotation of value, of which I shall speak shortly, while "immediate togetherness" does not. But structurally they are the same. If diverse elements can be immediately together, they are to that extent harmonious.

The fact that things are harmonious, however, does not mean necessarily that they are harmonious in all respects. Just as there are modes of harmony, there are modes of immediate togetherness. Many oil paints can be together on a canvass without being an harmonious picture. But they at last are harmonious in the sense that as physical objects they occupy adjoining and not coextensive places, etc. To achieve an aesthetic mode of harmony over and above the bare spatial or physical one require elements besides just the presence of paints, e.g. form, composition, color relation, etc. While the painted canvass of a bad painting has harmonious determinate being as a colored physical object, it does not have being as an aesthetically harmonious object: its elements are not immediately together in an aesthetic mode; rather their togetherness is mediated by spatial proximity, etc. If things fail to be immediately together in a harmony of a given mode, they can still be mediately and unharmoniously together in that mode through the mediation of a harmony in a different mode.

If diverse things cannot be harmonious together, because harmony just is not made that way, then they cannot be immediately together; rather they would be in whatever kind of contradiction is appropriate to the kinds of things they are, logical, existential, aesthetic, ethical, etc. Regardless of the contingency in the *why* of harmony, it is by intuition that we judge whether something is harmonious; it may be contingent that our cognitive nature is that way, but that is the way it seems to be.

A further qualification should be made to this point about the contingency of the why of harmony. To say that it is an arbitrary matter why harmony has the nature it does is not a commitment to the view that every harmony is arbitrary. Rather, harmony could be a transcendental property that is embodied in many different ways and modes in different things. It is conceivable that Plato is right in holding it to be embodied in various levels and various series of levels of purity. Whether this is true, of course, depends upon answering a host of metaphysical and cosmological issues. All we are committed to here is the view that harmony has many modes and is present in many structurally distinguished levels of determination. We have not spoken of the form of harmony itself, although we shall at the end; we have rather spoken of harmony as a transcendental property of determinate being which is present in harmonious things.

The third result I draw from the theory about harmony in determinateness carries us to the fourth level of the divided line; it has to do with harmony's connotation of value. Not only is the harmony of a thing that thing's unity, when it is taken as a concrete harmony, i.e., as one including and actually harmonizing the thing's components, it is the very nature of that thing as a determination of being. Now there are some things, for instance human beings, that have elements which commit the things to achieving or embodying a certain mode of harmony that is not actually achieved. For instance, people are committed by the elements in their natures which give them responsibility to achieve a mode of moral harmony that is rarely if ever achieved. People are harmonized in many modes, e.g. as physical objects, as capable social agents, etc., but often they are not harmonized as moral people, as creative people, and in various other modal characters. The *true* nature of man is a harmony of many modes of harmony, some of which are not achieved in actual life; hence few if any people fully embody the true nature of the human potential although the elements of the actual harmonies they have commit them to it. The true nature of humanity is thus an ideal, as are the more circumscribed component harmonies to which people are committed but fail in fact to embody. Other things are related to ideals in other ways, as artifacts are related to externally imposed ideals, a legal case to the ideal of judgment according to law, etc.

Whatever is an ideal for something which is committed to embody it but actually does not, in itself is a value, even when achieved. This suggests the thesis that harmony *per se* is value, and that the harmonies of things are values, whether embodied or not. A thesis of this sort is mere suggestion until it has been worked out in detail.[6] It has *prima facie* plausibility with respect to harmonies like the ideal nature of actualities and the harmonies implicit in aesthetic objects as aesthetic values. It is even plausible with respect to mathematical harmonies which exhibit the values of elegance, economy, articulateness, etc. To demonstrate the thesis with regard to the harmonies in things which seem to lack their appropriate value is even harder; to do this it would be necessary to work out in detail the various possible relations between the harmonizing nature of a determination and the harmonies of its constituent parts. The thesis does accord with the traditional view that whatever is has being and that evil, which is the failure to embody some specially appropriate being, is still dependent or resident in some actual being which has its own value.

Even if the full speculative extent of the theoretical connection of determinateness and harmony has only varying degrees of *prima facie* plausibility, nonetheless it gives considerable support to my main thesis. That is the thesis that harmony is of the nature of immediate togetherness of diverse elements. Since experience can be interpreted in many ways and explained by many mutually exclusive theories if taken in small enough doses, the best that a theory about something like harmony can do is to recommend itself as the most appealing line to follow. The nature of philosophical appeal is a problem much neglected. But at least it is fair to say that it involves aesthetic criteria of adequacy to the subject mater, elegance as a theory, and promise to fulfill the philosophical responsibility of men. Let the case then be rested for the moment that harmony is immediate togetherness, and that we do indeed know many such harmonies. This gives considerable plausibility to the thesis that we have a faculty of intuition.

JUDGMENT AND INTERPRETATION

The task of accounting for the apparent fact of intuitive knowledge with a theory about a faculty of intuition should be undertaken in the most economical way. What economy means for a philosophical approach is something that combines simplicity of theoretical structure, ease of belief and naturalness of suggestibility with appropriateness to the subject matter and elegance of formulation. Two alternative hypotheses put forward their candidacy for the prize of economy. On the one hand it would seem that it would be the simplest, easiest, most natural, appropriate and elegant state of affairs if it were the case that *all* judgments involved intuition. And on the other hand, the same virtues could be claimed for the thesis that the faculty of knowledge is specialized into many kinds and modes each appropriate to its special kind of object.

The historical difficulty with the first kinds of thesis, namely that all knowledge is of some one kind, is that it has often been the tool of vicious reductionism. For instance, the view that all knowledge is either sense perception or analytic reasoning about relations between ideas, while it has great classificatory force, has been shown to be grossly insensitive to the rich and varied texture of cognitive experience. The alternative difficulty with the second kind of thesis, namely that judgmental knowledge is many things, a different thing for each kind of object known, is that while it may be very sensitive to the richness of experience it simply lacks explanatory power. Philosophical understanding should, as Kant pointed out, reduce something to some kind of unity, although it should stop short of vicious reductionism. The latter thesis has the further difficulty of putting concerns of knowledge so posterior to the cosmology and metaphysics which determine what kinds of things there are to know, that the lesson of critical philosophy which modern thought has taught us cannot be applied in any salient form. Even if we are not Kantian, as I am not, we cannot ignore the value of reflection on the faculty of knowledge as a check to more "realistic" speculations.

When confronted with two alternative lines of approach, each claiming economy but each promising difficulty, the most economical move is to hold to both sides, each in a form that is compatible with the other. Hopefully it can be shown that the difficulties with each alternative are really sins of omission rather than commission and that what is omitted by one is fulfilled by the other. Banking on economy I shall maintain both theses.

I shall begin by arguing that every judgment involves knowledge of intuition of harmony. The plausibility for this comes from the suggestion made above that every determination of being is a harmony of other determinations. Every judgment has an object, although not necessarily a "real" object; the object of a judgment may be some other judgment or an object of "second intention" or some sort of meta-linguistic entity. But in all these cases the object of the judgment is determinate, and hence has a harmony. This thesis reflects the scholastic doctrine that being is the first object of intellect, where being is interpreted as the determinate being described above.

Next I shall argue that the specific place of harmony in the judgment plus the peculiar mode of harmony involved make all the difference that one may desire between kinds of objects of knowledge and the faculties of knowledge appropriate to them. Although it is true that a careful classification of the faculties of knowledge must wait upon a metaphysical and cosmological discussion of the kinds of objects known, my general thesis can be illustrated with some examples that show the diversity possible.

Philosophers nowadays are fairly well agreed with Peirce's view that knowledge in particular and experience in general are inextricably bound up with signs. In fact, it may even be agreed, though not so unanimously, that any specifiable element of conscious experience, any specifiable cognition, is at least a sign with an object and some significance, whatever else it may be. Most relevant to our present concern, it is agreed that *judgment* is of the nature of interpreting with signs, that a judgment itself is a sign and that it takes its subject and predicate as signs. Peirce put the point in a way vague enough to be acceptable: "A proposition has a subject (or set of subjects) and a predicate. The subject is a sign; the predicate is a sign; and the proposition is a sign that the predicate is a sign of that of which the subject is a sign."[7] On the same level of acceptable vagueness, it can be agreed that a judgment is the assertion or affirmation of a proposition. Therefore, to know something judgmentally, which is what our thesis is about, is to think with a complex sign which asserts that a component predicate sign interprets the same object that the relevant subject sign interprets. If we can show that judgment with signs involves intuitive knowledge of harmony, and can explain how and why, then we will have given our account of the thesis that judgment always involves intuition.

Now we must ask what a sign is. Again, Peirce is both vague enough and precise enough to be acceptable as a start.

> A sign . . . is something which stands to somebody for something in some respect or capacity. It addresses somebody, that is, creates in the mind of that person an equivalent sign, or perhaps a more developed sign. That sign which it creates I call the *interpretant* of the first sign. The sign stands for something, its *object*. It stands for that object, not in all respects, but in reference to a sort of idea, which I have sometimes called the *ground* of the representation. "Idea" is here to be understood in sort of a Platonic sense . . .[8]

Peirce is well known for his defense of the view that thinking, or especially judgment, is triadic; that is, he holds that the interpretant or proposition asserting the predicate sign of the subject sign's object, is a triadic relation. But there seem to be four things in his definition of sign: The sign itself, its object, its interpretant and the respect or ground. What is the respect? It cannot be the sign's object, for it is the object which needs interpretation in some respect. The respect cannot be identical with the interpretant, for the interpretant is the predicate which interprets the object in some respect; the same predicate may interpret other objects in other respects. Furthermore, the respect cannot be identical with the sign itself, for the sign is the actual mediating of the object and interpretant; the respect is far more abstract. But then the respect is not some determinate fourth thing; the relation is not quadratic over and above being triadic. For, if the respect were a determinate thing in between the object and the interpretant, the sign would first have to relate the interpretant to the respect and the object to the respect and then the two relations to each other; but the object would be related to the respect in some second respect, and the interpretant would be related to the respect in some third respect; and these relations in respects would be mediated by further relations in respects *ad infinitum*. Unless the interpretative situation can be articulated as a triadic relation or finite set of triadic relations no actual interpretation or judgment about an object can be made.[9]

One thematic lesson that is given encouragement by the discussion above is that whenever a togetherness of several things does not allow of infinite mediation in its unity an immediate togetherness or harmony is to be suspected. Furthermore, a judgment is a unified plurality, a kind of discursive harmony harmonizing its subject and predicate in a certain respect. Can this suspicion be borne out in the case of the unity of judgment or sign interpretation? What we are after is an account of the respect in which the sign asserts the interpretant of its object. It will not do to say simply that a judgment or sign interpretation is just the harmony or immediate togetherness of subject and predicate or object and interpretant in some respect, for it is the very respect that wants an account.

As noted above, however, a harmony of things always has a mode. That is, a harmony of things is always on a level relative to other levels of lesser constituent harmonies and of more inclusive harmonies. Furthermore, things with determinate natures can be together in a variety of modes. For instance, red paint and green paint can be together on a canvass in a mode of spatial harmony and also in a mode of aesthetic harmony. Their togetherness in each mode also in a mode makes them determinate with respect to each other in that mode. When paints are first put on the canvass they become determinate with respect to each other in the spatial mode of the canvass for the first time. If they are artfully put on the canvass they become determinate with respect to each other in an aesthetic way. If they do not attain harmony in an aesthetic mode we say that the canvass is ugly only because we expect it to have harmony aesthetically, not because it attains harmony in a contra-aesthetic mode. As Plato points out in the *Parmenides*, there is no form of ugliness.

It is no small coincidence that the word "respect" has taken on technical significance in two places in our discussion. We have said that things are harmonized when they are determinate with respect to each other. And we have said that a judgment takes place when, with a sign or proposition we interpret an object by an interpretant in some respect. With regard to the latter, we may now say that the respect in which a predicate interprets a subject's object, or the respect in which a sign ascribes or warrants an interpretant of an object, is the mode in which the predicate is together with the subject or the interpretant is together with the sign's object. The mode of togetherness is implicit in the sign which mediates between object and interpretant; but it is abstract. An object can be interpreted in many respects: this is to say it can be together with interpreting predicates or interpretants in many modes. An interpretant can be signified of many objects in many respects; this is to say it can be together as an interpretant with many objects in many modes.

It is necessary to remember that the modal harmony of signs in knowledge is a great specialization of the general considerations of modal harmony above. To be harmonized as object and interpretant is already a specialization of modes; not all harmonies are of this sort. Then there are probably some few general categories *à la* Aristotle, Kant, or Peirce that all modes of interpretative harmonies fall into; these further specify the modes. Finally the vast richness of possible kinds of judgments makes the modes even more specific. It is at this point that metaphysics, cosmology, art, science and many other disciplines, philosophical and otherwise, must be consulted for the compilation of an adequate catalogue of modes of interpretation. Let us lump all these problems and programs together for the nonce by calling those harmonies *semiotic* harmonies whose modes are such that one harmonized element interprets another in some respect, the respect being the mode of togetherness in which one stands for the other.

Further plausibility can be rendered this point by recalling our previous discussion of the connection of value with harmony. The harmony of many things in a given mode we said is a value for those things. With respect to the process of interpretation, value appears in the guise of goals or purposes of interpretation. To the extent that interpretation is subject to self-control we have purposes for interpreting things, and it is the purpose which selects the mode in which the thing is to be interpreted. To use Peirce's example, we interpret the stove as black because we want to know what color it is. (Many interpretations, especially those as regards color, are not subject to much self-control, for we have habits of noting colors without looking for them; but presumably the habit is established because some general value or purpose of noting colors is served by it.) Were there no such purposes, either conscious or habitual, permeating our interpretative life we would be at a loss to discover why we interpret in some respects rather than others. An interpretative purpose is the intention to determine an object in thought in the mode of harmony which is the respect in which interpretation is sought. A judgment, therefore, is a value which is the concrete harmony in the mode of interpretation intended.

It is fair to say now that all knowledge of judgments (knowledge that would be embodied in judgments about previous judgments) is knowledge of harmony and therefore intuitive. Whatever the grounds for the harmony in the judgment, be they empirical, analytical, postulative or whatever, the elements of the judgment are still harmonized. The only way in which the elements of the judgment may fail to be harmonized qua judgmental elements is if they fail to be harmonized in some semiotic mode. (If it were not the case that the meanings of "syntactics," "semantics," and "pragmatics" are as obscure and complicated as the subject their distinction is supposed to explain, we might say that any alleged judgment that is syntactically and semantically valid, though perhaps not pragmatically so, is a proper judgment with a semiotic harmony.) Any knowledge of a judgment, whatever else it might be, is an intuition of a harmony with a semiotic mode.

A judgment itself has an object, and it may be that not all objects of judgments are other judgments. Still it is the case that all objects of judgments, *qua* such objects, are asserted by the judgments about them to be harmonies. They are harmonies of the object indicated by the subject in the judgment with the object or feature contemplated in the predicate of the judgment. This is not the place to go into the various ways in which subjects can indicate their objects and the various ways in which predicates assign real properties to them. Since the relation between a judgment and its object is itself a complex harmony (one of pragmatics?) duly noted by higher level judgments, there are likely many complex modes in which subjects and predicates are related to their objects. These modes of harmony connecting judgments and their objects are the modes that articulate the correspondence between judgmental knowledge and its object. It is not possible today to maintain a correspondence theory of truth in any sense of simple mirroring, but correspondence in some general or formal sense, as Kant noted, is unavoidable. The semiotic modes of harmony in judgment are ways of asserting metaphysical and cosmological modes of harmony in the judgment's objects. This is to say that judgment articulates the determinate nature of its object and this determinate nature is a harmony of determinations. Therefore, any judgment has a harmony as its object and, whether true or false, lays claim to being an intuition in this general sense.

This general sense in which every judgment is an intuition has been rendered without recourse to the claim that an intuition is an immediate relation to its object. In fact, the relationship between an intuition and its object can be highly mediated. Before working our thoughts up into determinate judgments, the signs that go into them are greatly dependent upon previous signs for their occurrence, their nature and their function. Peirce may well be right that there is no sign in thought which is not determined by a previous sign. But when our thought does arrive at judgment the judgment is related to its object by the modes of correspondence; to the extent that these are modes of harmony, whose elements are immediately together, it might be said in this sense that any judgment is in immediate relation to its object. But let this not be confused with what Peirce meant, which was that the immediate relation is a surd. Rather, immediate relation is a harmony which, far from being a surd, we have just seen to lie at the heart of any intelligibility.

Our conclusions can be expressed in a common sense way. Any judgment is a grasping of its object to be such and so, whatever highly mediated reason there might be for grasping it that way. This grasp is a taking of the object to be immediately what it is. This is intuition in the general sense. So long as we remain on the level of general intuition, the judgments all have a fallible form. For, we can always ask whether the object is really as the judgment says it is. If the defense of the judgment is that the object must just be seen to be such and so, as the judgment says it is, then this is a move from the general sense of intuition to a more special sense.

INTUITION AND PLATO'S DIVIDED LINE

We come now to the second half of the thesis stated at the beginning of the previous section, namely, that judgment, and hence intuition, has a special form or nature for each of the several kinds of objects known. Thus, for instance, intuitive knowledge of the aesthetic value of a picture is intuition of a different sort from the intuitive knowledge that a law applies in a particular case; and both of these are quite different from the knowledge that a particular apple is red, which hardly seems like intuition in a special sense at all however much it is intuition in the general sense. It is hopeless to try to classify all the kinds of objects of knowledge in a literal way without appeal to some selective principle of epistemology which would say *a priori* what could be known. But whereas that procedure might be very fine for dealing with objects on the general level where kinds of knowables are not distinguished, it is viciously prejudicial on special levels where the knowables are distinguished. A proper classification must wait upon metaphysics, cosmology, science, art and all the rest of the cognitive and appreciative disciplines to reveal their findings.

The thesis that intuition does mean several special things, however, can be illustrated by use of myth, as it were. I shall take Plato's distinction of knowables according to the levels of the divided line and indicate different ways in which intuition is involved on each level. It must be remembered that not only is this use of Plato merely illustrative but also that Plato himself thought of his distinction as vague and imprecise.

On the lowest level of the division are what Plato calls images, whose chief characteristic is that they are discrete, separated out of experiential contexts and combinable in ways that do not reflect either experiential or theoretical structures.

Consider both a fragment of a dream episode and something we hit upon in a musement. We think them for reasons of association and their features are determined by previous signs. But in the former case the influence of rational and prudential reason is negligible, and in the latter case the influence of habitual trains of thought is cast aside as much as possible. Still, in both cases there is a determinate nature to the episodes, however absurd it might seem in light of the practical connective tissue of experience and the predictive probabilities and deductive necessities of theory. This determinate nature is something grasped in judgment and is a harmony of sorts; therefore it is grasped by intuition. It is instructive to ask how this intuition is fallible. Of course, memory of the episode is fallible, but that is not the point. Furthermore, the modes of harmony entertained in the episodes may not be possible either in experience or in theory, but that again is not to the point. The only way in which a dream judgment may be wrong intrinsically is if it is inconsistent with the bizarre rules or modes of harmony presupposed in the episode. If there are no such rules, then the episode is merely a passage of images and there is no judgment involved. But dreams do seem to involve at least quasi-perceptual judgments, and this means that there must be at least enough continuity from dreamed object to dreamed perceptual interpretation of the object for the judgment to be accurate or not. Daydreams and musement illustrate this much better than night dreams where analysis is encumbered by censored memory.

Consider also creative imagination. It takes place within the context of some problem to be solved. But the problem does not present rules for its solution and discrete bits of imaginative states of affairs are proposed as hypotheses. The criticism of the hypotheses takes place according to criteria after the work of imagination. But the suggestions themselves have a determinate character which can be considered in themselves. Thus a painter might suspect that coloring an area green would improve his picture; the idea of green color for the area is a determinate suggestion that can be contemplated. That is, it can be though of in intuition. The idea of a green area might be wrong in its relevance and wrong in its value as a suggestion, but these errors are beside the point here. The only way in which a suggestion of creative imagination could be wrong internally is if it is not really possible, that is, if it contains within it some hidden inconsistency.

These illustrations suggest the following remark about intuition concerning images in general. Imaginative intuition is the grasping of certain features together in a mode of harmony which bears no intrinsic connection with other or wider or more generalized modes of harmony. In most senses of error, imaginative intuition cannot be said to be fallible. But it is fallible in the sense that the mode of harmony uniquely constitutive of the intuited manifold may directly contradict itself. This means simply that an erroneous imaginative intuition would not have the proper form of intuition; its alleged harmony would be no harmony at all. The objects of valid imaginative intuition are sheer possibilities: sheer in the sense that they might not be possibilities for anything concrete to realize since they might be unconnectible with anything on heaven and earth; and sheer in the sense that if the logical depths of their consistency is probed beyond the surface presentation they might even then be seen to be self-contradictory. Perhaps it would be more accurate to say that an imaginative intuition itself is not fallible; rather a later judgment which alleges a judgment to be an imaginative intuition might be mistaken. The continuity of imaginative intuitions with identifying judgments is a far more complex problem than meets the eye, however, and our suggestions here should be tentative.

Plato's second level of knowledge deals with experience whose objects are mainly existents that are casually effective and connected. The kinds of judgments we make on this level are too numerous to get a representative sample. Let us consider only two kinds, perceptual judgments and prudential judgments.

In a perceptual judgment there is asserted a harmony of at least two forms, the indicative form of the subject and the attributional form of the predicate. But over and above this is asserted the harmony of the physical embodiment of the predicate form with the physical object indicated by the subject. In experiential judgments of perception the truth alleged is a kind of correspondence. Even if it be the case that we would say the perception is highly conditioned by our own physiology or structure of consciousness, the perceptual judgment contends that there is something in the object which is a proper object of our judgmental elements and which is to be represented by the way we do indeed represent it. To judge that an apple is red may involve the claim that we see the apple redly; but it also involves the claim that there is something in the apple which is properly to be perceived by our redly seeing. Perceptual judgments intuit the nature of the object perceived as something corresponding to the harmony in the perceptual judgment. But it is presupposed here that the modes of correspondence between the signs in the judgment and the elements in the object which they represent are proper. That is, it is presupposed that the harmony of correspondence is such that the meanings by which we interpret the signs in the perceptual judgments will accord with the object as perceived in other guises and contexts.

It is for this reason that we say, acknowledging that perceptual judgments are largely beyond our conscious control, that our perception is trustworthy only under standard conditions. For instance, if part of the significance of the red color of an apple is that it indicates ripeness, then the mode of correspondence involved in perceiving the apple to be red should allow us to infer that it will taste ripe; the proof will come in the taste perception. If the apples are really green and are sold under red cellophane or under red lights, then these are nonstandard conditions of perception. The real greenness in the apple would be whatever is in the real existent which is casually connected with that in the existent which we would taste as sour. Perceptual intuition is fallible in that the modes of correspondence between the judgment and object may be improper for the meanings of the signs in the judgment to be applied to the object in coherence with other perceptual judgments.

Prudential judgments are much more complex, since part of their intrinsic nature is to be conclusions of deliberations that take account of many other kinds of judgment. They require that the actual state of affairs be accurately described and understood by perceptual judgments, judgments as to the law-like behavior of things, etc. They require that an ideal or norm be grasped in some way. And they require that the elements of in the present state of affairs be conceived as rearranged in a proportion or measure that has just enough of each thing, not too much and not too little, to best embody the ideal.

This conception of the rearrangements of elements in a normative measure is a kind of schema relating the norm and actual state of affairs. The conception must be hit upon by imaginative intuition, and it should be determined to be a real possibility, given the present state of affairs. But at the heart of prudential judgment lies the judgment of normative measure, that is, the judgment of what is just enough of each element that must go into making up the future state. Now the schema or conceived state of measured arrangement has a structure which forms the conception. Once the structure is accepted as normative there is a certain deliberation involved in determining the means to achieve that structure in reality; but this is not what I am calling prudential judgment. Prudential judgment is judgment of the proper measure or proportion that would best accord with the norm. This is intuition in the good old fashioned sense that the structure of the harmony in the judgment is also seen to be normative.

Philosophy after Plato has sorely neglected the analysis of this kind of intuitive judgment and therefore we have no generally accepted account to draw upon. Its analysis would have to proceed much farther even before we could tell a myth about it. But a word can be said about its fallibility. There are many ways in which the imaginative and generally descriptive judgments that go into prudential deliberation may be fallible, as we have already discussed. And there is a way we have yet to discuss about how intuition of the norm is fallible. The peculiar fallibility of prudential intuitions of normative measure, however, is that the mode of harmony in the conceived schema may not be one which harmonizes all the elements of the actual state of affairs that have degrees of intrinsic importance. That the schematized conception does justice to the norm is something that must be just seen. But that the schematized conception acknowledges the intrinsic importance of the individual harmonies in the elements it brings into larger harmony is something about which we are often mistaken in practical prudence. For, it is easy to submerge the individual values in the things to be harmonized as a whole so as to arrive at a mode of inclusive harmony that is too simple. The fault of most prudential schemes is that they are too simple and lose values which they might otherwise embody. This is especially true of that prudential thinking which finds its norms in ideologies and preconceived codes of values.

Plato in the *Statesman* classifies the king, the best example of one who uses what we have called judgments of normative measure, as someone whose knowledge is closer to the theoretical than to the applied. This was because the king's knowledge deals with norms and with the actual state of affairs understood in theoretical fashion. In the *Theaetetus*, however, Plato uses prudential judgments as involved in the fabric of practical experience to refute the claim that all knowledge is just perception. In consonance with his latter employment of prudence I have treated prudential judgments as being on the second or experiential level of the divided line. The peculiar fallibility pointed out with such practical prudential judgments is one peculiar to the experiential domain.

There are, however, other kinds of fallibility which attend those portions of judgment of normative measure that are properly on the theoretical or dialectical levels. There is a fallibility, for instance, even in judgments of harmony which must be "just seen." To say as we have that the peculiar fallibility of intuitions of normative measure in the practical or experiential sphere is that too simple a mode of harmony may be attempted in the schema for the proper fulfillment of the lesser harmonies to be united is not to acknowledge all the kinds of fallibilities present. Rather, it is only to point out the one peculiar to normative measure on the practical level. There is a purer factor in judgments of normative measure to be found on higher levels.

The top two divisions of the divided line are much harder to interpret than the bottom two. But since our purpose here is not to be exhaustive we shall illustrate our point about the plurality of kinds of intuition by reference to three kinds of judgments which Plato would call knowledge. First we shall cite judgments of formal cohesion, which belong on the third or theoretical level. Second we shall cite judgments of formal evaluation, evaluation according to self-constituted norms; it is ambiguous whether Plato would put this on the third or fourth level, but we shall let it mark the transition. Thirdly, on the level of dialectic, we shall consider judgments which apprehend norms as such.

By *judgments of formal cohesion* I mean judgments that formal, structural, or conceptual elements hang together in some way because of their very nature and not because of some external medium. Mathematics affords obvious examples, as does formal and conceptual theory construction. Judgments of formal cohesion are judgments that the object, which in this case may be just the aggregate of formal elements, is structurally harmonious. There are many modes of such hang-togetherness, even on very abstract conceptual levels; in a logical theory some elements are harmonious in a mode of compatibility, others in a mode of entailment or perhaps co-entailment. And so forth. In a judgment of this sort, the subject of the judgment indicates all the elements structurally harmonized; the predicate indicates the harmony in question, i.e., the harmony of the proper mode.

The mode of harmony of the subject and predicate is one of a more general mode than the one contained in the predicate; it is a semiotic mode which corresponds to the most general mode of immediate togetherness. To judge things to be formally cohesive is to judge in a mode which commits the judgment to say that the cohesion of the elements is just their very being. To judge that things are formally cohesive is to judge that this is just the way they are. Where the previous intuitive judgments we have analyzed had objects either that were not real except as thought in the judgment or that were real apart from the judgment but only represented therein, judgments of formal cohesion have as their objects things which are what they are irrespective of any thought about them but which are exactly what they are thought to be. For the first time we come to judgments of the being of the objects.

Judgments of formal cohesion are immediate in the sense that the contemplation of the elements indicated in the subject allows one just to see their harmony. While misunderstanding of the formal elements contemplated might be cleared up by argumentation no argumentation can deduce, induce or probate the conclusion of harmony. Nonetheless, such judgments are fallible. For however immediate the appropriateness of the subject and predicate for each other, the assertion of them together is itself a sign mediating between the two. Finite knowers must separate the subjects harmonized from the harmony we recognize in them in order to assert the identity. This very separation insures the fallibility, for we might ascribe the harmony contemplated in the predicate to a subject that in fact is not harmonized. Peirce's question returns: how do we recognize that an intuitive judgment of formal cohesion is indeed such a true recognition of the harmony? Of course there is a feeling of certainty, a sense of "Aha! It is so." But as experience has shown this feeling has all to often come at the wrong time. To judge whether an alleged judgment of formal cohesion is a true one, or whether it is a mistaken judgment, requires further deliberation. This further judgment must be more complex, since it must repeat the first judgment in order to check and it must also judge that its repetition is an accurate repetition. Furthermore, if some concrete doubt about the formal cohesion has been raised, the criticizing judgment must handle that too.

The answer to Peirce's question must be that the faculty of judging whether a given judgment is an intuition of formal cohesion is: (a) intuitive in the sense of the first judgment and (b) discursive in comparative and perhaps argumentative senses. But this faculty is also fallible. Never do we get an infallible judgment that a judgment of formal cohesion is correct; but never can there be such a judgment that does not in some way look again to what the original judgment was about. We must judge from long experience whether a judgment of formal cohesion is correct, and experience only gives probability. The probability that the Pythagorean theorem is as reason sees it to be is very high, higher in fact than any mathematical articulation of what probability means. The probability of certain other intuitions of formal cohesion is not so high. But this does not vitiate the point that they are indeed intuitions, judgments of that which must be just seen to be so.

The possibility of error is introduced into intuitions of formal cohesion by the mediative force of judgment itself. But what kinds of mistakes are possible? Setting aside errors that come from an unruly and indiscriminate will which asserts harmony of formal structures without reason, mistakes in the intuition seem to be of two sorts. On the one hand we can mistake the nature of some of the elements alleged to be harmonized; on the other hand we can mistake the mode of harmony appropriate to these elements. Usually both work together. The notion of the appropriateness of a mode of harmony cannot be eliminated from the analysis of judgments of formal cohesion, for the mode of harmony must be appropriate to the formal elements harmonized. Appropriateness is a normative notion, and this brings us to the consideration of normative judgments. Some of the fallibility of judgments of formal cohesion stems from the normativeness involved in such judgments.

Evaluative judgments mark the transition to the level of dialectic. There are many kinds of evaluative judgments; but let us consider here those which evaluate candidates for ideal forms. As in prudential judgments when matters of concrete experience are evaluated, the formal structure of the real existents plays a large role in their ideals which we seek to determine. Some kinds of evaluation deliberate about means to ends; but these are not the kind to which attention is being called here. Nor do we mean to treat evaluations where particular cases are subsumed under laws; this is closer to prudential judgment. Rather, the evaluative judgment to be considered here is that which evaluates a form, a cohesive structure, in terms of whether it is an ideal for other formal cohesive structures.

Determining the ideal form is like the judgment of normative measure which we discussed above except that in the present case it is pure rather than applied. That is, the real thing given in this case is a cohesive formal structure. It does have a harmony, at least in the minimal mode of compatibility, for we recognize its formal articulation. For instance philosophical anthropology and all the sciences may give us a formal theory of the nature of man. As a formal theory it should be consistent and presuppose perhaps several modes of harmony. But philosophical anthropology and science do not tell us what the ideal man is; they do not tell us what the ideal form of man is. In common experience we make many appeals to such ideal forms, especially to the forms of those things we have a hand in making.[10]

How do we go about determining the ideal form for a formal structure? My interpretation follows Whitehead's view in *Adventures in Ideas* fairly closely, elaborating some of his suggestions; if this is not the only way to arrive at conceptions of ideal forms, it is at least one way and it affords an example of intuitive judgment. In any given formal structure or conception, such as in certain mathematical axioms or in a theoretical conception of human nature, the structure combines several formal elements in a harmony that has at least minimally some mode of compatibility. Each one of these formal elements is itself a harmony in some mode in its own right. For instance, people are so structured that certain elements of our being harmonize to form our sensual erotic life, and other elements (or some of the same in new combinations) harmonize to form our intellectual life. But perhaps the overall harmony descriptive is not of sufficiently complex a mode that the harmonies of erotic concerns and intellectual concerns can reach *their* highest modes; perhaps a person's erotic and intellectual life coexist by partially frustrating each other. The ideal form of the human must then be conceived as a harmony of the same elements that the descriptive form harmonizes but in a mode of sufficient complexity that the harmonies of the elements can attain their highest modes. This is to say, the ideal form of something must allow for the ideal fulfillment of all the elements which it harmonizes. Presupposed here, of course, is that we have a clue to the ideal forms of the contained elements. This is not a vicious presupposition, however, since we are not arguing that the ideals of the contained elements are strictly to be deduced from the ideal of the whole.

Determination of the ideal of the whole is more complex than we have indicated. For, an ideal form which allows for the ideal realization of the lesser harmonies is likely to call for intervening modes of harmony that relate some but not all of the elements in the descriptive structure. For instance intellect and will, perhaps, must be harmonized and the erotic life and discipline also harmonized, before a sufficiently complex mode of harmony is possible for the harmony of intellect and the erotic life. The ideal form then would have to allow for the realization of two lesser modes of harmony, not just one. Furthermore, these two lesser modes perhaps have relations to each other for which there is an ideal harmony making the ideal whole even more complex. Considered as a process of coming to know an ideal form, the moves we have discussed so far would probably lead to a reevaluation of the kinds of harmonies ideally to be sought for the lesser elements. Both love and intellect would probably have opened to them far more complex modes of harmony in the light of the total ideal person than we would have expected at first. One has only to read the development of the concept of the ideal person in the *Republic*, from the appetitive person to the just person, to see how noble just appetite alone is.

Implicit through all this shifting calculus in the determination of ideal forms is the norm of harmony. The ideal is that form which best harmonizes the constituent elements of the thing of which it is a form so as to bring those elements individually to greatest harmony. To determine this requires the use of the art of normative measure, this time in a pure and formal fashion, not in application to concrete existents. For we must measure the mixture of the elements so that we have just enough of each for both individual and collective enhancement of harmonious modes. One cannot explain the normative character of an ideal form simply in terms of a collection which allows for the highest possible modes of harmony for its parts; what makes the measured collection an harmonious structure is the norm which it schematizes to the given descriptive forms.

Knowledge of the pure norm itself is the problem of dialect to which we shall turn shortly. Knowledge of the ideal form which stands between the pure norm and the structural form is a kind of intuition. In fact, it is a double-sided intuition. On the one hand it must identify the structure of the ideal form as a possible transformation of the structure of the descriptive form. On the other hand it must identify the same structure of the ideal form as a harmony in the highest possible mode which allows for the highest possible modal harmony of all the constituents; that is, it must identify the ideal form as ideal. Both sides have their analogues in prudential judgments. That we have a faculty for judging or recognizing harmonies of this sort is evident from experience, since we do it all the time. As Jonathan Edwards pointed out it is quite conceivable that we should be creatures without such a faculty; but as matter of fact we have it. Furthermore, the judgment identifying a structure as an *ideal* form is an immediate kind of thing: we either grasp that it is the proper harmony, or we do not. But as Plato showed in nearly all of his dialogues, this is an eminently fallible faculty, for there are few things we are more often wrong about than ideals. Constant dialectic is our only protection against this fallibility.

In what does the fallibility lie? There is always the ordinary fallibility in recognizing whether any concatenation is a harmony; but this is not the peculiar fallibility plaguing determination of ideals. Rather the peculiar fallibility is that we are apt to settle for the wrong mode of harmony in the ideal. The mode of harmony in the ideal form is wrong if it is not such that it harmonizes all the constituent elements of the thing according to their individual ideal modes. We often settle for modes of harmony in our ideals that repress, subjugate or pervert certain of the elements in the structure idealized. The fact that the mode in the ideal we do settle on is indeed a harmony and the fact that it does probably enhance the modes of harmony of some of the constituents tempts us mightily to think it is the best possible mode. Only a dialectic which reminds us of the neglected ideals of the constitutive elements, a dialectic characteristic of moral deliberation and illustrated in its various kinds by Plato, corrects the fallibility of our intuitive faculty for determining ideal forms.

The level of dialectic *per se* is one of the hardest Platonic notions to interpret. Plato's own descriptions are strangely evasive. But this is for a reason. According to the divided line diagram in the *Republic* on each level the faculty of knowledge is to be distinguished from the appropriate object. On the third level, for instance, the faculty is that of recognizing theoretical or formal structures, and structural forms are the object. On the fourth level the faculty is the method dialectical thinking (how does Plato describe that?) and the objects are supposed to be the pure values which make some formal structures ideal and others not so ideal. But any object of knowledge must be determinate, as we have seen; for otherwise we could not know it to be what it is in contrast to what it is not. Yet to be determinate is to be formal or structural, and hence the only objects of knowledge possible on the level of dialectic can be the ideal forms considered as ideal, what we have just discussed.

Nonetheless, the aim of knowledge on the dialectical level is not to know which forms are ideal but what it is in them which makes them ideal. Dialectic aims at knowing the form of the good or harmony *per se*. Yet since this normativeness of harmonies never can appear pure as an object, we can only grasp it in determinate forms. We may consider the ideal forms in terms of each other, ordering them in hierarchical fashion according to which have modes of harmony that include the ideal modes of the others; this is perhaps what Plato meant when he described dialectic as the treating of the ideal forms as hypotheses which we lay down as steps of a ladder up which we ascend to the Good. But the Good cannot be an object of knowledge without becoming determinate and hence a form. And for any form, we may ask what it is that makes it ideal; any form of which we can ask this question cannot be the pure good.

At this point we must recur to our previous distinction between two questions: the question whether something is a harmony and the question is why it is so. This distinction can now be rendered as follows: there is the question whether some form is the ideal for that of which it is alleged to be the ideal, and there is the question why its harmony which makes it ideal has the structure it does. Intuition in the various senses we have discussed can determine whether a given form is an ideal by determining whether its mode of harmony allows the ideal modes of harmony of its constituents. The ideal has the structure it does because that is the structure which harmonizes the ideal harmonies of the constituents. But this does not explain *why* the ideal's structure is a harmony. As we have been doing, it is possible to articulate the metaphysical structure of harmony *per se*, but such an articulation, treating harmony as a determinate form, can never answer the question *why* harmony has that structure. That which makes harmony have the structure it does can never be a determinate object of knowledge, for the harmony which it is supposed to explain is constitutive of the most elemental nature of intelligibility in an object of knowledge. Yet, since it is a contingent fact that harmony has the differential and normative structure it does, harmony would not be at all unless it were created to be what it is. Therefore, Plato was most accurate in the *Republic* when he described the form of the Good as that which creates the intelligible forms which are objects of knowledge.

Dialectic requires no kind of intuition different from those we have described so far. Using those kinds of intuition it enables us to determine the formal structure, including the ideality, of all possible objects of knowledge. For, there is nothing which dialectic in principle cannot do to articulate the structure of any harmony if our previous argument was right that all knowable things are determinate and that determinateness requires, and in fact consists in, the harmonizing of other determinations.

The aim of this chapter has been to defend the notion of intuition interpreted in a certain way. My two specific theses are that we have a faculty of intuition and that this faculty is fallible. I first argued that experience shows that we do have such a faculty. Intuition was identified with the faculty of apprehending an object that involves harmony. Then I illustrated this faculty with kinds of knowledge our experience exhibits on four stages of Plato's divided line. In passing, a theory of harmony and determinateness was sketched. Next I attempted to give a philosophical account of the faculty of intuition exhibited previously. I developed the view that every judgment whatsoever is intuitive in the general sense that it is a grasp of harmony. Finally I distinguished several kinds of intuition according to Plato's division of the divided line and discussed special senses of intuition or graspings of harmony involved on various levels. No attempt was made to list kinds of intuition exhaustively; our list was only suggestive. The fallibility of each kind of intuition listed was discussed.

Like most Platonic undertakings, the defense of these theses is tentative. Nevertheless, it is plausible enough to make a suggestive extension of the theory of interpretation developed so brilliantly by Peirce.

NINE

Whitehead and Pragmatism

THE ENTANGLED LEGACIES OF PRAGMATISM AND PROCESS PHILOSOPHY

PRAGMATISM AND PROCESS PHILOSOPHY should not be viewed as alien schools of thought at all but as tangled with one another in many common causes throughout twentieth century philosophy. At Harvard from 1924 until his death, Whitehead was in the academic and cultural home of Charles Peirce, William James, Josiah Royce (the Absolute Pragmatist as he called himself[1]), Ralph Barton Perry, C. I. Lewis, William Ernest Hocking, and Willard Quine. Among his most important graduate students were Charles Hartshorne and Paul Weiss who edited the *Collected Papers of Charles Sanders Peirce* at Harvard while Whitehead was teaching there. Hartshorne says that his move to the University of Chicago from Harvard put him in close personal and intellectual touch with Dewey and Mead. Dewey, from the pragmatists' side, was enthusiastic about Whitehead's philosophy, reviewed it, and contributed a major article to the Library of Living Philosophers volume on Whitehead. George Lucas has traced many of the entanglements of Whitehead with the pragmatists.[2]

In many respects, pragmatism and process philosophy, especially in the early years, worked the same side of the street, defending:

- realism against idealism[3]
- realism in the other sense against nominalism[4]
- the importance of experience in a broader sense than British empiricism[5]
- the possibility of metaphysics in the grand tradition though in revolutionary forms critical of the tradition[6]
- the importance of philosophy for public life rather than as an academic subject alone (as it tended to be on British, German, and French models of philosophy)[7]

- the meaning of truth as correspondence[8]
- the criteria of truth as pragmatic (some pragmatists are more careful with this distinction than others)[9]
- fallibilism and the method of hypothesis over against foundationalism[10]
- all of the above in considerable self-conscious cooperation over against both Anglo-American analytic philosophy and Continental philosophy which were dominant in the English-speaking academic world throughout the last two-thirds of the twentieth century, with the result that pragmatism and process philosophy together were marginalized in academic philosophy from the 1960s onward[11]

This having been said, there are some crucial *cultural* and *class* differences in the origins and trajectories of process thought and pragmatism. Although these may not be politically correct to mention, they are important for understanding the distinctions between the schools, especially in the minds of recent representatives. Whitehead was an upper-class Anglican, and so was Hartshorne; Harvard seemed their due.[12] If that religious upper-class sense of intellectual place has slipped a bit in process-Methodists such as John B. Cobb, Jr., and myself, it should be remembered that Methodists are fallen-away Anglicans with more spirit but less class. Although not all process philosophers are theists by any means (consider the important anti-process-theism work of Donald Sherburne[13]), most process philosophers are also philosophers of religion or theologians. The ambiance of Whitehead's thought is that of high civilization in which religions play defining roles. The "adventure of ideas" relates to civilization, not society.

The pragmatists related more to society than to civilization. This is least true of William James, a true Boston Brahmin, though it is still true of him. Charles Peirce was an utter cultural failure at the Boston Brahmin role, despite being an Episcopalian, deeply religious, theologically imaginative, and filled with as much Greek and Latin as Whitehead.[14] Of the other Harvard philosophers who might be called pragmatists, Royce was also an idealist and is usually classified that way rather than as a pragmatist, and the same was true later of Hocking.[15] Perry was too close to James to reach out fully to the naturalism and social reform interests of pragmatists of his generation such as Dewey and Mead. Lewis and Quine narrowed pragmatism toward logic, not social relevance.[16] Pragmatism in mid-century flourished in the unpolished Midwest, and in New York with all its immigrants, including especially Jews such as Ernst Nagel and Sidney Hook. Thinkers who want to change the world through social reform and education can quickly latch on to pragmatism in some form or other but have a hard time thinking of process philosophy as a practical guide for change-agents.

Although some pragmatists have been theists, and Dewey's *A Common Faith* is an important positive theological contribution,[17] pragmatists have generally thought of themselves as naturalists. To many who came from Orthodox Jewish or low-church conservative Christianity, naturalism means anti-supernaturalism which in turn means anti-religion.[18] Whereas process thinkers have tended to identify religion with its very sophisticated expressions, pragmatists have tended to identify it with its least sophisticated expressions. Both are motivated by sensibilities of class-background, I suspect, as much as by philosophical considerations; therefore on the whole they have had opposite responses to theism and religion. Properly to understand the origins and trajectories of pragmatism and process philosophy, it would be important to pursue these cultural issues in much greater detail, though I shall not do that here.

One more introductory remark needs to be made, namely, that both process philosophy and pragmatism are products of the early twentieth century and a great deal has changed since then. First, both of those schools inspired major thinkers who would not identify with the school itself but would claim their own philosophies in which the schools have impact but not determining identity. Paul Weiss was Whitehead's most important student in the same sense that Aristotle was Plato's; he started from the possibilities Whitehead gave him for speculative thought and has gone his own unique and brilliant way.[19] So too, Justus Buchler was a Peircean pragmatist, but surely went far beyond Peirce.[20]

Then the evolution of generations within the schools has produced such novelty that even those closely associated with the lineages have gone far beyond the original motifs. Think of the multivolume systems now being published by Frederick Ferre,[21] George Allan,[22] and Joseph Grange[23]—all process thinkers in some sense, but far from orthodoxy. Think of the philosophy of culture of the late David L. Hall,[24] or the aesthetics of Elizabeth Kraus[25] and Judith Jones[26].

The pragmatist side is harder to identify in a consistent lineage, although the marvelous system of Sandra Rosenthal in *Speculative Pragmatism*[27] and various essays is a clear extension of Dewey and Peirce, and also James and Mead. The lineage of pragmatism is hard to track in part because it ramified itself so quickly outside of academic philosophy into social and political theory and practical educational theory.

But an even more important block to tracking the pragmatic lineage is the current popularity of Richard Rorty's neo-pragmatism which rejects the systematic or metaphysical elements in pragmatism both in principle and in nearly all the points listed above it has in common with process philosophy.[28] Thus instead of a realistic philosophy of nature it has an idealism of conversation,[29] instead of a realism of generals or habits it has what David Hall calls "default nominalism,"[30] and instead of truth's nature as correspondence and criteria as pragmatic it holds to a kind of persuasive-coherence theory of rhetoric.[31] Instead of opposing analytic philosophy's evisceration of experience as interaction, neo-pragmatism builds on the "linguistic turn."[32] Instead of opposing Continental philosophy's tendency to translate experience into narratives and texts rather than nature, it builds a super-narrative of Western philosophy, justifying "strong misreadings."[33] About all that's left of classical pragmatism in neo-pragmatism is anti-foundationalism, an expansion of British empiricism to include (not nature, but) other points of view, and a strong commitment to philosophy as a contributor to public life.[34] The great irony is that neo-pragmatism deletes nearly everything from classical pragmatism except its epistemology, and the very heart of pragmatic epistemology is a criticism of the Western tradition for being too epistemological.[35] Moreover, without its realism (in both senses) and its speculative metaphysics to help correct bias, pragmatic epistemology focusing on fallible knowledge vulnerable to experiential correction degenerates into rhetoric and the power of convincing narratives. That is a decisive rejection of pragmatism's naturalism and appreciation of science. This is not to say that neo-pragmatism is wrong—I believe it is mainly wrong whereas David Hall believed it is mainly right—only that it skews understanding the lineage of classical pragmatism. The above points have been footnoted so obsessively to prove a point: Where pragmatism has any interesting connection with Whitehead is precisely in the elements of pragmatism rejected by neo-pragmatism. Rorty writes:

> I myself would join Reichenbach in dismissing classical Husserlian phenomenology, Bergson, Whitehead, the Dewey of *Experience and Nature*, the James of *Radical Empiricism*, neo-Thomist epistemological realism, and a variety of other late nineteenth- and early twentieth-century systems. Bergson and Whitehead, and the bad ("metaphysical") parts of Dewey and James, seem to me merely weakened versions of idealism—attempts to answer "unscientifically" formulated epistemological questions about the "relation of subject and object" by "naïve generalizations and analogies" which emphasize "feeling" rather than "cognition."[36]

As to Peirce, Rorty says his "contribution to pragmatism was merely to have given it a name, and to have stimulated James."[37] What I am concerned about in this chapter is the relation of Whitehead to classical pragmatism, perhaps even better called "paleo-pragmatism" to avoid confusion with neo-pragmatism.

One more element of the philosophical situation needs to be mentioned that has changed since the founding days of process philosophy and pragmatism, namely, that the philosophical public now includes the traditions of South and East Asia, as well as (though to a lesser extent) Islam. Although both Whitehead and Dewey wrote about Asian thought, and Dewey made an important visit to China, although both schools' idioms have been used extensively to translate Asian philosophy for Westerners, and although both of those authors would heartily approve of the more nearly global public for philosophy, it was not their public. Their ideas were not shaped in dialogue with Confucianism or Nyaya. Contemporary process philosophers and pragmatists operate within that larger public, even if not so well as they should in all cases. David Hall's philosophy, especially in the books written with the Sinologist Roger Ames—*Thinking Through Confucius, Anticipating China*, and *Thinking from the Han*, is an outstanding example of process philosophy (and neo-pragmatism?) elaborated in a context including East Asian thought in terms Whitehead never thought about.

Finally, our present situation includes many thinkers who have developed their own positions, showing deep indebtedness to both process and pragmatic thought, but who would never be thought to "belong" to either school, contemporary heirs of the independence of style of Weiss and Buchler if not of their philosophies. One thinks of Steve Odin whose first book[38] used process philosophy to engage Hua-yen Buddhism critically on the issue of time and whose second book[39] used the pragmatism of George Herbert Mead to engage the Japanese conception of the self. Or one thinks of the system of scientific naturalism of David Weissman who draws equally on Whitehead, Dewey, and Wittgenstein, but not to the satisfaction of any defenders of orthodox lineage.[40] Or Robert S. Corrington, a Whiteheadean, Heideggerian, Peircean "ecstatic naturalist:"[41] no Deweyan pragmatist would be ecstatic, no Heideggerian would be a naturalist, and no Whiteheadian would accommodate the strong rejection of final causes in ecstatic naturalism.[42] For an interesting analysis of thinkers such as these, see George Lucas' "Outside the Camp: Recent Work on Whitehead's Philosophy."[43]

The moral to draw from this long introduction with a gazillion footnote citations is that Whitehead's process philosophy and Peirce's pragmatism together have produced a vital group of philosophers who cannot be identified as merely process thinkers or pragmatists. Although many in the group have interacted also with analytic philosophy, Continental philosophy, and neo-pragmatism, by and large the group enlarges on the general areas of agreement between process and pragmatism cited at the beginning.[44] It is out of a strong sense of appreciation and continuity with these heirs of process and pragmatism that I raise the following issues to extend the debate.

My purpose in the remainder of this chapter is to engage a contemporary debate concerning continuity and time that might well illustrate some of the integral tensions between Whitehead and pragmatism. Then I shall argue that those tensions illustrate a deeper intuition about time and eternity that both Whiteheadians and pragmatists fail to grasp. And finally I shall explore the implications of this intuition (into creation *ex nihilo*) for assessing pragmatism and process philosophy on time and its significance.

TENSIONS REGARDING TIME AND CONTINUITY

Sandra Rosenthal has argued in several places that the decisive difference between pragmatism and process philosophy lies in their treatments of the continuity of time.[45] Both schools stress process over substance, to use the old polemical categories. They emphasize the temporality of all things (well, maybe not eternal objects) and reject idealist themes such as an eternal absolute or a Whole inclusive of all time. Rosenthal points out, however, that their metaphysical analyses of temporal continuity are different, and arise from fundamentally different intuitions of things.

To summarize a well-known process theory, Whitehead held that an emerging occasion comes into being, defining its present/here temporal/spatial scope, and when it is fully definite with regard to its extension and all other possibilities, it stops becoming and simply is, past. Whitehead was ambiguous regarding the status of a finished occasion. Perhaps it simply is what it is, with an achieved actual reality in itself, such that any subsequent occasion has to take account of it; I hope that is what Whitehead meant. Or perhaps a past occasion has no reality except insofar as it is prehended by a subsequent present occasion, with the result that all reality is either in God or is present reality, residing objectively in an emerging prehending. The latter view has a somewhat weakened sense of continuity because everything gets packed into the present somehow or other, with the past occasions losing any sense of independent or in-themselves reality. This latter view is attractive to people who emphasize relationship to the point of saying that things have no reality except their relations. But I think in the end it will fall back to an idealist notion of *totum simul*.[46] The process analysis of time that Rosenthal examines is the former view, that there is a continuity between present emerging occasions and past, finished, fully definite occasions, a continuity that consists in the past being prehended into the present.

How the past is prehended into the present to provide continuity is not an easy doctrine for which there is consensus among process thinkers. Jorge Nobo has the most detailed examination of this question, though his own answer is not the popularly received account.[47] Rosenthal is a master of these debates and her articles are to be consulted on the topic. With regard to continuity in the process view of time, however, she focuses on two central points common to all the approaches.

First, for all interpretations of the process account of continuity, the past is prehended into the present by, and hence continuous with, the present concrescence which harmonizes the many past elements into one. As she puts it in all her articles cited, continuity in the process model is a matter of "the coming together of" diverse past elements. The basic Whiteheadian "intuition," as she calls it, is that process consists of harmonization, beginning with diversity and adding to the diversity with a new harmonizing entity.

This is, of course, the Category of the Ultimate in *Process and Reality* as expressing itself in the issues of temporal continuity.

The second point central to all Whiteheadian positions is the interpretation of time's directional arrow in terms of the definiteness of the past. A present occasion is present and emerging precisely because it is not fully definite, and "when" it achieves full definiteness the urge for definiteness is "satisfied" and the occasion becomes past. Within an emergent present occasion there are no earlier and later stages, though a genetic analysis of the occasion can give logical stages. Only when the occasion is past does it have a definite temporal (and spatial) dimensionality. Only when it is past can it be prehended, and there must be finished definite past things to prehend in order for a present moment to emerge ("subjective unity" in Whitehead's categoreal terms). Time's arrow is defined by the order of prehension. Anything that can be prehended is in the past of the prehender, anything that can prehend an occasion is in the future of that occasion, and all the things that neither can be prehended by an occasion nor can prehend it are simultaneous with it. Thus there is a sharp discontinuity between fully definite prehendable occasions and emergent prehending occasions, and a total indeterminateness of temporal relation among occasions where no order of prehending-prehended exists. Rosenthal's question, relative to pragmatism, is whether the continuity of prehension is sufficient to overcome the discontinuity of the prehended-prehending relation when it comes to accounting for the actuality of time's passage.

The pragmatic theory, she points out, takes such a different tack as to be attributable to a different fundament intuition. Whereas the process intuition is "the coming together of," the alternative pragmatic intuition is "the emerging out of." For pragmatists in various ways present time is characterized by the growth or extension of what has been into what is emerging and will continue to emerge. For Peirce, this is at the heart of the doctrine of Thirdness.[48] It appears in James, Dewey, and Mead in their biological metaphors and a great many other elements, as Rosenthal lays out. On the pragmatic analysis, emergence has no sharp breaks. It is a process of infinitesimal growth or accretion, and the direction of causal action is from the past to what emerges from the past's burgeonings. This contrasts with the Whiteheadian reversal of the classical direction of causation: for Whiteheadians, it is the causal power of the emerging present that integrates into actuality the diversity of past potentials.

The pragmatic theory of infinitesimal continuity in emergence contrasts also with the Whiteheadian discontinuity in the order of time's flow. For the pragmatists, Rosenthal points out, the past is only relatively definite, and indeed can change as what emerges from it gives it new overall character. Pragmatism therefore entertains a rather extended specious present in which the orders of earlier and later are not fully set. Present nature might not be entirely "blooming, buzzing, confusion," to use James' phrase, but neither does it exhibit a sharp distinction between finished and new. Rather, present time for pragmatism, on Rosenthal's accurate account, is the reality of the act of emerging, wherein there is no discontinuity or even distinction regarding definiteness between that from which the emergence comes and that which emerges as new. Within the extended moment of present time, what emerges comes from what is sometimes not settled. Whereas for process philosophy, continuity requires separate and discontinuous acts of concrescence to bring the past together in continuity with the present, for pragmatism the very meaning of present emergence is a continuity of creativity.

ETERNITY AND TIME

Rosenthal rightly says that, despite my other protestations of pragmatic allegiance, I am on the process side in this "great divide," as she calls it. There are several reasons for this. One is that, agreeing with both process philosophy and pragmatism that the present involves (indeed requires) novelty, I believe that novelty consists in part in a reaction to the past. The past must be fixed, wholly definite, in order to be objectified in reaction. A later thing cannot come after something unless there is something definite to come after. The arguments for reaction come from Peirce's theory of Secondness. But Whitehead had the better theory to show how reaction is possible. It requires, among other things, energy in the reactor over against the object of reaction, hence a discontinuity in time's moment's acts of creativity or concrescence.

Another reason I am on Whitehead's side are all the sentiments in existentialism now validated in critical theory about the importance of otherness. Consider some kinds of otherness. Present time is not really a swarmy reaching out into the past and future, Husserl's retention and protention notwithstanding, but rather a time when the past is dead and gone and the future is not yet. Self-conscious realization of present time should be filled with amazement, and helplessness and loneliness. I don't agree with those who say that only the present is real. On the contrary, the past is very real in determining parameters for the present, in having a value that is obligatory for the present to respect, especially in human terms, and in being normative for continuing identity and moral life. The future too is real as determining the stage in which our present actions have consequences, and thus lays its own kind of norms upon present action. Though real, neither past nor future are presently real, and the present does not inhabit them as it does its own arena. Augustine's ontological shock at this was right on.

Another sense of otherness is that there are really different things in the past, each with their own integrities and somewhat autonomous careers. These things often have contemporary otherness as well, and have future stories not to be reduced to any present experience. So I reject the pragmatic sense of a monolithic past unfolding emerging elements, though that perhaps is an unfair characterization. Rather, the diversity of things is given and ought to be acknowledged, and the integration or harmonizing of the diversity is an achievement: sometimes it doesn't happen. The deep tragic element in passing time is that so many things are distorted when harmonized in the present or lost altogether when the harmony fails.[49] The pragmatic idiom fails to catch that metaphysical tragedy. The process intuition of "the coming together of," which sometimes does not come together, or does so at an oppressive price, is far better.

Nevertheless, there is a deeper intuition in these matters than either the pragmatic "emerging out of" or the process "coming together of," namely, the intuition of making, "creation *ex nihilo*." Creation *ex nihilo* is something like a reversal of the "coming together" theme, for it denotes a creative act which results in a determinate plurality of things which are really different from one another and are inter-defined so as to be different. Each created thing has its own essential features, and it also has the features by which it is conditioned by or conditionally defined by the other things, so that the different things are determinately different from one another. As products of creation *ex nihilo*, created things are determinate and partly defined in terms of one another, but radically new: without the creative act there is nothing, and with it there is the plural world, a point that will be expanded in most of the subsequent chapters.

Creation *ex nihilo* picks up on the pragmatic intuition that something new emerges in present process. But pragmatism fudges the issue of whether the new is already contained in the old. If it is, as Aristotle argued in saying that process is the reduction of potency to act by the act in efficient causes (a point carried on in early modern popular science), then there is nothing really new.[50] But if there is something new, whatever is new was not contained in the old and its appearance necessarily is *ex nihilo*. Pragmatism should acknowledge a continuous input of creation *ex nihilo* if emergence is continuous. "Emergence" really means "*ex nihilo*" because what emerges is not in that "from which" it emerges. The "from which" is a fake except in the sense of denoting the earlier state plus those elements in the present that are not new. As mentioned, however, pragmatism has difficulty distinguishing the new from the old in present time. In his famous "Neglected Argument for the Reality of God," Peirce clearly adopted the creation *ex nihilo* hypothesis to account for the togetherness of the three realms of reality, Firstness, Secondness, and Thirdness, thus seeing the point of this critical advance.[51]

The advantage of process philosophy in locating the causal power of harmonization or "coming together of" in the present is that it underscores the novelty in the emergence of a new occasion. There is a new individuated harmony that did not exist before; before there was only a disjunctive harmony. Each new occasion combines the old, namely the data prehended, with the new, namely new subjective forms individuated to the new satisfaction.

Without something new, there is only the old disjunction. But if there is something new, the new is combined with the old, and whatever is new was not there before. The new in every occasion, insofar as it is not among the data prehended, is *ex nihilo*. Every occasion is an instance of some new creativity *ex nihilo*. Process philosophy is in a good position to indicate the experiential cash for this in its general interpretations of the subjectivity of human experience. Ordinarily, process philosophy, however, has emphasized that experience is the creation of new *order* out of the old prehended things. It would bring out its existential potential, however, by emphasizing the experience of the creation of *new* order, with the *ex nihilo* surprise of the new in the spotlight.

Process philosophy and pragmatism are together in not grasping the implication of creation *ex nihilo* in their emphasis on novelty in process. Why? I believe there have been two reasons. The first is a failure of nerve, if I might put it bluntly, in the face of the insight into novelty: it would seem that novelty is intelligible only as derivative from something old or higher, the Aristotelian point generalized. So most Whiteheadians think that what explains has to be some high principles, a rationalist position. The creation *ex nihilo* theory by contrast says that ultimately what explains is the location of the creative decisions or acts of makings: understanding is not reduction to principle but grasp of an act that makes. If philosophers do not admit that grasp of a making-act is explanatory, then every novelty will be a mystery on top of determinism, whether emergent or concrescent.

The other reason pragmatism and process philosophy draw back from creation *ex nihilo* is the theistic history of the notion. The idea of creation *ex nihilo* here is highly refined, but it arises out of a distinctive theological tradition. That theological tradition is directly opposed to the theory of God in process philosophy, and so I clearly and systematically reject process theology in its classic forms.[52] Process philosophy's polemic against God as creator of all determinate being coercive blinds it to any serious notion of divine creation, and also to the brute creativity in the bitsy novelty in individual actual occasions. For its part, pragmatism has generally been allergic to serious theology that owns up to an institutionalized tradition, as noted above. The exception is Peirce, who was a theist and defended creation *ex nihilo*.

So I propose that creation *ex nihilo* is a deeper intuition than either "the coming together of" or "emerging out of," and indeed is necessary to acknowledge the novelty both process philosophy and pragmatism want to affirm.

CREATION, ETERNITY, TIME, AND CONTINUITY

Large matters remain to be settled, however, to sort the functions of creation *ex nihilo* within continuous temporal process and the characterization of it as giving rise to a plurality of different though related things. Here the theological resonance of the concept comes to time's flow. My hypothesis is that the theory best expressing the deepest intuition is that everything determinate is created in a single creative act. "Everything determinate" is a loaded phrase. I define determinateness in terms of the essential and conditional features of things mentioned above. To be a thing is to be a harmony of essential and conditional features. To be created is to be in a context of mutual relevance with everything with respect to which a creature is determinate; mutual relevance means that things not only can condition one another but can integrate their conditioning features with their respective essential features which are not mutually conditioning.

Think of just one instance of the generality of this claim. The modes of time, the past, present, and future, are different from one another but obviously determinate with respect to those differences. Process philosophy and pragmatism give somewhat different account of the three modes, but would agree with the general point. The togetherness of past, present, and future cannot be temporal. That is, the past is not earlier than the present, nor the future later. Temporal things are earlier or later than one another because of the nontemporal togetherness of the modes of time. The modes of time all have essential features and also conditional features defining their relations. So, to review briefly only a process philosophy model, the past is essentially fixed actuality, the present essentially spontaneous creativity, and the future essentially pure form. The past has form (and value) as a condition from the future, and it has increasing growth or extension as a condition from present temporality. The present has actualized things as potentials for new actuality from the past, and structured possibilities as conditions from the future. The future has actualized things from the past that give conditional structure to its form, and has a continually differentiating kaleidoscope of possibilities as the condition resulting from present decisions. This quick theory does not have to be swallowed whole for the point to be seen that the togetherness of the temporal modes is very definitely not temporal but eternal. Eternity, as the ancient Western tradition and I use the term, does not mean static form but that ontological togetherness that makes the passage of time possible for temporal things. The singular act of creation *ex nihilo* does not take place in time at all but rather creates time itself, a theological position as old as Origen and Augustine.

Pragmatism and process philosophy are quite right, within this view, to say that time unfolds in a creative process with indeterminacy and novelty. Because it is not temporal, the singular act of creation *ex nihilo*, does not determine anything in advance except in ways that the past partially determines the present which has its own novelty. This obviates the process criticism that a creator-God predetermines what happens. Within a present moment, supposing a process model, creation *ex nihilo* is finitized to be the creation of something new out of the prehended past, a new combination of old and new. Supposing a pragmatic model, creation *ex nihilo* is finitized to effect the emergence of novelty out of the rest of the emergent process. Although these remarks do not settle a theory of novelty within time, they at least indicate that such a theory needs to account for bits of creation *ex nihilo* functioning to bring the old and new together into something that has continuity but is also novel.

For all its emphasis on creativity, process philosophy has fallen into the idiom of time's flow as the ingression of order. Rosenthal's image of "the coming together of" describes this accurately. There is no metaphysical necessity in this, of course. Each occasion is a prehensive unification of its world in utter independence from its contemporaries, and it might well be that the only subsequent occasions that can harmonize the contemporaries are of trivial importance—things lost in a puff.[53] But the effect of the process conception of God has been to emphasize continuous, or at least repeated, inputs of order, a hedge against entropy. Even Lewis Ford's great reconception of process theology conceives God as future, only inputting order.[54] Peirce shared this confidence in creeping Thirdness.

Yet is not chaos as deep a feature of the cosmos as order? Creative novelty so often seems blind, to go nowhere. How do we reconcile the trajectory of order that results in the human habitat with the billions of failed experiments with life, the species lost, the planets blasted, the stars gone to super-novae? How do we face the fundamental realities of human life, a species not in a garden but cast in the wilderness to scrabble brief lives through work and pain, with a God who is an order-monger? Creation *ex nihilo* recognizes the unregulated, free, divine act whose lifeboats of order in oceans of chaos are leaky just like our own lives. The God of process theology is too small for real religion, too domestic. Creation *ex nihilo* represents a God whose power is infinite and whose character is constituted by the creating, a God shown as much by chaos as by order. Perhaps pragmatism rejects the too-small God of order and fears the Creator *ex nihilo* who cannot be controlled because it hopes to control events that emerge from what we manage. Peirce alone of the pragmatists subordinated the managerial impulse to wonder and awe, and he did so because he had a semiotic theory open to chaos as well as order.

In sum, I have argued that process philosophy and pragmatism share much, disagree over the fundamental intuitions regarding continuity in time, as Rosenthal has shown, and both miss out on a deeper intuition about the true infinite scale of creativity. As a result, though their common ground and internal debates might be the place to begin in the current philosophical situation, their outcomes are tragically superficial. How can we have survived the twentieth century and entered the Third Millennium without knowing that our being is grounded in the Act that creates our cosmic doom as well as destiny, whose name is Chaos along with Order, and with whom is to be absolutely lonely as well as loving and beloved?

TEN

Philosophy of Nature in American Theology

EARLY AMERICAN THEOLOGY was very European, of course, advanced by people born and educated in Europe.[1] The situation was far more complex than can be analyzed here. Nevertheless, the common emphasis in Reformation thought was on God and the human drama of redemption, with far less appreciative thought given to nature. The enthusiasms of early modern European science, like a magnet, drew discussions of nature away from the theological realm to a scientific language alien to the biblicistic orientation of Reformation church theology. To be sure, the appeal to nature was made in order to explain the lower desires of human beings, and Calvinist thought developed its idea of creation in terms of God-given orders of nature, today such an embarrassment because of apartheid. By the time of Kant, however, most European intellectuals agreed with Kant that only science knows nature, philosophy knows about knowledge, including scientific knowledge, and that "philosophy of nature" is an oxymoron, or, worse, an unmodern holdover of medieval thought. Recent European Protestant theology, say, in the work of Barth, Pannenberg, and Moltmann, acknowledges the importance of nature in the doctrine of creation, but has been much more concerned about the redemption of the human sphere. Where nature has been taken seriously, as Pannenberg has tried to do, it is not understood in sophisticated ways that learn from the sciences. At best, nature provides analogies for thinking about the human, as in Pannenberg's attempt to describe the Holy Spirit as an energy field.

JONATHAN EDWARDS

What a surprise, then, to discover that American Protestant theology has had a very strong notion of nature from the earliest days, for instance in the work of Jonathan Edwards. Edwards (1703–58) was educated at Yale and served pastorates mainly in Massachusetts where he wrote most of his theological and philosophical works. He died of a smallpox vaccination shortly after taking office as president of Princeton University. Edwards was precocious to a high degree, entering college at the age of twelve. While in college, or before, he produced a series of descriptive "naturalist" studies, on insects, the soul, rainbows, and being.[2] The striking theme of these essays is their emphasis on the beauty of their subjects. This theme is developed further in his "Notes on the Mind," written during his senior year in college when he was sixteen or seventeen in which he sought to modify and develop John Locke's theory of perception so as to explain the perception of beauty with a theory of harmony and balance.[3] His late work, *The Nature of True Virtue* (written in 1755) is one of the most extraordinary pieces of philosophical ethics written in the modern period.[4] It begins with the carefully argued claims that human virtue is some kind of beauty, that beauty is seen in a kind of perception, and that virtue is not conformity to rules or the result of rational thinking from principles. His theory of the perception of beauty had been developed his whole life. The heart of human virtue is what he called "consent to being in general," by which he meant a kind of intentional harmonizing of the self with the whole of being, or with the part of being at hand. The harmonizing derives from a cultivated appreciation of the beauty in being. The human virtue in question then is the beauty of the relation between the person and the object, which he explains in terms of the details of "consent." Because of the harmonious interconnections of all objects, the real object of virtuous orientation is the whole world, plus God its creator. Virtue is thus an aesthetic way of being in the world with an orientation to being as such. For Edwards, to be is to be a harmony, and in harmony with other beings. A harmony has value, and therefore all of nature, as well as the human realm which he did not distinguish much from its larger natural context, has value.

Thus Edwards introduced into American theology (and philosophy) a conception of nature very much at odds with the mechanistic, materialistic, value-free conception that came to dominate the European Enlightenment and that set science in opposition to Christian theology. He was an avid reader of Isaac Newton and the scientists of his time, as well as Locke, and he considered the scientific approach to nature to be a kind of piety that he himself practiced. The deterministic laws of nature claimed by the science of his day, he took to be among the elements of harmony in nature, though by no means the only ones. The reason the scientific study of nature is a kind of piety is that the beauty and value science finds in nature itself inspires reverence and awe and also reflects the beauty or glory of the Creator. Edwards conceived of nature to be rationally structured (reason articulates harmony), intrinsically valuable in ways that could be sorted by sorting the connections of harmonies, and knowable through a kind of aesthetic scientific rationality.

It never occurred to him to see science as requiring a bracketing of value. Although he did not have a vision of the full mathematizability of scientific knowledge, he would have found that congenial to his view that value consists in the elements of harmony he believed mathematics to articulate. In this regard, he was a true Platonist. Far from sensing any opposition between science and theology, Edwards thought the former was an appreciative theology of nature and the latter an extension of science's kind of appreciative inquiry beyond nature to the human realm within nature, to the world's Creator, and to the harmonious relation between the two.

This cluster of themes—that nature is harmoniously structured, that it is intrinsically valuable, that knowing nature involves appreciating its value, and that science and theology are connected and mutually supportive—characterizes the American tradition in the thought of Ralph Waldo Emerson, Charles Peirce, William James, John Dewey, Alfred North Whitehead, Paul Weiss, down to our contemporary systematic philosophers of nature and religion such as George Allan, Frederick Ferre, Joseph Grange, David Weissman, and myself.[5] Several of these people would not count themselves as theologians, and two, Weiss and Weissman, are Jewish (the rest are Protestant Christians in one sense or other). I will discuss some of these thinkers below.

Now Edwards was a rather orthodox, if spectacularly imaginative, Calvinist theologian of the Eighteenth Century, reflecting the major themes of Calvin and writing in the language of Reformed theology.[6] His main preoccupation was with redemption and he was a pivotal revivalist preacher in the Great Awakening.[7] In Edwards' view, the great themes of creation and divine providence were linked: creation serves providence, which itself serves God's free glorying in the divine nature. The divine nature is to create a glorious world that glorifies its Creator: glory, like (or the same as) beauty and value, is a function of harmony. The essential divine harmony is in God's creating the world with the providential design for expressing divine glory. Given the fall of human beings, providence requires redemption, which is the restoration of harmony within the world, which in turn restores the harmony between the world and its Creator in which the divine glory consists.[8] Edwards can be read as an extreme aestheticizing and Platonizing of John Calvin while being true to the main part of Calvin's theological doctrines.

One of Calvinism's major issues, of course, is how to tell whether one is saved. This is an especially urgent issue during times of religious revival such as Edwards'. Perhaps his most original book was *A Treatise Concerning Religious Affections*.[9] The plot of the book has three main steps. The first is to argue that the reality of religion (salvation) is the difference it makes in a person's heart, or "affections." This is to say, religion is mainly a matter of experience, to use the later word (Edwards called it "experimental religion"). Saved Christians should have loving affections. The second step is to observe that any private feeling or sentiment can be counterfeited by the Devil.

Therefore, the fact that a person feels that they love others, or have the sincere belief that they do, might be a delusion. Edwards had delightful contempt for what he called "mere wouldings," that is, what a person "would do" if the person were to act on the inner inclination. The third step, consequently, is to lay out a scheme for telling whether one's affections are real by seeing how they play out in actual practice. Edwards developed twelve "signs of gracious affections" that connect biblical notions of spiritual causes of affections with actual changes in life and behavior. The significance of this plot is that experience, for Edwards, is not a mere epistemological notion of what appears in consciousness, as it was for many of his European counterparts such as David Hume. Rather, for Edwards, experience is a matter of will and action as much as aesthetic appreciation or sensory vision, hearing, etc. Of course, this sense of experience has been characteristic of the American tradition right down to pragmatism, which defined it in great detail. Dewey called experience "transaction," and "interaction." Moreover, in Edward's *Religious Affections* the tests for the genuineness of affections is plainly pragmatic, although of course he did not know that word. He cited the biblical dictum, "by their fruits you shall know them" (Luke 6:44; Galatians 5:22), a notion referred to regularly by the classical pragmatists. The informal pragmatism that runs through American philosophy of nature and theology is Edwards' legacy.

For all his dated brilliance as an Eighteenth Century Calvinist theologian, Jonathan Edwards set a decisive direction for the course of American philosophical theology in its thinking about nature. With the European tradition, Edwards and his heirs took nature to be knowable by modern science, about which all were enthusiastic. Against the main line of the European tradition, Edwards and his heirs took nature to be intrinsically valuable and as analyzable in aesthetic terms that do not conflict with science. Science, for the Americans, does not have to prescind from the aesthetic element in knowing and inquiry. Science, for this and other reasons, is congenial to theology (although the various Americans construed theology differently), contrary to most other traditions of theological thought. Furthermore, all this is because experience is construed, following Edwards, as involving a continuity of intention and action, with aesthetic responsiveness to the world and its problems.[10] This American conception of experience has for centuries stood in opposition to the European approaches associated with British Empiricism, Kantian transcendentalism, and Husserlian consciousness-oriented phenomenology.[11] In a much briefer fashion, I can indicate how Edwards' themes resonated with some of his heirs.

RALPH WALDO EMERSON

Whereas Edwards was an early Eighteenth Century orthodox Calvinist revivalist, most of his life the pastor of a congregation, Ralph Waldo Emerson (1803–1882), exactly a century younger, was an early Nineteenth Century

Romantic, raised and eventually ordained in the distinctly unorthodox Unitarian Church. He resigned his ministerial orders in 1832 on the grounds that he did not believe in the regular practice of the Eucharist. The rest of his life he was a writer and lecturer, and was known as the major founder of New England Transcendentalism. He took the title "Transcendentalism" from Kant whom he read at an early age and, most fortunately, totally misunderstood.[12] For Emerson, the shame of ordinary life is that people commonly filter their experience through what other people teach them to experience.[13] Yet the human soul has an affinity with what he called the "Oversoul," or God.[14] He called upon people to foreswear doctrines, rituals, and second-hand knowledge to develop what he called "an original relation" to reality.[15] Not only is every finite soul a part of the Oversoul, so is all nature.[16] Emerson was a philosophical idealist and a nature-romantic. He believed that engagement with nature was a far better way to engage the Oversoul, which is our true reality, than to read books about God. Moreover, he believed that the American experience, close as it was to the wilderness of nature, bred a more courageous engagement of "original relations" than the overly digested and bookish European experience of his time (he traveled in Europe and developed strong opinions on the matter). He adored the genius of great persons, but warned that this can be appreciated only after one has attained one's own original relation with reality: then one can understand the genius in other people's original relation.[17]

Emerson's version of Edwards' philosophy of nature relative to science, value, and God, is expressed in the following:

> The natural world may be conceived of as a system of concentric circles, and we now and then detect in nature slight dislocations which apprise us that this surface on which we now stand is not fixed, but sliding. These manifold tenacious qualities, this chemistry and vegetation, these metals and animals, which seem to stand there for their own sake, are means and methods only—are words of God, and as fugitive as other words. Has the naturalist or chemist learned his craft, who has explored the gravity of the atoms and the elective affinities, who has not yet discerned the deeper law whereof this is only a partial or approximate statement, namely that like draws to like, and that the goods which belong to you gravitate to you and need not be pursued with pains and cost? Yet is that statement approximate also, and not final. Omnipresence is a higher fact. Not through subtle subterranean channels need friend and fact be drawn to their counterpart, but, rightly considered, these things proceed from the eternal generation of the soul. Cause and effect are two sides of one fact.[18]

Although the ontology is quite different from Edwards, the themes about nature, value, and science relative to theology are clear extensions of Edwards thought. Like Edwards, Emerson construed experience, not on models of mirroring nature, but as transformation of soul.[19]

THE PRAGMATISTS

The American pragmatists are comparatively well-known in Europe and can be discussed more briefly. The difference between Emerson and the classical American pragmatists, Charles S. Peirce (1839–1914), William James (1842–1910), and John Dewey (1859–1952), was that the latter were decisively shaped by ideas of evolution. Where Edwards and Emerson had talked about knowledge, and about how it is fallible, a pragmatic theme, Peirce, James, and Dewey talked about inquiry. The essential idea is that inquiry is a strategy for making knowledge evolve by setting up experiments in which good ideas are naturally selected and bad ideas are discarded as nonadaptive. For all of them, experience is driven by human purposes (like the purposes of other animals interacting with their environments) and the structures and values of nature come to be recognized as nature is purposively engaged. For none of the pragmatists is value something projected onto value-neutral nature by human intention. On the contrary, the projections we bring to nature through our culture and semiotic systems are regularly corrected by nature's value-laden reality. All the pragmatists emphasized the importance of science for making experience experimental, so that misconstruals of the world are corrected as quickly and painlessly as possible. Pragmatism is sometimes viewed by Europeans, with some justification in certain texts of William James, as saying knowledge is nothing more than believing what gets you ahead with your purposes. Peirce, however, emphasized the importance of inquiry to determine which purposes are worth having, and they turn out to be those that know reality most comprehensively and truly so as to love it. Peirce was a serious scientist, graduating *summa cum laude* from Harvard in chemistry; he published far more scientific papers than philosophic ones. Yet he called his philosophical vision "Evolutionary Love."[20] Peirce's own philosophy is filled with technical terms too abstruse to develop here. Suffice it to say that he thought that logic is a species of ethics (ethics for the mind) and that ethics is a species of aesthetics (the beauty of human action). These are all Edwardsian themes. As to the connection between science and theology, the most succinct statement of Peirce's theory of scientific inquiry is in his essay, "A Neglected Argument for the Reality of God," which also contains his proof of God.[21] James was a psychologist, the first to set up a scientific psychology laboratory in America, and was most known in his day for his psychological writings. Of the three classic pragmatists, James was the most inclined to use language congenial to British empiricism because he approached nature through its psychological effects. But in his later writings he was clear that, for him, experience is prior to the distinction between experiencer and the experienced.[22] John Dewey was not a laboratory scientist, although his theory of scientific instrumentalism was very much about laboratory science. Yet he generalized the notion of instrumentalism in the following way. Human experience, he said, is a matter of enjoying the qualities of interactions. Yet some qualities are bad, and the good ones are precarious. So human beings lace experiential enjoyment with experimental conscious inquiry so as to have better quality experience. Like the others, the fundamental categories are aesthetic. The function of instrumental inquiry is to learn the natural joints of reality so that it can be engaged in the most satisfying ways. Dewey was not a theist of any ordinary sort, as both Peirce and James were; nevertheless, his *A Common Faith* related his theory of experience and nature to theology and affirmed the same connection between science and theology that Edwards (and Emerson, Peirce, and James) did.[23]

ALFRED NORTH WHITEHEAD

Alfred North Whitehead (1861–1948) was born an Englishman and had a distinguished career in the United Kingdom as a mathematician and academic administrator; he was best known there as the collaborator with Bertrand Russell on *Principia Mathematica*. Most, though not all, of his philosophical works were composed in the United States, however, where he came to teach at Harvard in 1924, retiring in 1937. His work, known as process philosophy, has an enormous following among American philosophers and theologians. His two most famous graduate students, Charles Hartshorne and Paul Weiss, were the editors of *The Collected Papers of Charles Sanders Peirce* very early in their careers, and he was a friend of John Dewey. Whitehead was a speculative metaphysician, far more abstract and systematic than any of the pragmatists. He noted in *Science and the Modern World* that the common sense metaphysics of substance or atomism supposed by early Twentieth Century science could not explain how mathematics could apply to things.[24] So he developed an astonishing new metaphysical theory emphasizing relationships, or what he called "prehensions," that could account for this.[25] Whitehead was an avowed Platonist and saw structures as mathematizable harmonies, picking up on the same language Edwards had used, though I do not know whether Whitehead ever read Edwards. Whitehead's conception of nature was that it is composed of actual entities, each of which actualizes a specific value by integrating all the past entities it grasps in prehensive relations. This complicated picture of the world—like Peirce's, too technical to explain briefly—is a clear version of Edwards' conception of nature as a set of harmonies with beauty and value. Whitehead had a technical way of accounting for aesthetic judgment. Whitehead's theology was very different from Edwards'. Instead of a Calvinistic "immense" God, Whitehead's is finite, and interacts with the world, prehending each actual entity after it comes to be and offering to each actual entity coming into being a pattern for it to use in achieving the value of integrating all it prehends. In no existential sense does God create the world, for Whitehead, only urge order upon it. Yet like Edwards' conception,

God's interesting nature comes in the relation with the world, and the value in the world is that which the actual entities of the world achieve one by one as they employ divine patterns to direct their coming to be. Some of Whitehead's most eloquent writing is about how God and the world are in a reciprocating relation.[26] Whitehead's theory of actual entities coming to be by prehending past entities into themselves, and then determining subsequent entities to take them into account in their own arising, is a technical way of saying, in the human sphere, that experience is causal and interactive, not a matter of a field of consciousness. Whitehead's theory is an exquisite, Twentieth Century, academic rendering of Edwards' main themes that were pointed out above.

The moral of this story is that the American tradition, or at least the part of it associated with the figures mentioned here, offers a striking resource for contemporary theology. The situation in Protestant theology is radically different from what it was a generation ago. In the days of Karl Barth it was plausible to think Christocentrically, and to tell "the Christian story" as if it were God's story with hardly a mention of the Hindus, Buddhists, Daoists, Confucians, Muslims, and shamans. Now that is wholly implausible. The Christian story, which Barth claimed was above religion and culture, is in fact just one religion modifying a family of cultures, and Barth's arbitrariness is embarrassing to Christians who relate as brothers and sisters to non-Christians. Moreover, the whole story of humanity and human cultures itself is limited to Earth, a small planet in a small solar system in a small galaxy in a cosmos so vast that its Creator must be truly glorious! The drama of sin and redemption, and the saving acts of Jesus Christ, are tiny local phenomena, however important they are to us living within the locale. Theology's responsibility to acknowledge and respond interpretively to God cannot take much of its orientation from our local drama, however much it needs also to interpret that local drama. Rather, theology needs to take its basic orientation to God from nature whose vast scale and intricate subtlety are only now becoming clear to us. The theology that had taken its basic orientation from history is no longer plausible. Our theology needs to start with nature, and find the human place for sin and redemption within that.

The fruitfulness for the American tradition of philosophy of nature for theology is apparent. From Edwards on, nature was conceived on a cosmic scale, in metaphysical terms expressive of notions of harmony that in principle could be given mathematical articulation. Human beings were seen as arising within nature, with objective values in nature that are somewhat continuous with human purposes and intentions. Experience was conceived as dynamic action and reaction, not in dualistic terms as a kind of mentality alien to the nature science knows. Science does not necessarily conceive its object to be alien to human nature, value, and intention, but in fact can be instrumental to advancing the human place within the world. Moreover, science is a proper part of theology, for the American tradition, a way of knowing God in creation. American philosophical theologians differ in their use of pious language in theology, but all those discussed here have seen science to be a help to theology, not a competitor.

The general traits of the American vision of nature and its role in theology, of course, do not by themselves constitute a viable theology. Much needs to be done to develop an understanding of creation that is built around the best knowledge we have of the cosmos created. Similarly, our theology of human nature needs to work through the inquiries of biology and neuroscience as well as its traditional venues of history, culture, and the arts. It is possible, indeed customary in our time, to have a philosophy of nature that represents science as requiring nature to be conceived as value-free and alien to the human. Yet that philosophy of nature, so alien to theology, is not necessary, because the American tradition presents an alternative from which to work. Contemporary theology that develops this American tradition is a promising way forward.

PART III

Realism in Religion and Metaphysics

ELEVEN

Concepts of God in Comparative Theology

CONCEPTS OF GOD IN COMPARISON

THE OBVIOUS PROBLEM with concepts of God as cross-cultural comparative categories is that some religions do not have them, or conceive gods in relatively trivial ways. To appreciate why this is a problem, however, it is important to see why concepts of God are so attractive for comparative purposes. The main reason is that, at least for the monotheistic religions, the categories spelling out divinity refer to what is religiously most important. God is the center around which all other religious elements move. Whether conceived in metaphysical ways as creator or in existential ways as judge, savior, lover, goal or eschatological Finisher, God is conceived in the monotheistic religions to be the most important reality for human life, concepts of which determine more of all the other religious notions than any of them directly affects the concepts of God. So naturally comparative theology ought to be able to recognize what at least some religions take to be the most important reality and compare religions in respect of it. If a religion cannot be compared to others with respect to what it takes to be most important, the comparisons that are left seem trivial. Religions can be compared on their respective attitudes toward eating popcorn, but so what? Religions can be compared with respect to their moral codes, but, without connection to the concepts of God, moral codes fail to be religious for the monotheistic traditions. The same is true regarding many other things in respect of which religions can be compared: without connection to God, the comparisons seem to distort the heart of religion, for the monotheisms.[1]

Monotheisms do not have a monopoly on God. Most forms of Hinduism have important conceptions of God. Many recognize a pantheon of gods, but usually with a hierarchical order; their theological traditions usually affirm a sophisticated monotheistic reality underlying a variety of apparent manifestations. Advaita Vedanta is even more intensely "mono" than most forms of West Asian monotheism that suppose some duality between God and the world. In East Asian religion, concepts of the Dao, the Great Ultimate, Heaven and Earth, Principle, and the like play roles similar to concepts of God, similar enough that comparison is fruitful (if also seductively treacherous) to lay out similarities and differences.

Of course it has long been recognized that God is conceived differently in different religions. More recently we have become conscious of the fact that radically different conceptions exist within the same religion, marking out different and perhaps conflicting roles. Perennial philosophers, for instance, have pointed out Neo-Platonic-like similarities of strains within Judaism, Christianity, Islam, Advaita Vedanta, and other religions, while noting that each of those religions has other strains that reject the perennial philosophy.[2] Most theistic religions have very personal conceptions of God as well as highly impersonal conceptions, often in conflict for use in interpreting sacred rituals and texts.[3] Sorting these different concepts and their various roles within religious practice is the very stuff of theological comparison.

The attractiveness of concepts of God to the great Western comparative projects of the nineteenth and twentieth centuries is understandable. In fact, comparing pantheons was of interest in the ancient Western world as well as in India. Part of the Axial Age phenomenon analyzed by Jaspers was a consciousness of the culturally transcendent character of otherwise conventional notions.

Nevertheless, important forms of Buddhism, such as the Theravada, do not have concepts of God or gods. Popular forms of Buddhism have thousands of gods that are religiously trivial compared with monotheisms. Although some forms of Mahayana Buddhism treat Emptiness as something like a theistic category of the absolute, other Mahayana forms such as the Madhyamika deny ontological reference to ultimate or absolute realities. For Buddhism, the main point of the religious practice is to find release from suffering, according to the Four Noble Truths, and any realities that might aid that are religious only as expedient means to release. High-powered concepts of divinity are usually thought to be inexpedient.[4] If concepts of God are important comparative categories for religions, then Buddhism turns out to be not a religion, or only a deficient one. This is a disastrous result for the intended objectivity of scholarly theological comparison.

The case of Buddhism has highlighted the bias of comparative work that originates in the Western world. To put the point simply, with minimal oversimplification, Western comparativists' enthusiasm for concepts of God was revealed to be a strong prejudice that the monotheist, mainly Christian, conceptions of God define religion itself. When dealing with non-monotheistic religions, this Western comparative project has treated their basic notions as "analogous" with conceptions of God, as illustrated above. As mere analogues with God, Brahman and the Dao are poor versions of the prime analogate of their referent. Hegel made the best case for this way of thinking when he analyzed a wide range of conceptions of religions' objects according to their roles in a large dialectic culminating in his version of Absolute Christianity. For all his insights into the intricate structures and relations among religious ideas, however, his project is now rightly recognized as arbitrary apologetics for his own religious heritage: Buddhist, Vedanta, and Confucian dialectics would have the gradings of other religions turn out to be quite different.

The reaction in many quarters against the dominance of concepts of God in Western cross-cultural theological comparison has been to demonize the very project of theological comparison. That project seems to illustrate the folly of logocentrism and fuel the oppressive distortions of orientalism. The better part of scholarship, according to this reaction, is to eschew theological comparison and work on micro-studies of particular religious texts and circumstances. The absurdity of this reaction is that one cannot say that a comparative approach distorts unless one has some more basic comparative perspective within which to stand. To say that a comparative project imposes alien categories, such as those of God on non-theistic religions, presupposes a comparison between what the categories say about the religion and some other more privileged information about the religion. So the more honest strategy for correcting bias in comparison is to find ways of comparison that are vulnerable to correction for bias. This requires taking a deeper look at comparison.

THEORETICAL ISSUES IN COMPARISON

The deeper comparative question to ask about concepts of God is, in what respects do they interpret reality?[5] Comparison is always in some respect or other. The clichéd joke about comparing apples and oranges turns on the supposition that one should compare items with respect to being different kinds of apples, or different kinds of oranges; the joke does not work if the intent is to compare apples and oranges with respect to being different kinds of fruit. The "respect" in which things are compared is the "comparative category" being used. Confusion about the respects in which things are compared, usually occasioned by misleading relations of language, lies behind many theological confusions.

Respects or categories of comparison are not mere conceptual tools whose instrumental worth lies within the comparative project or scheme. Rather, comparative categories aim to pick out the respect in which the items compared themselves interpret reality. Thus, the interpretive context and purpose of comparison rests on a more basic interpretive relation that in turn illustrates a more general notion of interpretation.

The more general notion, I propose, is best understood in terms of Charles Peirce's theory of semiotics, discussed in detail in chapter 7 above. In

Peirce's theory, an interpretation takes a sign to stand for an object in a certain respect. An interpretation is an existential act, a way of engaging the object by means of the sign that represents it in a certain respect. If the object is a river, for instance, "brown" represents it in respect of color, "southward" in respect of direction of flow, "in the Midwest of America" in respect of place, and "Mississippi" in respect of name. The context and purpose of interpretation determines the relevant respect in which to interpret the river. To say that a sugar cube is both white and sweet is not a contradiction because those attributes interpret it in different respects. To say that God is both love and light is not a contradiction because, presumably, those attributes stand for God in different respects. Is the uneasy compatibility of God's alleged justice and mercy also to be adjudicated this way?[6] To answer the question requires becoming more precise about the respects in which they stand for God in given interpretations.

Since the unhappy "linguistic turn," we are accustomed to think of all signs as mental or linguistic entities.[7] From this we tend to think of the objects and further interpretants of signs also as mental or linguistic entities, and before long people are saying that everything is a "text" because we cannot talk about anything at all that is not itself a sign or referred to as a sign. Peirce, however, argued rightly that things in the world are really and extra-mentally related to one another according to semiotic patterns. A brute action according to a physical law he regarded as the effect standing for the cause in respect of the physical law, with the interpretation being the new situation. I let slip the cup that falls to the floor and breaks: the breaking cup stands for my slip in respect of the law of gravity and the whole event is the interpretation. To continue with that example, my wife's glare interprets the slip in respect of my inattentive manners, and the host's rush to mop the coffee, muttering that he'll fetch another of his great aunt's antique cups, interprets the slip in a complex, double-meaning respect that both levies and lightens blame in a social situation. In matters of religious thought, we can ask about the respects in which the concept "God" interprets reality and we can alternatively ask how God, so conceived, interprets reality. The latter means to ask what God means in respect of what and for what or whom. For instance, God means Creator in respect to the existence of the world for the monotheistic religions; God also means Judge in respect of the ultimate worth of nations and individual people, for those religions, etc. In monotheistic categories, God belongs to the categories that mark out the respects in which God is significant for, that is, interprets, one thing or another. God is interpreted by those categories, and we should understand that those categories are the respects in which God is interpreted for certain interpreters.

Peirce's is a realistic view of truth in interpretation. Not all theistic religions interpret God in the same respects. Moreover, the conceptual categories are at best wise stabs at getting the real categories or respects of interpretive relation right. Nevertheless, in respect of the world's existence, either God is its creator or not, and this does not depend on how theistic theologies think about it. The philosophic problem for theology at this point, of course, is that even asking the question to be answered realistically depends on our historically contingent concepts to frame the question. To ask about the world's contingency supposes some conceptual metaphysics or other, and there are many among which to choose that give different versions of contingency.

So, interpretive theology, necessary to produce theological concepts to compare, needs to control for three dimensions of its context. First, it has to ask the realistic questions: is God or is God not the creator of the contingent world? Second, it has to ask the hermeneutical questions: does the theology at hand have adequate categories to interpret the realistic situation, for instance understanding contingency? Third, how do the cultural values and purposes of the theological interpretive project at hand select and control for the respects in which it aims to interpret reality, and can these be justified as the best?

To summarize this section, a general Peircean notion of interpretation has been cited that points up how a theological interpretation aims to interpret its object, e.g. God, in certain respects, e.g. the contingency of the world. Two different religions or theologies can be compared only where they are found to have concepts interpreting the same object in the same respect.

OBSERVATIONS ABOUT ULTIMACY

We are now almost ready to ask in what respects concepts of God interpret their objects so that we can compare the concepts. A linguistic confusion needs to be dealt with first. "God" is both a common noun and a proper noun. When we speak of monotheisms, "God" as common noun is common to all. The Jewish conception of Yahweh, the Christian Trinity, and Muslim Allah are overlapping but somewhat different proper names for the common noun with different theological conceptions and symbol systems. "Brahman," "Dao," "Emptiness," "Buddha Nature," and "Heavenly Principle" are also common nouns in a sense, with different conceptions within each family of religions that use those titles as proper names, and they all are somewhat like. To minimize confusions, in what follows, "ultimacy" or "the ultimate" will be used as the common noun of which various concepts of God, Brahman, Dao, Buddha Nature, etc., are versions to be compared. The restated topic of this essay, then, is the role of concepts of *ultimacy* in cross cultural comparative theology.[8]

In what respects do concepts of ultimacy interpret their object? To answer that question with the formulation of a proper hypothesis, three observations are in order: an historical one, a point about two senses of ultimacy, and a metaphysical observation.

The historical point is that in all or nearly all the great religious traditions with a traceable history the earliest representation of the ultimate were highly personalistic or personified. That is, the ultimate was represented as a super human being with an intensification of human powers beyond the ordinary, and the world was conceived as the product of super-human making. Usually, the ultimate was one super being among others, though superior, as Zeus to Apollo, Yahweh to the other gods who should not be put before him by the Israelites, Shangdi the Chinese sky god, Indra, Vishnu, Dyaus or some other top god in Indian pantheons. These ultimates were conceived as intensely personal, like human persons only more so. They were thought to have places within the cosmos and to interact with human and other personal beings as well as natural forces.

As the great religions developed, the highly anthropomorphic images of the ultimate were supplemented if not supplanted by less anthropomorphic concepts. Within the history of Israel, the Yahweh of the Ten Commandments was to be put first among all the gods by the Hebrews because he was their own god (not necessarily because he was better than the gods of the Egyptians and Canaanites—a point which had to be proved in battle); the God of the creation narratives, on the other hand, is absolutely supreme; the God of Second Isaiah was Lord of all nations, not only Israel; the God of Job was to be conceived expressly beyond human categories; and the God of St. John was both love and light, not loving and illuminating only, but love itself and light itself. Within the first centuries of Christianity, God the Father was conceived on the model of the Neo-Platonic One beyond being and distinction; for Thomas Aquinas God is the Pure Act of Esse. In Indian religions Buddhism was, among other things, an anti-anthropomorphic reaction against the personifications of divinity in the Vedic traditions. In Chinese religions both early Daoism and Confucianism took form by explicitly denying the anthropomorphism of the early Shangdi worship, which they took to be superstitious, although later Daoism returned to decidedly anthropomorphic models. To use the rhetoric of the Western monotheisms, the danger with the anthropomorphic concepts is that they become idolatrous, mistaking something non-ultimate for the ultimate.

In all these traditions, after the Axial Age when the cosmos came to be considered as a whole, the ultimate as unitary, and human beings as individuals defined before the ultimate rather than in terms of their land and kin, a spectrum of rhetoric was maintained with extremes of anthropomorphic personification of the ultimate and of abstraction of the ultimate to principles or something "beyond" definition.[9] But the religions took their classic rhetorical forms by fixing on some portion of that spectrum. The Western monotheisms fixed on the rather anthropomorphic rhetoric of God as a player in an historical narrative. Liturgies, songs, and stories emphasize the personal aspects of God. In Judaism, that narrative strongly defines the people Israel. In Christianity the salvation-history theme has always been strong, especially since the rise of Biblical reformation thought that suppressed metaphysical medieval theology; strong anti-anthropomorphic elements also exist within Christianity. In Islam, because of the very great importance of combating idolatry, the anti-anthropomorphic elements predominate, although the rhetoric of Allah as a person remains.[10] In India, the reconstitution of the Vedic and Upanisadic traditions as "Hinduism" over against Buddhism included extremes of the non-anthropomorphic "principle" concepts, as in Advaita Vedanta, although it also kept highly sophisticated personalistic conceptions, as in Ramanuja's Vishistadvaita Vedanta. Buddhism, for all its anti-anthropomorphism in concepts of the ultimate (to the extreme of denying ontological reference entirely in Madhyamika), returned to personalistic notions in devotion to bodhisattvas such as Avaloketeshvara or Guanyin. For whatever reason, the Indian religions occupy a broad expanse across the middle of the spectrum. In China, the triumph of anti-anthropomorphic and anti-supernatural Confucianism and Daoism in the early Han dynasty was a major cultural/political transformation. The center of rhetoric of those traditions is highly abstracted or devoted to principles rather than personification. Nevertheless, even Confucianism with its rejection of Shangdi insisted on waiting for the mandate, i.e. will, of Heaven, and Daoism developed into elaborate cosmologies with pantheons in its medieval period. The religions usually called theistic are those whose center of rhetoric comes from the anthropomorphic end of the spectrum, whereas the religions that are not theistic take their center of rhetoric from the other end.

The observation about two senses of ultimacy is this: whereas the bias of thinkers from monotheistic traditions is to give an ontological interpretation of ultimacy—an ultimate being or ultimate ground or principle, the bias of thinkers from some other traditions is to give an anthropological interpretation of ultimacy—religion as an ultimate quest for release from suffering, from ignorance, or perhaps from disharmony. Where the ontological ultimate is construed to be a reality or characteristic of reality, or something really transcending all that (bearing in mind the mystics), the anthropological ultimate is a characteristic of a life process, a drive, a quest, or something like that. Usually the two are connected and religions have only predominant biases. The ultimacy of the ontological God in the monotheistic traditions determines an ultimacy to human life and its obligations, guilts, and redemption. The ultimacy of self-realization, attunement, and religious virtuosity in the East Asian religions has to do with the nature of the Dao, the principles of Heaven and Earth, and related ontological matters. The ultimacy of the quest for enlightenment, release from suffering and rebirth, and the achievement of nonattachment, as well as the ecstasies of worship in the various religions of India are all related to the ontological characters of things. For most of the religions of India, the ontological characters include ultimate realities. For the forms of Buddhism that deny ontological ultimates, that denial still is based on a reading of the ontological characters of things, e.g. Emptiness, pratitya samutpada.

Paul Tillich has been explicit in tying ultimate ontological reality to ultimate concern, his phrase for the anthropological ultimate. In one of his most important essays he distinguishes

> two ways of approaching God: the way of overcoming estrangement and the way of meeting a stranger. In the first way man discovers *himself* when he discovers God; he discovers something that is identical with himself although it transcends him infinitely, something from which he is estranged, but from which he never has been and never can be separated. In the second way man meets a *stranger* when he meets God. The meeting is accidental.[11]

Tillich calls the former way "ontological" and the latter "cosmological," which differs from my usage here. Here the way of overcoming estrangement is the anthropological ultimate and the meeting with God as a different being is one version of the ontological ultimate. Tillich's point is that the latter is flawed. The way of overcoming estrangement, however anthropological on our account, is the way of connecting with ontological ultimacy, on his view. In comparative perspective, it must remain an open empirical question whether the anthropological and ontological ultimates are to be so happily connected. A properly vague hypothesis to connect them will be presented shortly.

The metaphysical observation is the hypothesis that ontological ultimacy partly, though not exclusively, has to do with the problem of the one and the many. The problem of the one and the many has several versions. One version is to start with a recognized plurality and ask how these are ultimately unified so as to be possible together. This version is well expressed in Neo-Platonism and the Perennial Philosophy. Another is to start with fundamental unity and ask how the plurality of things there seems to be is possible or actual. Non-dualist theologies treating plurality as illusion and the origins-from-non-being philosophies of East Asia express this version. The more general statement of the problem is to account for how the world can be both many and also have the unity it does. The existence of a somewhat unified manifold is a puzzle at the heart of reality. Ultimate reality is what makes possible both plurality and unity together.

One consequence of this for theology is that candidates for the ontological ultimate need to constitute the ground of one and many together and not merely be one of the many, or the one apart from the many, to be discussed at length in chapters 12 and 14. If the alleged ultimate were one of the many, for instance God as a being among others, or a one apart from the many, for instance a Neo-Platonic One apart from its emanations, then that which contains the alleged ultimate plus the rest, or makes possible their togetherness, would be "more ultimate."

The different religious traditions have various ways of formulating the problem of the one and the many. The hypothesis here is that many of those ways are attempts to recognize and articulate the real one-many structure of things. So, most traditions contain pressures to criticize inadequate formulations of the one/many character of ultimacy. The Yahweh among other gods in the Ten Commandments is too small; so is the Yahweh whose justice and mercy treat only Israel. In fact the monotheistic interpretation of creation came quickly to be that anything that could be distinguished from any thing else, hence both parts of the many, cannot be the ultimate. The medieval principle that God must be simple, common to many Muslim, Christian, and Jewish theologians, was perhaps not so much derived from love of Aristotelian notions of perfection as from the fact that internal complexity would make God different from things with different complexities and hence only one of a larger many. The Indian appreciation of fundamental unity exerted constant pressure to treat the many gods as manifestations of deeper underlying realities, however diverse their functions. The Buddhist emphasis on pratitya samutpada, variously interpreted, resisted attempts both to reduce the perceived many to substantial unitary realities and to reduce the unity of phenomenal experience to separate integral units with their individual own-being. The East Asian intellectual environment resisted any attempt to identify a single determinate ontological cause for things, often saying that things arise from non-being, or indeterminate nothingness. The ontological pluralism of the Confucian tradition, accounting for nature as the result of Heaven and Earth combined, was unsteady in respect of the unity of the two ultimate principles, with Zhuxi claiming half-heartedly that Heaven (Principle) produces Earth (Material Force) and Wang Yangming, his rival, saying that all is Principle. The struggles between those two schools of Neo-Confucian philosophy should be read as grappling with how not to be idolatrous with the problem of the one and the many.

AN HYPOTHESIS ABOUT THE RESPECT IN WHICH CONCEPTS OF ULTIMACY INTERPRET REALITY

An hypothesis can now be formulated about the respect in which concepts of God or versions of the ultimate interpret reality. Concepts of ultimate reality, within the semiotic systems of their culture, stand for that in reality in respect of which human life is to be considered as having ultimate significance. "Ultimate significance" means whatever value or meaning a person or group has in a context that is not qualified by any larger or alternative context, though the value in question might be made up of the contributions of many sub-contexts internal to the ultimate one. This hypothesis can only be proved or substantiated by a thorough review of religious notions of the ultimate, a task of a lifetime. The following portions of this chapter shall just gloss the hypothesis.

A tension always exists between recognizing the culture-bound or historical character of all conceptual constructs and recognizing that these are aimed to be really correct by those who use them and that they evolve through complicated corrective processes of engaging reality in their terms. All concepts, of course, are indeed culture-bound and historically developed. The hypothesis reflects this in the extreme vagueness of the phrase, *that in reality in respect of which human life is to be considered as having ultimate significance*. In pre-axial age religions, for instance, concepts standing for reality in that respect might be a system of totemic animals that gives one's tribe identity and pre-eminence relative to the tribe over the hill. Genuine pagan pantheons, in which different natural functions are governed by different gods with no supreme god, define ultimate human significance as responsive to the many gods in their functions. Axial age religions of the sort mentioned earlier have both subsidiary conceptions of the cosmos as a whole that bound the context of significance, and subsidiary conceptions of the individual as given significance relative to that cosmic context as well as to more local contexts such as family and territory. Different Axial Age cultures bound the cosmos differently. Ancient China conceived it as a great blob of *qi* structured according to macrocosmic and microcosmic yin-yang patterns.[12] The ancient Near East conceived it as a hierarchy of planes with somewhat different causal structures and different kinds of agents (angels of various orders, demons, etc.). Similarly, different conceptions of individuality exist, related differently to the respective conceptions of the cosmos. As a rough generalization, virtuosi in East Asian religions aim at attunement to or harmony with the ultimate context of the cosmos, virtuosi in South Asian religions aim at enlightenment with respect to that cosmos, and West Asian virtuosi aim at righteousness or justice, although all models are present in each of the cultures with some configuration or other. Comparative ethnography can trace the various configurations.

The other side of the tension is that religions cope with the realities of their situation. Religious conceptions guide people in the most pervasive aspects of their lives, shaping their behavior by the contours of the conceived ultimate context and the priorities of ultimate significance (about which more shortly). Reality is a hard teacher. If a society's conception of the cosmos does not countenance the existence of the barbarians, and they suddenly appear over the hill, the conception has to shift; if the conception says the higher celestial planes are filled with angels but better science finds hot rocks in the void, the conception is corrected, albeit often with difficulty. Sometimes not facts per se but considerations of intellectual elegance correct conceptions of the ultimate. The argument above to the effect that a God conceived as alongside the many is not as ultimate as whatever includes both God and the many is an example of the reality of the structure of intellectual possibility correcting conceptions inadequately thought through (an example at least for those for whom deep thinking is important). However different religions might be in their conceptual structures, their adherents intend the conceptual structures to be true to reality and not merely what their group happens to think. Only recently have people argued that being faithful to an ethnographic conceptual/behavioral scheme can be substituted for making a case for the nonarbitrariness of a group's views.[13]

Human value or significance is conceived in many different ways within and among the world religions. The focus of the hypothesis is on *ultimacy* in value. People are valuable in many obvious ways: for what they contribute and do, for the roles they play in society and history (often defined by family roles), for how they are regarded within their society and the influence they have, for their achievements of personal character, integrity, intellectual or artistic accomplishment, and so forth. Cultures define these forms of human value variously, though with many overlaps that support conditions for universal morality. All of these values are relative to time and circumstance. Is there not some context in which a person, or group, simply *is* the sum total of values (or disvalues) achieved and significances for others and the world? This is a reformulation of the question of the anthropological ultimate: what is it that defines a human being ultimately?

Confucianism and Daoism, and in part Chinese forms of Buddhism, say that all of one's values (and disvalues) are ultimately contextualized by the ways one harmonizes with the processes of reality. They disagree about the relevant processes, Confucianism emphasizing social ones, Daoism natural ones, and Buddhism mental ones. They agree, each in its own ways, that the ultimate meaning of one's life is how, where, and to what degree one's harmonizing with the processes gives one the power and identity of the cosmos (appropriately defined).[14] Indian and other kinds of Buddhism take release from suffering to be the immediate goal of human life, with practiced detachment as the means. What makes release from suffering ultimate, however, and not just an analgesic experience, is that suffering itself results from a vast ontological mistake of misidentifying what is real; enlightenment in Buddhism is not so much about an ontological object but about enlightened ones being ultimately right ontologically.[15] West Asian religions focus more on the processes of living justly than those of harmony or enlightenment, though all are present. Ultimate matters in justice are often symbolized by persons and communities being judged by God as by a king. Even when the anthropomorphic symbols are dismissed for more abstract transcendent ones, the ultimate concern of Jews, Christians, and Muslims is to be justified before the ultimate as a means of praising God. The Christian logic is to say that God in Christ presents people as justified before God, even when they do not deserve that.

The hypothesis about the respect in which conceptions of the ultimate represent their objects can relate the spectrum of conceptions of the ontological ultimate from highly personified forms to abstract ones to the distinction between the ontological and anthropological ultimates. The hypothesis refers to *that in reality in respect of which human life is to be considered as having ultimate significance*. "That in reality" is the ontological ultimate. The anthropological ultimate determines the respect in which "that" is taken to be ultimate. This point is easy to make in the case of those conceptions of the ontological ultimate that fall toward the personifying end of the spectrum. The human interest to attain ultimate harmony, enlightenment, or salvation with respect to righteousness easily personifies the conditions in reality that determine how that is possible. Confucians wait upon the mandate of heaven, Buddhists appeal to Guanyin or think about understanding Emptiness as approaching Buddha-nature, and monotheists pray to God for deliverance and salvation. Petitionary prayers in all religions suppose a cry from the bottom of the heart for what is ultimately most needed and important, and such a cry is addressed as to an interpretive listener.[16]

Conceptions of the ultimate focused more toward the abstract or transcendent end of the spectrum are just as much interpretive in terms of the anthropological respect, though they might not seem so at first. For those theological traditions that have sensed or articulated the logic of the one/many formal criterion of ultimacy, the character of the anthropological ultimate has been keyed to the ontological conception. One's ultimate quest has to do with relating to the ground of the one-and-many configuration of the cosmos, conceived as best one's culture can. The conception of that which answers to the anthropological quest for ultimacy is that which defines the ultimate context in which one's ultimate value or significance is to be found.

The extremes of the ontological/anthropological distinction would seem to lie outside the generalization just made. The extreme ontological side is characteristic of those traditions with detailed and explicit discussions of the one and many problem, such as Buddhism, several forms of Hinduism, and Christianity and Islam. In these traditions, hypotheses about how the one/many character of the world is grounded can be formulated without any reference to human life. They can be phrased in modern evolutionary terms as compatible with the possibility that no human life would have arisen at all. They can be purely metaphysical theories or hypotheses that would affirm what they do irrespective of any human significance. Nevertheless, they would not be taken to be religiously interesting as referring to the ultimate unless they shaped the anthropological quest for what is ultimately important; that shaping comes in the presentation of the grounding of the one and many in life. The metaphysical hypothesis shapes the sacred canopy, as Peter Berger puts it, in terms of which life has ultimate meaning (or no ultimate meaning on some conceptions).[17]

The extreme of the anthropological ultimate might be in some Theravada and Madhyamika Buddhist theologies that concentrate exclusively on human mental transformations and positively reject the value of any ontological hypotheses. This would seem to be a successful abandonment of all ontological ultimates. Nevertheless, those forms of Buddhism do have ontological hypotheses, namely, that nothing in reality has its own-being and that all phenomena reduce to the relativities of pratitya samutpada. The Buddhist ontological hypotheses deny that there is any ontologically ultimate object such as a God, Brahman, the Dao, or any transcendent creative source or principle. Yet it is precisely that total absence of any ontologically ultimate object that is the ontological reality in respect of which human significance is to be found: the lack of own-being is what makes nonattachment the ultimately important way of dealing with suffering. The ontological conception that nothing has ontological own-being needs to find its place on the spectrum from personifying to abstract conceptions.

We come finally to say how concepts of God or the ultimate legitimately can function in cross-cultural comparative theology. Concepts of God and other names for the ultimate articulate what exists in reality that gives human life ultimate significance. Some kinds of secularism and atheism say that life indeed has no ultimate significance, and when developed with articulate sophistication these views say why reality does not sustain any ultimate significance for human life. Comparison needs to be able to point out cultures whose ontological views preclude anything that might give ultimate significance. As noted already, some forms of Buddhism conceive of ultimate reality as lacking ultimate objects, gods, or principles, yet as having a truth condition that defines the ultimate path of detachment; ultimate peaceful detachment, released from the bondage of suffering, is possible for these Buddhist views because nothing ontological is absolute enough to be worth attaching to. Some interpretations of ultimate significance might not seem very ultimate at first glance. To have a God-given purpose seems more instrumental than ultimate. To achieve a certain standing in a community might not seem ultimate. Yet for some cultures, things like that are significant because of how they relate individuals and communities to God or some other version of the ontological ultimate.

Comparative projects can ask religious (or anti-religious) cultures what they conceive in ontological reality that orients ultimate human significance. Some will answer with gods that govern the real, others with a creator God or Principle or Dao that orients ultimate human significance. The comparative process can say how each of these theologies specifies the vague category of the respect in which the respective ontological reality conveys human significance. Then those various specifications can be compared, saying which ones are in agreement or disagreement, how they overlap or fail to connect, and how some theologies are positive about the ultimate and others deny it.

Of course, at the same time that such comparisons of concepts of the ultimate is being carried on, attention must be paid to different conceptions of ultimate human significance. That is as broad a topic as that of comparative gods, and not to be addressed here.

The thesis defended here about the respect in which concepts of God or the ultimate represent their objects is an hypothesis. It has been proposed as a way of integrating an otherwise confusing and politically hot discussion, and have indicated some of its power to bring religions into comparative perspective without bias or saying that they have to be alike to be compared. This proposal about comparison works as well with differences as with similarities. Nevertheless the defense of the hypothesis here has been only suggestive. Honesty requires listing some potential difficulties for it.

- Given the structure of the hypothesis, comparativists need a steady sense of what ultimate human significance is. There is not such a thing now, and therefore the investigation is struggling with two variables that define one another. Nevertheless, we have come to know that all of our comparative categories can be called into question, and that of ultimate human significance is no exception. It should have its turn as the topic.
- Monotheists might argue that only highly personified conceptions, those customarily called God, are important enough to be candidates for comparison, and that the more abstract conceptions such as Dao or Principle fail to articulate the intensity and seriousness of the ultimate category. The hypothesis can be defended against this complaint by showing how those more abstract notions in their turn define ultimate human significance.
- Because worship is the primary way of relating to the ultimate in many religions, the reference in the hypothesis to ultimate human significance is misplaced. Conceptions of God, it might be argued, represent ontological reality in respect of what is worthy of worship. The hypothesis, so the criticism goes, focuses too much on the human subject to define the ultimate and too little on the glory of the ultimate itself. The defense against this objection would have to show that ultimate human significance derives not from some finite human need but from the character of the defining ultimate ontological reality. The advantage to the reference to ultimate human significance is that it explains why the respect of interpretation of reality by means of concepts of the ultimate is ultimately important, reflecting the anthropological ultimate.

These and other objections need to be thought through before much confidence can be put in the hypothesis sketched here. The hypothesis is vulnerable to correction as that probation is made.

TWELVE

Some Contemporary Theories of Divine Creation

CLASSIFICATIONS OF CONCEPTIONS OF GOD

BUILDING UPON THE DISCUSSION in the previous chapter, conceptions of God further can be classified conveniently into two rough sorts, those that conceive God as a determinate entity, and those that conceive God as the ground of being, not a determinate entity within or alongside the world.[1] The determinate-entity conceptions accord immediately with anthropomorphic images from popular scriptures, and are represented with extraordinary philosophical precision in our time by process theology.

The ground-of-being conceptions sort into a further subdivision: fullness-of-being conceptions and *ex nihilo* conceptions. Fullness-of-being conceptions, such as in Neo-Platonism and Thomism, and perhaps Kyoto School Buddhism, conceive God to be beyond finite determinateness, and hence indeterminate in a strict sense by virtue of simplicity and by having no contrast term.[2] As the pure fullness of reality, God is conceived to create the world by some kind of diremption or introduction of negation that finitizes elements of the fullness of being, *creatio a deo*.[3] Although strictly speaking indeterminate, the fullness-of-being conceptions are sometimes thought to possess, in an eminent and infinite way, some characters such as goodness, unity, and beauty that apply determinately to finite things.

Ex nihilo conceptions of God as ground of being claim that God is the creative act that gives rise both to the world and also to the divine nature as creator. Apart from creating, God has no determinate nature, nor an indeterminate eminently full nature, although the act of creating determines a divine nature. Symbolizing the act of creation as will, it is sometimes said that the divine will determines the divine nature, a claim made about Duns Scotus in contrast to Thomas Aquinas for whom the divine nature determines the divine will.[4] Radical Orthodox theologians such as John Milbank read this glorification of will as the root of all evil in modern thought, inevitably leading to nominalism.[5] Nevertheless, I believe the *ex nihilo* ground-of-being conceptions to be the best hypothesis in our current situation, and I do not think that Scotus' realistic theory of common natures, expressed in modern form by philosophers such as Charles Peirce, necessarily reduces to nominalism.[6]

Another way of distinguishing the fullness-of-being from the *ex nihilo* ground-of-being conceptions is to say that the former conceive God as symmetrical, the latter as asymmetrical. Symmetry symbolizes wholeness, completeness, that which is settled completely in itself, and to which references is made in explaining other things. Mathematicians resonate with the sensibility that when you have everything in equilibrium, in balance, nothing more needs to be said. Asymmetry in this context symbolizes the arbitrariness of will, the fact that the divine act of creation produces a particular singular world, and is itself singular. The intellectual piety of symmetrical conceptions fosters a repose of mind. The intellectual piety of asymmetrical conceptions fosters a restless inquiry, an empirical questioning to find out just what world God creates, and what God as creator does and is in particular. The symmetrical views have the problem of understanding how a symmetrical ground of being can break symmetry to create an asymmetrical world. The asymmetrical views, by contrast, expect an asymmetrical world and have the problem of explaining how natural selection eliminates unreinforced elements so as to have the vast regularity and stability that the world exhibits. As the appeal of symmetry is to mathematicians, the appeal of asymmetry is to artists and humanists for whom the thisness, the Scotistic *haecceity*, if you will, of a complex singular universe exhibits the most dense and valuable reality.

In what follows I shall remark first on process theology's conception of God as an example of the determinate being sort, arguing against that. Then I shall develop the contrast between the fullness of being and *ex nihilo* ground-of-being conceptions, arguing for the latter. The *ex nihilo* conceptions need further technical development, which I shall sketch along the way. Finally I shall remark on some of the implications for spiritual life of the different conceptions.

PROCESS THEOLOGY

Process theology is greatly to be revered in our time because it derives from the ground-breaking work of Alfred North Whitehead, who demonstrated against a powerful Kantian tradition that metaphysics is both possible and necessary in this age of modern science.[7] Although it was Charles Peirce who formulated the anti-Kantian argument that metaphysics is hypothetical, it was Whitehead who worked out a detailed system illustrating that. The argument from *esse* to *posse* is one of the best.

Whitehead conceived God to be an everlasting actual entity that prehends every finite actual entity as soon as it becomes definite, and that supplies initial aims to each emerging occasion to guide its transition from subjective unity to subjective harmony; the technical details of this are not germane to my present argument. An interesting contrast Whitehead saw between finite actual entities and God is that the latter is infinite in its conceptuality but finite in that all its actuality is prehended from the state of the world moment by moment.[8]

A difficulty was noticed in Whitehead's conception early on, namely, that because God is conceived never to finish and hence never to be definitely actual, there is no way in which finite actual entities can prehend God. Unlike finite entities which finish their coming-to-be in order to be prehended, God never finishes coming-to-be and hence is unavailable as something actual and definite to be prehended. Less obviously, God can never finish prehending one finite actual occasion so as to be able to move on to another—the order of time cannot be quite real within God.

Charles Hartshorne addressed this difficult with an alternative, though closely related conception of God.[9] For Hartshorne, God is a society of actual entities, each of which has finite duration, allowing of being prehended when definite and able to pick up on the things that have occurred since the previous divine entity prehended its world. This neatly solves Whitehead's problems but occasions its own difficulty. No guarantee exists that a divine actual entity within the society will be succeeded by another divine entity. Each divine entity is conditioned by absolute metaphysical requirements, but those requirements need an actual entity within which to reside, according to process philosophy. No overarching entity holds those metaphysical requirements over the transition from an earlier to a later member of the divine society, the very point that prompted Whitehead to make the single actual entity of God everlasting so as to embrace all dates of temporal actual entities within its absolute primordial eternal nature. To say that an emerging divine entity prehends the metaphysical requirements from its predecessor does not help, because the prehender has the freedom to prehend them negatively.

These issues have been debated in great detail, with many imaginative variations. Lewis Ford, for instance, has altered the process view to say that God is the reality of the future, constantly framing possibilities for emerging actual entities. Joseph Bracken has been perhaps the most imaginative in developing a Trinitarian process theology based on the idea of societies of Persons. I want to lodge an objection to all the process theological conceptions of God as a determinate entity, however, based on an argument about the one and the many.

In process thought, any complex thing, from a single actual entity to an organic society of societies of actual entities to relatively unorganized adventitiously meetings of trajectories of processes, is to be understood by identifying the decision-points that have gone into their constitution. A decision-point—that is my language—is where an act of creativity adds some novelty that resolves the things prehended into a new definite actual harmony. Each actual entity has its own subjective decision-point, but then each thing it prehends had its own objectified subjective decision-point, and so on *ad infinitum*. Whitehead called this the "ontological principle."[10] One of its consequences is that, whereas the metaphysical principles of process philosophy capture the intellectual impulses of rationalism, the need to understand particular things by looking for their salient decision-points captures the intellectual impulses of empiricism. Whitehead brilliantly recognized the singularity of the universe, and the need to understand things in their singularity, as well as to express the general summary patterns of our cosmic epoch.

Now, the basic metaphysical situation, according to process philosophy, is God and the world bound in processes of interaction as governed by the metaphysical principles. The most abstract statement of this, prescinding from the distinction between God and world, is the Category of the Ultimate; the more fleshed out statement is the philosophical cosmology itself as detailed in *Process and Reality*.[11] That metaphysical situation is complex, combining God and world. Therefore, the ontological principle would oblige us to ask what decision or decisions constitute that complex situation. Whitehead did not ask that question, deferring instead to the myriad decisions of entities within the metaphysical situation.

Should we not say, to repair this lack, that there must be an ontological decision-point of creativity that constitutes the complex basic metaphysical situation? This ontological creative act must be singular because the difference between multiplicity and unity arises only with the creation of the basic metaphysical situation. The ontological creative act must be eternal because time and its unfolding are among the created elements of the basic metaphysical situation, and it must be immense or nonspatial because spatiality is similarly created.[12] Decision-points within the metaphysical situation can be called cosmological because they are governed by the metaphysical strictures of the philosophical cosmology; the decisive creative act of the basic metaphysical situation can be called ontological, by contrast. Whereas cosmological decision points employ prehended antecedent actual entities and integrate them into new definite entities by adding novel elements, the ontological decision-point has no antecedents and thus creates total novelty. The ontological decision-point creates *ex nihilo*. The analogy between finite actual entities and the ontological decision-point, which I would call God in preference to the troubling concept process theology calls "God," is positive in that both involve the coming-to-be of definite novelty. The limit to the analogy is that finite actual entities add novelty to prehended entities that function as potentials, whereas the ontological creative act is all novelty, with no antecedents and no potentials.[13] Aside from the nature the ontological act takes on in creating the basic metaphysical situation, the act is indeterminate. This is to say, the ontological act is not another thing over against the world which would create a new complexity. On the other hand, it is not the finite things in the world by themselves as if they could be together without being created together ontologically.

Process theologians might argue that the basic metaphysical situation, although complex, is absolutely primary.[14] By definition, the ontological principle cannot demand that a creative decision is required to produce the basic metaphysical situation in which the ontological principle resides as a norm. Nevertheless, if that metaphysical situation is the ultimate context, then it does demand that all complexities be understood in reference to decision-points, and it is left with the unexplained surd of the complex situation itself. The ontological creative act does not itself have a determining structure other than the ones it establishes in the created basic metaphysical situation. All it has is its creativity of making novel things, namely the world with its complex metaphysical situation. The rationalism of seeking explanations of complexities in decision-points comes together with the empiricism of finding the ontological decision-point in a unified dialectical and mystical inference to the ontological creative act, or ground of being.

Process theology can avoid this move simply by refusing to ask the ontological question of the complex basic metaphysical situation. This is to say, it can refuse to take the problem of the one and the many seriously beyond its theory of how emergent entities unify their prehended contents. It can affirm one or several of its conceptions of an absolute but determinate and finite God, and decline to address the question of why or how there is anything at all. But then it would have to admit to a far more profound arbitrariness than one expects from process thought. It would suffer from neglecting a helpful way to join the grand tradition of God as creator that otherwise is precluded from its conceptions of the finite determinate God who works only by lures.

Now I want to make a stronger argument against process theology that applies more generally to all conceptions of God as a determinate being, though I will use process cosmology as illustration. What is involved in determinateness as such? A thing is determinate when it is this rather than that, itself rather than some other. My hypothesis about this is that a thing is a harmony with two kinds of features. It has conditional features by virtue of which it is related to other things with respect to which it is determinate, and essential features by virtue of which it has its own-being with existential location and in terms of which it integrates its conditional features. Both conditional and essential features are equally necessary for a harmony, and we should not be misled by language to think that the essential ones are somehow more important. For a thing to be determinate other things must exist with respect to which it is determinate, so that determinateness requires a multiplicity of things. Process philosophy illustrates this hypothesis in that the things prehended in an actual entity are conditional features while the subjective elements involved in integrating them, elements that are spontaneous to the emerging entity relative to what is given in the past, are the essential features; the resulting definite actual entity is the harmony of both. Relative to process conceptions of God, the primordial nature is the essential element of God and the concrete nature made up of prehensions of finite entities is conditional.

Now here is the problem of the one and the many. Different harmonies are related in cosmological ways by their assorted conditional features. But each harmony requires the togetherness of both its essential and conditional features to be itself, and thus to be able to function conditionally with respect to other things. Therefore, there must be some ontological context in which the essential features of different harmonies are together that is the ground for the possibility of things conditioning one another cosmologically. Traditionally in Western philosophy, that ground for determinateness is being, and it makes possible the relations of unity and multiplicity among the determinate beings. Obviously, this ground cannot be determinate, for then a yet deeper ground would be needed to relate it to the determinate things it grounds. If the ground were simply indeterminate, mere nothingness, it could not function as the ontological context in which harmonies are together as involving both their essential and conditional features. My hypothesis, the classic idea of creation *ex nihilo*, is that the ground is the act of creation that immediately makes the harmonies in whatever relations they have with one another.

As illustrated in process theology, the essential spontaneity in finite actual occasions needs to be together with the primordial nature of God in a deeper way than can be given by the alleged prehending of God by the finite entities and vice versa. Indeed, God cannot prehend finite entities without using the eternal objects of the primordial nature, and finite entities cannot prehend other entities, including God, without the essential functions of subjective spontaneity. The ontological ground of the singular, fundamental creative act is necessary for a (Whiteheadian or Hartshornean) process God and other actual entities to be in process relative to one another. To put the point more generally, any conception of God as a determinate being with some essential features that are not derivative from conditional relations with the world needs to be related to the world by a deeper ontological ground that creates them together so that they can interact. If it be said that the world derives wholly from a creative act of a determinate God and that no ontologically prior ground is necessary for the relation between the two, then this is to admit that the creating God is not determinate with respect to the world apart from creation, which then reduces to the creation *ex nihilo* position.

GROUND-OF-BEING THEOLOGIES

So far I have argued against process theology as an instance of a theological conception of God as a determinate entity, and have done so with an argument that generalizes to all or most conceptions of God as a determinate entity. For things to be determinate, they need to be grounded in an ontological act that creates them together, even when their togetherness is a matter of unfolding through time. Now I want to consider the distinction between fullness-of-being and *ex nihilo* conceptions of the ontological ground.

A distinct advantage of the fullness-of-being conceptions is that the created world participates in finite ways in the reality, which usually also means the value, that the full-being God has. This is so, for instance, on Neo-Platonic conceptions, Thomistic conceptions, and even on the Buddhist conception of nonbeing as pure fullness developed by thinkers such as Nishitani. The world thus has divine being and value, however limited that is in finite form. In Neo-Platonic and Perennial Philosophy conceptions, there are levels of reality, and yet even the levels most distant from the transcendent fullness of being have some derivative positive reality and worth.

The chief difficulty with the fullness-of-being conceptions as a class, however, comes in the interpretation of how God so conceived can create or ground the determinate multiplicity in the world. It would seem that creation would consist in making only negations or limitations so as to break up portions of the fullness of being into finite bits. Any positive reality in the finite world could not be new at all, since it is part of the original fullness of being. The only novelty in creation must be the negations that delimit the infinite into the finite. But what could it mean to create a pure negation? The negation must be pure, because any mixed-in positive reality would be antecedent within the fullness of being and therefore could not be created. Even more puzzling is the question of how pure negation plus pure being give rise to determinate being at all. Pure negation is as utterly indeterminate as pure being. Hegel knew this at the beginning of his *Lesser Logic* when he said that to get determinate being out of being and nonbeing one has to postulate becoming as well. Yet the world of becoming is precisely what requires determinateness in the first place: to become is to move from one determinate situation to another, as process philosophy has so exquisitely shown.

So I suggest that the fullness-of-being conceptions have a general flaw in intelligibility: they cannot account for how God as the fullness of being creates something determinate. This is to say, a situation of pure symmetry, to use the earlier language, cannot account for how the symmetry can be broken into something asymmetrically particular that derives from symmetry. Symmetrical processes within time's flow can give rise to asymmetrical results sometimes because those processes are always within a larger context that is asymmetrical with respect to the symmetrical processes. But it is difficult to see how ontological grounding by a symmetrical source can introduce asymmetries that constitute a particular determinate world. To conceive of creation *a deo* is to suggest that the only thing that distinguishes the fullness of divine being from the finite world is newly made nothings.

By far the simpler hypothesis is that divine creating gives rise to determinate things that have positive being and definite negations or limitations together. In fact, to make something new is to make something determinate, which involves a determinate mixture of being and nonbeing. If one allows the notion of making, for the creation of novel things, then creation of something determinate out of nothing is the simplest way to go. To disallow the notion of making something new, to say that out of nothing, nothing comes, is to deny divine creation, and is to be stuck with surd novel pure negations that somehow are supposed to delimit the fullness of being into finite chunks. Therefore, the creation *ex nihilo* conceptions of God as ground of being are preferable to the fullness-of-being conceptions.

This conception is hard to swallow, I admit, because we have a kind of elementary folk-psychology assumption that only determinate agents can do things such as create novel worlds. Perhaps you follow my arguments for rejecting a straightforward conception of God as determinate, but something of the determinate agent notion still seems to attach to the fullness-of-being conceptions of God as ground of being. Although not exactly determinate, because literally not finitely this rather than that, the fullness of being can be conceived as really real, purely good, unified with pure simplicity, and so forth. Although God so conceived is understood to be the ground of determinate being, God so conceived is also attributed those virtuous traits in infinite form apart from creation. So when we try to rationalize our folk psychology, we sometimes think that God can be worshipped as really real, purely good, simply unified, etc., without reference to creation. Actually, however, the fullness of being can be conceived to have those determinate traits only by extrapolation from the finite determinate versions of those traits in the world. God cannot be conceived to be apart from creation and still have those infinite full traits because the trajectory of moving from the finite to the infinite is not a finite continuum. The trouble with all analogies of proportion or proper proportionality is that the distance between the infinite and finite is infinite, and therefore breaks all continuity of extrapolating from the finite. To give teeth to the claim that the fullness of being is really real, purely good, simply unified, etc., apart from creation, it would be necessary to sneak back in some notion of God as a determinate being apart from creation.

So I appeal for a serious consideration of the primitive notion of making, of creating, wherein something determinate arises that is new relative to what existed before. In the instance of ontological divine creation, the creative act starts from nothing and gives rise to all determinate things, including the determinate indeterminacies of time's flow and human freedom. We can understand this by analogy with human beings, yet with a different analogy from that which says that God as an agent must have a nature with which to act, just as human beings have a nature with which they act. The analogy I propose, and mentioned earlier, recognizes that, in human affairs, what is most interesting about us is not what is given us in our environment, and in our biological and social heritage; what is most interesting is what we do with that. Our moral character develops over time through the countless decisions, mostly small but some big, that are our novel contributions to the given elements of our lives. Although we make only very small advances *ex nihilo* on what is given, God as the ontological creator of the entire metaphysical situation has nothing given and makes the positive reality of the entire cosmos. Whereas our freedom of creative making is extremely constrained by given elements, God's is wholly unconstrained. God the creator *ex nihilo* is the creative act whose terminus is the singular world, whatever that is. To know God's nature, then, requires knowing the world created. To understand the world, not only in its determinate nature, but as created out of nothing is to understand God in the act of creation.

The radical character of the eternity and immensity of the ontological creative act needs to be underscored. We see from the world that time does flow, for instance. Therefore, the divine creative act terminates in a metaphysical situation in which every date has a present emergent reality, a past fixed reality, and a future reality whose formal structure as possibility shifts with every change in which date is present. Eternity is the togetherness of the past, present, and future, and that togetherness is not temporal. God is never only at a now. The dynamism of the divine life is not temporal, like the dynamism of our lives. Rather it consists in the fact that in eternity every date is in the mode of present creativity, every date is in the mode of past fixedness, and every date is in a kaleidoscope of structural possibilities relative to the changes of present emergence. To get our minds around that dynamism of eternity is extremely difficult, and it is easier to imagine God as a determinate temporal being who might interact with us like other temporal beings do. Nevertheless, for the metaphysically minded, the complex theory of God as the act of ontological creation *ex nihilo* can serve as a sign for engaging God. That engagement embraces both the delight in divine presence found in each determinate thing and the mystic's awe at the act itself that makes ontological novelty.

PIETY AND CONCEPTIONS OF GOD

I suggested just now that conceptions of God can be used as signs by which we engage God. This is no innocent suggestion, but this is not the place to defend it. I wish to conclude with some observations about the piety or mode of engagement of God that is associated with the kinds of conceptions of God mentioned here.

Determinate-entity conceptions lend themselves to pieties of justice and righteousness, supposing that the world has something of the divine intent or nature inscribed within it but also with serious problems of being out of alignment. So, piety is ordered toward bringing the world, at least in our neighborhood, into closer alignment. Process theology is a paradigmatic example of this, with its emphasis on God's struggles with the evils of the world, limited to offering remedial lures but without the power to zap the evil directly. Human beings in their piety are coworkers, cocreators with God of a world that might be improved.

Fullness-of-being conceptions of God lend themselves to a piety of appreciation of divinity throughout all the world, in nature and in individual human beings, for everything in the world is a dirempted version of God's fullness. At the same time, this piety longs for the greater richness of the fullness in God, and hence is a bit impatient with the determinately limited reality and value of finite things. Mysticism in this kind of conception of God as the fullness of being tends toward the merging of the finite into the infinite. Perhaps Plotinus' flight of the alone to the Alone is a bit dramatic, but it points to the piety of repose in divine fullness.

Creation *ex nihilo* conceptions also lead to a piety of appreciation of beauty, value, and even divinity in the world, but not as derived from a purer, fuller version of those elements in God apart from the world. Rather, the piety of this conception is marked by wonder and surprise at the world God creates. God creates a world of determinate harmonies, which are valuable and beautiful. This piety takes quite seriously the observation in Genesis that God creates this and that and sees that they are good. They do not have to be good because of some antecedent divine nature. In fact, God makes the divine nature good by creating a good world. That the world is not entirely good also has implications for the divine nature. The piety of creation *ex nihilo* theologies is not oriented to repose so much as to inquiry into what world God actually grounds and the celebration of it. Because the divine nature is constituted by the product of the divine act, this is a radically incarnationalist theology. The mysticism in this piety is awe at the power of making, at the ontologically creative decision itself, and the vast togetherness of all the parts of creation in the divine eternity and immensity.

I confess that I worry about whether these fundamentally different pieties might be more determinative of the theologies we hold than the arguments we give for the different conceptions. For arguments' sake, I hope that the arguments lead us to develop pieties rather than the other way around.

Permit me to conclude by offering an answer to John Wippel's question, Why there is anything at all rather than Absolutely nothing.[15] Part of the answer has to do with interpreting the question. It cannot mean to ask, for what purpose the world is created, because purposes are among the things created, being determinate. I take it that the question asks, rather, what makes the difference between absolutely nothing and the world of some-things. The answer I would give is that the divine creative act is what makes the difference.

THIRTEEN

Descartes and Leibniz on the Priority of Nature versus Will in God

THERE SEEMS TO BE a resurgence of interest these days in the philosophical problems concerning God's transcendence of the world and his immanence within it.[1] In large measure this interest stems from the impact on the general philosophical community of the work of Professors Charles Hartshorne and Paul Tillich. Both men have succeeded in making the interest possible by treating the notion of God in a philosophically respected way and in making the interest potent by keeping their philosophical treatments in touch with the living concerns of religion. Yet the positions represented by Hartshorne and Tillich apparently differ in important ways. It is the purpose of this paper to raise some issues that bear upon their disagreements by elaborating a famous dispute between Descartes and Leibniz. While the earlier philosophers phrased their arguments in terms of the problem of divine creation and the later philosophers have a different focus, there is a striking continuity of issues.

TEXTS AND ARGUMENTS

Although both Descartes and Leibniz held to a theory of divine creation, they disagreed as to the priority of will versus understanding in the Creator. On the side of the priority of the will, Descartes argued:

> . . . it is self contradictory that the will of God should not have been from eternity indifferent to all that has come to pass or that ever will occur, because we can form no conception of anything good or true, of anything to be believed or to be performed or to be admitted, the idea of which existed in the divine understanding before God's will determined Him to act as to bring it to pass. Nor do I here speak of priority of time; I mean that it was

not even prior in order or in nature, or in reasoned relation, as they say [in the schools], so that the idea of good impelled God to choose one thing rather than another. . . . Thus that supreme indifference in God is the supreme proof of his omnipotence.[2]

Defending the priority of understanding, Leibniz answered directly:

I know that it is the opinion of Descartes that the truth of things depends on the divine will; this has always seemed absurd to me. For thus the necessity of the divine existence, and therefore of the divine will, itself depends on the divine will. Thus it will be a nature prior, yet posterior to itself. Besides, the principle of necessary truths is only this: that the contrary implies a contradiction in terms. . . . Since then the incompossibility of contradictories does not depend on the divine will, it follows that neither does truth depend on it. Who would say that A is not non-A because God has decreed it?[3]

Obviously, Descartes would say that A is not non-A because God has decreed it, since it is of the essence of his position to maintain that God created not only the particular logical possibilities but the structure of logical possibility itself. Leibniz' rhetorical argument, however, is accompanied by two non-rhetorical objections that must be taken into account.

The first is that it is self-contradictory for truth to depend on the divine will, since among truths is the truth of God's necessary existence; God's necessary existence cannot depend on his will because his will depends on his existence and his existence is necessary existence. Two rebuttals to Leibniz' argument seem to be possible in Descartes' behalf.

In the first place, it must be admitted, with Leibniz, that God's will must depend on his being, for otherwise it would not be; nonetheless, God's necessary existence can be a product of his will if the will created the intelligible structure that defines necessary existence. It would not be the case that God's being would change with this exercise of will; rather, necessary existence would come to be as a possibility (or even a necessity, if the ontological argument is true). This rebuttal is especially forceful for positions like Leibniz', which define necessary existence in terms of self-contradiction in the possibility of the contingency of God's existence.

In the second place, Leibniz can be rebutted by arguing that the truth of the divine nature and existence is not truth in the same sense as the allegedly created truths or the truths of created things. For truths in the latter sense are essences, in contrast to existence. But in God, not only are essence and existence not to be distinguished, as most everyone admits, but the distinction itself is simply inappropriate on a Cartesian view. The distinction of essence from existence is only in the created realm, posterior, as it were, to God. It is not that essence and existence come together in God; rather their meaning applies only to the created realm. This is the insight of Tillich's position, that God is not just the unity of finite distinctions but is beyond them altogether.

Leibniz' second argument against Descartes is that a necessary truth is sufficiently grounded if there is a contradiction in its contrary and that the incompossibility of contradictories does not depend on the divine will. What could it mean for the incompossibility of contradictories to depend on God's will? Only that there is another possible world, which God could have willed into existence but did not, in which contradictories would be compossible. But the definition of "contradiction" is the incompossibility of terms; therefore, such a world could not be possible after all.

This argument, however, begs the issue, from the standpoint of the Cartesian voluntarist. For the heart of his position is that the possible worlds are created in their very possibility; the possibility of the possible worlds is created. This includes within the realm of the created things even the principles common to all possible worlds, in the language of Hartshorne. Hence, Leibniz' argument does not appreciate the extent of the claim involved in Descartes' position, although to be sure Descartes did not spell it out this far.

The remarks up to this point underscore a basic contrast between the prior-will and the prior-understanding positions: if the will is prior, it is indifferent to the logical restraints of the understanding;[4] and if the understanding is prior, the will is indifferent to nothing.[5] The result of this is that, so far, there is no common ground from which to adjudicate the positions. Before pressing on to attempt an adjudication, however, a further aspect of the dispute should be brought out.

It is important to note how careful Descartes was to say that not only truths but goodness as well is created by God's will:

> We can form no conception of anything *good* or true . . . the idea of which existed in the divine understanding before God's will determined Him to act as to bring it to pass. . . . Thus, to illustrate, God did not will to create the world in time because he saw that it would be better thus than if he created it from all eternity. . . . On the contrary, because he worked to create the world in time it is for that reason better than if he had created it from all eternity.[6]

Against this, Leibniz argued three things. The first is that, if "the works of God are good only through the formal reason that God has made them," then "he would be equally praiseworthy in doing the contrary."[7] On what grounds, then, could we praise God for what he has done? Descartes' obvious answer is, because what he has done is good. *Anything* God would have done would have been good, precisely in virtue of that formal reason, and there would be grounds for his praise in any case! Since Descartes' position is to deny a standard external to God, praise and blame of God most certainly cannot rest upon it.

Leibniz secondly argued that to say God created goodness is to hold Thrasymachus' view that might makes right. This position, Leibniz claimed, confuses right and fact.[8] According to it, God could not be distinguished from the devil.[9] Descartes, however, could reject the analogy between exercising power without the restraint of norms and God's exercise of creative power; for, while power should be exercised for good or ill *when* in a context with standards external to it, when there is no such context, as is the case with God's creative will, it is no criticism to say that it is arbitrary. Descartes' very theory is that the fact of God's creation is its right. Of course, a positive defense of Descartes' position would entail showing that to be good is precisely to be created, a much harder proposition; but these remarks defend him from Leibniz' attack. A third argument of Leibniz is harder to cope with. "Every act of willing," he said, "supposes some reason for the willing and this reason, of course, must precede the act."[10] If, then, a reason precedes the act of willing, "the good pleasure of God is ruled by his wisdom."[11] Moreover, the *freedom* of will consists in its willing the good. "Indifference arises from ignorance, and, the wiser a man is, the more determined he is toward the most perfect. . . . This shows at once how there may be a freedom in the Author of the world, even though he does all things determinately because he acts on the principle of wisdom or perfection."[12] The will of both God and man is determined by a good external to it, and the difference between God's will and man's, though great, is only one of degree.[13]

To this Descartes went so far as to agree that,

> *as to man*, since he finds the nature of all goodness and truth already determined by God, and his will cannot bear upon anything else, it is evident that he embraces the true and the good the more willingly and hence the more freely in proportion as he sees the true and the good the more clearly, and that he is never indifferent save when he does not know what is the more true or the better."[14]

But, contrary to Leibniz' view that indifference comes from ignorance and that ignorance is bondage, Descartes claimed that indifference is compatible with freedom, though admittedly not of its essence. It is perhaps difficult to see what argument Descartes would give for admitting that the indifferent will on the human level is free, since he agreed with Leibniz that "we are free . . . chiefly, when a clear perception impels us to prosecute some definite course."[15] But whatever difficulty Descartes might have justifying indifference on the human level, he made it clear that,

> as to the freedom of the will, a very different account must be given of it as it exists in God and as it exists in us. . . . Thus the indifference which attaches to human liberty is very different from that which belongs to the divine.[16]

And indifference *is* of the essence of divine freedom. The upshot of this is that Descartes denied that the difference between man and God is only a matter of degree. Here again Descartes and Leibniz shared little common ground.

TRANSCENDENCE AND IMMANENCE

It is clear now that the conflict between Descartes and Leibniz on the priority of the will versus understanding is not in itself a genuine meeting of different views but indicates a more fundamental divergence. As to the priority conflict, they had no common ground and were hardly talking about the same issue; but as to the fundamental divergence they had hit upon a problem at the very heart of a theory of creation. And when the basic problem is brought to light, there is a large measure of truth in each position.

The basic problem is the old one that God is in some sense transcendent of the created world and in some sense immanent within it. And the sense in which God is characterized as creator is equivocal with respect to divine transcendence and divine immanence. It is inherent in the logic of the notion of creation, taken even in a rudimentary form, that it must have two moments, a moment when God is transcendent and a moment when God is immanent.

The term "moment" is a dangerous metaphor which needs clarification; its meaning has two sides of interpretation. On the one hand, the term has its temporal connotations when it indicates a stage in the dialectic of our understanding. As will be explained briefly in the following, one moment in the dialectic understands God by way of connection with the world; the next moment in the dialectic understands that, if God is in the peculiar connection of being the world's creator, then God in *aseity* must transcend even that connection. On the other hand, the term "moment" indicates a somewhat parallel order in being that runs, as it were, in the opposite direction from the order of our understanding. But this order in being is an order or ontological dependence, not an order of temporal succession, since time is an element of the world that comes along in the second moment. The numbering of the moments employed here follows the order of being and not the order of understanding.

In the first moment, when God is transcendent, if God is creator, then God's being in itself is *not* dependent on what he creates. To say that God's nature is so dependent would be to say that what God creates is equally as prime and irreducible as God; else it would not condition God dependently. But, since by hypothesis God *creates* the world, the world is not prime and irreducible. God, then, must be externally related to the world, transcendent of it, such that God's being in itself is not dependent on or conditioned by the world.

The world, however, receives its *most fundamental* condition in virtue of its relation to God, as it is God's creation and its being comes from God.

Hence the world must in some sense be internally related to God since it is wholly dependent on God. God is what God is in Godself, and the world is what it is by virtue of a relation to another, namely, to its creator.

It was to do justice to this first, transcendent moment that Descartes said "supreme indifference in God is the supreme proof of his omnipotence." On Descartes' view, apart from acting within creation, God in Godself pays no heed to truths about possible essences or standards of good creation, since there are none. It takes an unconditioned, indifferently free, and, from our perspective, arbitrary act of will for God *to put Godself in the position of being creator*, that is, in relation to the world (which God does by creating it). For God to be *bound* in *aseity* to be creator would be to limit God's omnipotence or complete being, the point Descartes underscored so well. Even when the world is created, we must, for the reasons cited, acknowledge God to be transcendent; else God would have insufficient being to be creator and would be conditioned from the beginning, in *aseity*, by what is created, by that which depends on God absolutely.

The second, immanent moment of creation comes as God wills the creation of the world and thus becomes creator. For God to have the features of a creator, there must be such a thing as the created product about which there are truths and which perhaps there are standards. As creator, God is conditioned by the essential features of what God creates, by the conditions of creation. Leibniz was right that, in order to be the creator, God must abide by the necessary truths for any created intelligible world, and God's actual product is to be measured by the normative standards God creates for it.

If there were not, in this second moment of creation, a conditioning of God by what God creates, there would be no grounds within the created world from which to understand God, no grounds for taking certain natural features as being marks of creation. For some essential philosophic purposes, if not religious ones, God must be understandable as an explanation in some sense of natural features. Otherwise, apart from wholly intuitive, completely nonnatural revelation, a dubious affair in itself, there would be no grounds for acknowledging God at all. This is the ineluctable truth in Leibniz' position, and to deny it would be to cut ourselves off, not only from direct experience and ordinary inference of God, but also from the most devious dialectical knowledge of God; for there would be nothing in the natural order testifying to God from which the dialectic could start and nothing in God in which it could terminate.

There is a sense, however, in which Descartes' truth is more basic and more often missed. Accepting the theory that God is the total creator of the world, it is not the case, as Leibniz might urge, that in the first moment of creation, when God is transcendent in *aseity*, the role of creator and the possible product stand over against God as possibilities. For, should they do so, they would condition God's *aseity* as much as an irreducibly prime world would. They are not possibilities that God could choose if God wanted; if they were, God would indeed need a reason for choosing them, and all reasons must be of God's own making. Rather, their being as possibilities comes by means of and depends upon God's creative act. What it would mean for God's original creative act to be other than it was is entirely unintelligible to us, since, as was argued by Descartes, intelligibility itself is the result of the willful act God performs.[17]

The problem of God's transcendence and immanence can be illuminated by an analogy. Just as a woman is only a woman and not a mother unless she has children, so God is wholly transcendent and in *aseity* not a creator unless God creates. And as a woman, in order to have children, must first be independent in herself of her children, so God, in order to be an immanent creator, must also be transcendent in Godself. As a woman makes herself a mother when she creates children, so God makes the divine nature that creator when God first creates. And with respect to understanding, as small children understand their mother only in her role as mother, so we understand God only as creator; but, whereas, children come to understand their mother more nearly in herself by multiplying the role contexts in which they see her, there is no other context in which we can understand God, since understanding is limited to this created context of intelligibility.

TILLICH AND HARTSHORNE AS DESCARTES AND LEIBNIZ

The tentative results of this discussion of Descartes and Leibniz have several consequences for the positions maintained today by Hartshorne and Tillich. Three of these shall be singled out for comment.

The discussion urges contemporary proponents of the ontological argument such as Hartshorne to consider the possibility that God's necessary existence stems from the peculiar character of the created project if that product includes intelligibility in general. This is not to suggest flatly that God is "necessary on the hypothesis of the world," though it does come close to suggesting that. The point is that, if the Cartesian side is right, God gives Godself the feature of necessary existence when God creates a world wherein necessary existence is meaningful; prior, logically, to the creation of such a world, God's being is beyond or irrelevant to the applicability of categories such as necessary or contingent existence, or even existence and essence.

What proponents of the ontological argument should consider in this Cartesian suggestion is *not* a threat to the validity of the ontological argument. For, all Descartes suggests is that God's necessary existence is entailed by the structure of intelligibility which is itself part of the created product. Whether the ontological argument works depends upon an examination of the structure of intelligibility, not on the status of intelligibility with respect to whether it is created or prime. Hartshorne has properly seen this truth in Leibniz' position.

Rather, what the proponents of the ontological argument should heed is what Descartes suggest about the *nature* of God. To claim, as Hartshorne does, that God *is*, in part, the necessary or undeniable element in intelligibility may be to confuse or to blur the distinction between the derivative nature God has, which comes from God's connection with God's creation, and God's being in itself. If Descartes is right, the ultimate thing to say about God in the divine *aseity* is that God transcends even necessary existence. And, if this is true, what God is "most essentially" or "most truly" or "in Godself" and without regard to self-given connections to other things is *not* the necessary element in intelligibility but what transcends and grounds that intelligibility.

God's transcendence of the determinate structures of being is a Cartesian point most ably defended in our day by Tillich. The dispute between Descartes and Leibniz bears upon his position in at least two ways.

In the first place, the extremity and philosophical heterodoxy of the position should be acknowledged. To claim that God is the ground of the very structure of possibility is to say that all determinations of being are created. Therefore, if being itself is conceived as the ground of even the most basic structures of being, as it is on Tillich's view, then to identify God with being itself is still to identify God through the divine connection with the world. The extremity of this view is that, because of God's nature as creator or ground, God must transcend even that nature, since that nature depends on a connection with the created world. But to know that the creator must transcend the divine nature as creator is still not to know anything about God as God is absolutely in *aseity*, for it is only to know something about what it is to be a creator, God's connectional and hence derivative nature.

The much noted extremity of Tillich's views on symbolism seems to stem from the extremity of his view on God's transcendence. To say that all statements about God are symbolic except the one that says God is being itself, and that even this exception may be symbolic too, is to acknowledge that God is the unconditioned ground or creator of all determinations of being, and that even the concept of unconditioned ground is conditioned by a connection with that of which it is the ground. A ground that grounds nothing is no ground, and if it does ground something, it gets its nature as ground from that connection. Yet, if God is the ground, then in Godself God must be independent of what God grounds, since what God grounds depends wholly on the divine creative act. And, apart from God's nature as ground, we know nothing of God, not even that God is independent of what God grounds, because that knowledge of God's independence is about what it is to be the ground, not about what it is to be absolutely apart from that nature.

This is implicit in Tillich's view of symbolism, although perhaps he could have made his view more palatable to the public if he had framed the issue in terms, not of symbolic versus literal knowledge, rather in terms of God in *aseity* versus God for us. But against this last suggestion it should be acknowledged that Tillich's theory of symbolism has served better than any contemporary alternative to keep before us an awareness of God's transcendence and mystery while at the same time articulating a sense of the presence of this mystery and transcendence in our lives. It is doubtful whether this would have been possible were he to give up the discussion of the symbols of transcendence in favor of a doctrine of God's immanent knowability.

The discussion of Descartes and Leibniz bears on the transcendence position, in the second place, to the extent that it forces thinkers such as Tillich to acknowledge the truth in Leibniz's view. This is the truth that, having accepted the derivative status of the determinations of being and the transcendence of God beyond what we may know, still the structure of the created world does testify to God on God's immanent side, that is, as creator. Furthermore, we only know God to be transcendent through the structure of what God transcends while being immanent. Consequently, far from disparaging philosophical arguments for and about God, be they ontological, cosmological, or any other, we should seek them out and develop them with all possible dialectical rigor.[18] This is a side of the transcendence position that was present in the medieval Augustinians but that is lacking emphasis today.

EXPERIENCE AND REASON

This discussion can best be rounded off with a general historical observation. Although we are coming more and more to recognize a great variety in the approaches and sensitivities of the thinkers of the medieval period, we linger with the sense that there was a striking unity of experience and articulation in the divines and philosophers of that time. Those who appreciated most the niceties of argument, insofar as this connects God with human knowledge, still had a sense for the mystery of God's transcendence; and those, like Richard of St. Victor, who dwelt most appreciatively with God's transcendence, still recognized the importance of the intellectual ascent. This impression may be faulty because of the vagueness of historical distance, but it nevertheless provides a contrast with the early period of modern philosophy. Descartes and Leibniz understandably had difficulty with the unity of their articulations, since they both were struggling to integrate the impact of modern science and scientific philosophy with the older heritage of problems and vocabulary. Yet we suspect that ambivalence of articulation was not the only problem with them; the novelties of the age most likely disrupted to a high degree the comprehensive fabric of their religious experience. Descartes seemed genuinely overwhelmed by the brute fact of the structure of the "natural light," and Leibniz seemed experientially honest when he said Descartes' opinions about this were absurd to him.

In our own day, the comprehensive fabric of the religious *experience* seems to be in the remaking. To take as an example the affairs of Protestantism in the last hundred years, the appreciation of the immanence of God in liberalism, with the cosmological approach of personalism, has given way in the arena to the transcendence emphasis of neo-orthodoxy.[19] And these days, neo-orthodoxy is being called to task for its disparagement of the work of the intellect presupposed in its own position. The former move is from the immanent to the transcendent, while the latter shows the truth of immanence in transcendence. These moves in the theological arena more likely are responses to the pervasive experience of the day that to intellectual argument as such, although to be sure there has been plenty of the latter.

What are needed now are the philosophical categories to articulate the more or less general consensus or religious experience which acknowledges both the transcendent and immanent moments of God. Both theology and the consistent living of religion require that this be done. Of course, this conclusion assumes that it is philosophically legitimate to maintain as true some elements of both the immanent and transcendent position. All that has been shown in the above sections is that Descartes' view of God's transcendence can be defended against Leibniz' attempt to reduce God to what Descartes would see as immanence only. That Descartes' theory can stand on its own or that Leibniz has any power apart from a criticism of Descartes has not been shown at all but has been taken to be something we would "like" to maintain to do justice to the experience of our day. Discussions like the present one can do no more than raise issues about the direction and emphases of our more systematic studies.

FOURTEEN

The Metaphysical Sense in Which Life is Eternal

INTRODUCTION: IMMORTALITY AND ETERNAL LIFE

CHRISTIAN TRADITIONS CELEBRATE two fundamental eschatological notions for ultimate human significance: immortality and eternal life.

Immortality vaguely means life in time without end, especially life after death.[1] In Second Temple Judaism, immortality was a somewhat contentious notion, with the Pharisees advocating a version of it over against the older biblical tradition that souls last a while after death but gradually dissipate in Sheol, a tradition represented by the Sadducees. The Pharisaic version of immortality was the resurrection of the dead, and Jesus gave a defense of it, according to Matthew 22:29–33. There he argued that God is the God of Abraham, Isaac, and Jacob, who died; but God is the God of the living, not the dead; therefore Abraham, Isaac, and Jacob must be resurrected and living still or again. This was in answer to the Sadducees' question about whose wife a woman would be in heaven who had married all of seven brothers. Jesus said her resurrected body would not be her own female one but rather an angelic, sexless body. Other Christians, such as Augustine, argued to the contrary that the resurrected immortal body would be recognizably our own, at some ideal age. There was also contention about whether resurrection to immortal life is a special gift to only some people, with others remaining dead, or is a universal condition such that unsaved people would have to be raised for immortal life in Hell, or perhaps for a sentence in Purgatory. Dualists believed that only the soul is immortal, while the body perishes. Reincarnationalists believed that the soul occupies one body for a lifetime and then passes to another for another lifetime, and so on. Some people, for instance Anselm, believed that all souls are created at the beginning of time and get one lifetime to live in earthly historical time.

Each of the major religions have some popular conception of heavens and hells where whole people, or at least their souls, go as they relate to God or the gods. Sometimes, as in most forms of Buddhism and Confucianism, these afterlife conceptions are for popular consumption only, with sophisticated thinkers rejecting them. Buddhists, after all, believe there is no intrinsic soul, and so there is nothing to go anywhere after life in pratitya samutpada. Yet a powerful need exists within every axial age religion to represent how finite creatures can be related to infinite ultimate reality. The dual appeal of most symbols of afterlife realms is that, first, people can be conceived to be themselves while freed from some restrictions of finite life, such as death, and, second, the ultimate can be conceived to be geographically and temporally located, so as to be approached, or fled.

Symbols of immortality have a hard time in late-modern consciousness, however. We know so much about how the mental and spiritual dimensions of life are functions of physical bodies that separable-soul dualisms are not very plausible. Moreover, unitary soul-body resurrection requires considerable bodily continuity for personal identity to remain continuous in immortal life, and the obvious decay of bodies threatens the plausibility of after-death resurrection. The images of afterlife immortality have some power as literary figures. Jesus used them that way, as in his imagined conversation between the rich man being tormented in Hell and Abraham who was cradling Lazarus on his bosom in Heaven (in Luke 16). But as straightforward literal answers to inquiry about how to conceive relations beyond this life between us and God, the symbols of immortality do not fare well among Enlightenment and post-Enlightenment thinkers in our time.

Images of eternal life, by contrast, vaguely affirm that finite temporal life is somehow embraced already within infinite eternal life. This is compatible with the view that there is also a resurrection to later life after death, all within temporal life. But it is expressed in the so-called "realized eschatologies" of the New Testament. The author of Ephesians says, for instance, that we have been made "alive together with Christ . . . and raised . . . up with him and seated . . . with him in the heavenly places in Christ Jesus" (Ephesians 2:5–6). The author of Colossians says "when you," (the Colossian Christians,) "were buried with him in baptism, you were also raised with him through faith in the power of God, who raised him from the dead. And when you were dead in trespasses and the uncircumcision of your flesh, God made you alive together with him, when he forgave us all our trespasses" (Colossians 2:12–13). "So if you have been raised with Christ, seek the things that are above, where Christ is, seated at the right hand of God. . . . Put to death, therefore, whatever in you is earthly" (Colossians 3:1, 5). The author goes on to list the behaviors of ordinary life that are incompatible with simultaneously being raised with Christ in heaven. For instance, "Do not lie to one another, seeing that you have stripped off the old self with its practices and have clothed yourselves with a new self, which is being renewed in knowledge according to the image of its creator (Colossians 3:9–10). Although there will be a later fulfillment of glory, already ordinary earthly life is embraced within the divine life. John's gospel suggests much the same thing when, in the Farewell Discourses, Jesus warns the disciples that their historical life will be filled with trials although Jesus has already overcome the world and will guide them through the Holy Spirit. Eternal life is the life we already enjoy, and our finite temporal lives are only abstract parts of this fuller eternal life. The more we become aware of the larger eternal context, the more of God's glory we see. This does not eliminate the need to dispose of the trash or wash the dishes, however. Nor does it say that history itself will get better, only that it will be shown to be not the whole reality.

The complicated issues of eternity and time are not transparent to popular religion. Nevertheless, the traditional images of eternity and eternal life are to be found in popular religion. Philosophers of the ancient world such as Plato and Aristotle were sophisticated about these ideas. Perhaps Plotinus, in the Third Ennead (at 7.11), offered the ancient metaphysical account that was most influential throughout much of Christian history. Eternity, he said is "Life in repose, unchanging, self-identical, always endlessly complete." Time is the result of Soul which stirs to make something out of itself, and thus produces succession. Brilliant as Plotinus was within a metaphysics appropriate for his time, time and eternity need to be conceived in a metaphysical system appropriate for our own time, cognizant of science, world history, and comparative theology.

In what follows I shall sketch a metaphysical theory of time and eternity consistent with a larger metaphysical position I believe defensible that involves the central notion of divine creation. Then I shall elaborate this into a metaphysical interpretation of the divine life of God. Finally, I shall say some things about what the eternal life of human beings might mean in relation to the divine life.

TIME AND ETERNITY: A METAPHYSICAL ANALYSIS

I turn now to the concepts of eternity and time. Eternity in the sense I mean is not something static within time, such as a form, although this is a popular use of the word "eternity" in contemporary metaphysics because of Alfred North Whitehead's phrase, "eternal objects."[2] On the other hand, eternity in my sense is not divorced from time and change. It can only be conceptualized in relation to time as that which makes temporal change possible. Eternity can be understood as the ground of time and change. Eternity includes time within it as a kind of abstraction from the whole of concrete reality that is eternal. There are three metaphysical ideas to be developed here: eternity as that which makes time possible, eternity as that which is time's real ground, and eternity as that which includes time within it such that the temporal location of things is but an abstraction of their true eternal reality. These ideas are the metaphysical topics of this and the following two sections.

In what sense does eternity make time and change possible? More simply, how is temporal change possible? Our first thoughts have to be about the nature of time.

To be real is to be changing.[3] Temporal change is not a succession of moments of static, fixed actuality, first one state of affairs, and then another. Rather, temporal change in any moment that can be marked off by a span of consciousness, or by any arbitrary temporalizing measure, is itself a movement, a changing. That change happens requires the recognition of three modes of time, which for convenience's sake we can call the past, present, and future.[4]

By the "past" in this discussion I mean things that are actual and fixed. They are finished becoming and cannot be changed, although subsequent events might alter their meaning and value. If we did not acknowledge the fixedness of the past, we could never say that anything changed from something earlier, that anything new occurred.[5] Novelty in this sense does not necessarily have to be free and unpredictable; it just has to be different if change is to take place.

By the "present," therefore, I mean the creative activity of moving from the past to something else. In relation to the past, present creativity is spontaneous. That is, it adds something that was not there in the past. If what present spontaneous creativity adds were already in the past, nothing would be different from the past.[6] Present spontaneity is conditioned not only by the past upon which it builds novelty. It is also conditioned by the future that gives forms of possibility. All the changing creativities of present realities need to be compatible with one another when they have finished their spontaneous becoming and are the coherent past relative to some later creative present. It is impossible that one creative change issue spontaneously in something that is incompatible with what some other contemporary creative change is doing spontaneously.

So by the "future" I mean those forms of possibility to which all spontaneous present creative changes must conform. The future is not actual like the past. It has no dynamic creativity or spontaneity of its own, like the present. The future can be *imagined* as alternative states of affairs like the past, but that imagination is not true to the formal constraints of future possibility. The future is normative: no change can take place that does not conform to what is formally possible in a field of possibilities that is formally normative for all present changes taking place. The future is also normative in the sense that forms have value; actualizing the forms is actualizing the value.

Permit me to mention one more level of metaphysical analysis of the modes of time, already implicit in what I have said. Each mode of time, the past, present, and future, has two kinds of features.[7] One kind is essential and gives the mode its own-being. The essential feature of the past is that it is fixed actuality. The essential feature of the present is spontaneous creativity. The essential feature of the future is pure form. The other kind of feature is what I call "conditional," and by that I mean the ways by which a mode of time is conditioned by the other modes. Each mode receives conditional features from the other two.[8]

The conditional features of the present are easiest to understand. From the past, the present receives completed actualities as the raw material or potentialities for creative change. The past gives the present that from which changes are made. From the future, the present receives the forms that are possible for spontaneous actualization, forms that are compatible with whatever other spontaneous changes might go on so that the result can eventually be a coherent past. Past potentialities and future possibilities are conditional features that make change in the present possible.

The past, in its fixed actuality, embodies form as conditional features, which it receives from the future. If the future did not have structured possibilities, no form could have been actualized to give the past its determinate nature. The past has complex values because those values resulted from actualizing the forms that were in fact actualized and not others.[9] For the past to have acquired formal structure with value, however, it had to receive the actualization of that particular formal structure rather than another from some present spontaneous creativity; this is the present's contribution of conditional features to the past. So the present contributes the growing edge of actualization to the past in a serious of continuous changes that actualize new things.

The future, for its part, would be pure, undifferentiated formal unity unless there were actual, different things that require formal integration. Pure form needs, as conditional features, diverse things to be formed in order to gain determinateness. Without diverse components, form is empty. So from the fixed past, the future receives the conditional diversity that gives its forms of possibility their determinateness. Because the present is always adding new actuality to the past, however, the present conditions the structure of the future to be changing constantly. If the structure of tomorrow as future allows for us to be in Frankfurt or Australia, and today we stay in Frankfurt until it is too late to get to Australia tomorrow, the future for tomorrow no longer contains the possibility of our Australian visit. The present gives the future the conditional feature of constantly shifting.

Note now that the possibility of any change requires the togetherness of all three modes of time: past, present, and future. For a present change to take place, a fixed past needs to exist from which to be different, the change adds something new to the past when it is finished, and the present implants the forms the change actualizes into the new past, excluding the possibilities it rejected. A change needs possibilities among which spontaneously to actualize a definite set that coordinates it with all other changes taking place. A change means that the future possibilities for things are also changed, because what had been possible before is no longer possible. Change takes place within time and requires the togetherness and mutual conditioning of all the modes of time. I say this in summary answer to my earlier question of how temporal change is possible.

The modes of time, however, are not themselves temporal or within time. They are not temporally related. The past is not before the present and future, or vice versa. The modes of time define the temporal relations of changing things within time. The togetherness of the modes of time is what I call eternity. Eternity is the complex dynamic reality of at least the three modes of time and perhaps space within which temporal change and motion are possible. Eternity does not have a present, past, or future, but is that within which temporal things have present, past, and future. This is the preliminary definition of eternity.*

One final observation needs to be made about eternity as the complex dynamic reality of the temporal modes together. Each of the modes is itself dynamic in a sense appropriate to itself. We are accustomed to thinking of the present as dynamic because of its creative spontaneity. The past, however, is also dynamic in the sense that time's flow continually adds to it, enlarging it, sometimes changing its meaning and value; the past is constantly growing with every new change. The future too is a kaleidoscope of shifting forms. Every new present moment changes what the future must supply forms to accommodate. Although the past, present, and future do not themselves change temporally, their internal dynamics make possible temporal change. The dynamism internal to the modes of time is a function of shifting dates of present spontaneous creativity.

ETERNITY IN THE DIVINE LIFE OF GOD

With this elementary discussion of time and eternity, it is now possible to move to a characterization of God the creator as eternal, embracing the temporal. The second metaphysical thesis about temporal change is that eternity is the causal ground of temporal change. The fact that eternity is the possibility of temporal change does not account for the actuality of temporal change. Suppose that temporal change requires eternity, as I have argued. What if there is no eternity? But there is temporal change. Therefore there is eternity, in something like the sense I have described. The further question, however, is why there is any of this, and I believe the answer is that there is a nontemporal, ontological generative power by which eternity gives rise to temporal change. Ontological "giving rise to" is not like temporal change in which novelty arises within time. I call change within time "cosmological."

"Ontological change" is that which gives rise to the conditions for the possibility of cosmological change, and ontological change is an eternal act.

Something unstable lurks around this metaphysical thesis, namely, that eternity as I have described it, the togetherness of the modes of time, is itself a kind of middle ground between (1) indeterminacy or nothingness which needs no explanation and (2) the temporal flow that my hypothesis about eternity explains. If we can ask why there is temporal change and answer, because there is eternity, we can also ask why there is eternity in the first place. To this, I believe the further answer is that there is a kind of ontological fecundity or creativity that moves from that which needs no explanation, namely nothing at all, the totally indeterminate, nonbeing, through successive layers of ontological reality to issue in the cosmological realm of temporal change that we know. Time's flow floats atop eternity's fountain.

Permit me to give a brief but technical argument for this last point, having to do with the metaphysics of the one and the many and connecting with the notion of God as creator. How is it possible for things to be different and yet related enough to be determinately different from one another to be together? Suppose that the concepts of essential and conditional features I used above to characterize the differences and relations among the modes of time can be generalized to characterize all determinate things. By virtue of their conditional features, things are related to one another. By virtue of their essential features they are different. The things are no more their essential than their conditional features: they are harmonies of both. Now the question of the one and many is this. How can the harmonies be together? Cosmologically, they are together by virtue of the various conditional features that connect them. But the conditional features would not exist in the harmonies without the essential features; the conditional and essential features of each thing must be harmonized together. Therefore, in some sense the essential features of the different harmonies must be together over and above the ways the conditional features relate them. I call this sense, "ontological togetherness." Ontological togetherness is the ground for the actuality of cosmological togetherness, as eternity is the ground for the actuality of temporal change.

Now I ask, in what can this ontological togetherness, this ontological ground, consist? If we answer with anything determinate, then we need to treat the relation between this determinate ontological ground and the determinate harmonies it grounds as itself just another relation between determinate things. And then we would need a deeper ground. And so on. So we have to say that the ontological ground is itself indeterminate. Nonbeing does not need an explanation, for it has no features to be explained. Yet it is related to that which needs a ground by making or giving rise to the determinate things. The essential notion here is making, or creating, or giving rise. The Western metaphors of creativity are greatly purified when turned to metaphysical use. They have to mean those acts which produce novelty. If the novelty is temporal, it arises from a past state of affairs. If the novelty is eternal and ontological, however, it arises from no state of affairs, from utter nonbeing. Whereas novelty within time is partial and conditioned both by past potentialities and by future possibilities, ontological novelty is utterly unconditioned and gives rise freely to all there is. I know of no other rational hypothesis than that of the eternal act or generation or fecundity by which that which is indeterminate, nothing at all, gives rise to the harmonies that are determinate, such as the modes of time and then all the harmonies within time's flow. This is to say that God creates *ex nihilo*, and that God as determinate creator is the result of the ontological act of creation.

God's singular creative act eternally results in the spatio-temporal world. The act is not in time, and it has no date. It gives rise to time and all the dates in their changing flows of past, present and future. God's act is singular because it creates all things together in their manifold relations, including changing temporal relations. God's act is not like a general principle according to which things are made, although within the created world are principles such as those that define harmony in terms of essential and conditional features, and that determine how harmonies include forms, components formed, existential location, and value.[10] God's act is singular in that it creates the particular world that exists, a cosmos that is not wholly unified or symmetrical, but asymmetrical and peculiar, the sort of thing one might expect to be symbolized by jealous Yahweh. The cosmos is not a totality in the sense that Kant worried about, but just the set of things and their various relations and lack of relation that have their eternal places in the temporal unfolding of the creation. Only order and regularity, not chaos, need to be explained, and the regularity of the cosmos is what results when conditions reinforce things so that they last or repeat, and the things that are not reinforced simply pass away without regular consequence. God is the singular creator of a singular universe, and for this reason I call my position a theism, although God is not a determinate being within or alongside the cosmos.

In fact, the created universe is the terminus of the divine creative act, not separate from it, but the act in eternal fruition. So God's character as creator comes from the singular universe created. The divine character, in the divinely created world, is the product of the divine creative act. Because everything determinate needs to have a creative ground for the essential and conditional features making it determinate with respect to other things, everything determinate is created. Therefore God has no character prior to or apart from creation (to use clumsy temporal and spatial metaphors). Some mystics celebrate the indeterminate God-head behind the creating God.

Nevertheless, there obviously is the created world and therefore God has the character of being creator of it. Many dimensions of this divine character have been discussed in the Christian tradition under the rubric of the Logos.

All the transcendental principles defining harmony are included within this, as mentioned above. But also the divine nature includes the eternal togetherness of the modes of time according to which affairs unfold within the temporal created world. Because of these, we can speak of the divine character as being God's life.

Within the divine character are all the dates of things as they are present, when they are spontaneously coming to be, some with decisive elements. This highlights the classical sense in which God is the spontaneous ground of the present, and has all things within the divine reality as they are present existents; Augustine liked this. Within the divine character also are all those things with future dates, and in their different futures relative to changing present dates of actualization the future structures of possibilities are always changing. The future is a vast kaleidoscope of changing patterns of possibilities governed by actualizing decisions. Within the divine character finally are all those things with past dates as they have just been actualized and as subsequent actualizations add to their meaning, value, and connections. The actual past is a singular, growing field of achievement.

The dynamism of the divine life, therefore, is the togetherness of three essential kinds of temporal dynamism: the spontaneous making of present time, the kaleidoscopic shifting structures of future time, and the growing accretions of past time. As I argued earlier, these are not separate modes of time, but work together through the conditional features they give one another to create change. So the dynamism of the divine life is really nine-fold, with the three essential dynamisms of present, future, and past brought together by the conditional features each gives to the other two. The present acts on the future to change what is possible, and it acts on the past to add new reality and meaning. The future acts on the present to give it possibilities for actualization and it acts on the past through the present to give it structure and value. The past acts on the present to give it potentialities to be worked into new actualities, and it acts on the future through the present to provide a multiplicity that transforms pure unity into patterns for unifying diverse things. The nine-fold dynamism of the eternal living God is radically richer than our puny temporal dynamism in which we get excited about present decisions and enjoyments with badly imagined futures and barely remembered pasts.

This concept of the eternal living God is extremely complicated and hard to bear within one's metaphysical imagination. To be able to hold it all in mind and use it as a name of God with which to pray, to use it as a sign with which to engage God meditatively, to turn it into a vision of God, is very difficult indeed. But I have done it on a number of occasions that are sacred to me. Perhaps one needs to be a practiced metaphysician to be at ease with this kind of sign. You can see why the tradition has been tempted all too often to find temporal analogues for God rather than holding on to the eternity of the creator. If God is like us, particularly if God is a person like us, then it is easier to understand and relate to God. But then there are all the implausibilities of God as a big determinate entity alongside the world, and the frustrations of theodicy when God is conceived as a moral person like us.

The conception of the eternal living God does not suggest that God is a person with subjectivity looking out on the world, listening to us as pleading objects, and playing finite roles within our history. Rather, that sense of personhood should be limited to the subject-object character of temporal life within the world. In order to understand the relation of human subjects such as ourselves to God, I recommend not attempting to conceive God on human analogies.[11] Rather, I recommend reconceiving human life on the divine analogy. This is to say, we should understand ourselves as not only temporal but also as eternal, the final topic to which I now turn.

ETERNITY AND TIME IN HUMAN LIFE

The matters of temporal change are themselves abstractions from the larger ontological reality that includes the eternal act of creation. Ordinarily we think of our present reality, now, as our concrete and real existence. The past is gone, however influential it is in the present. The future is not yet, merely a set of possibilities for what we do now. The past and future seem abstract to us now, not as real as the present, and according to many philosophers we only represent them, we do not directly engage them. All change takes place in a present moment of changing. The past has stopped changing and the present has not yet begun to change. Nevertheless, according to the arguments I've rehearsed earlier, change itself requires a kind of interactive togetherness of the past and future with the present. Moreover, the past is always changing in the sense that it grows as new changes become past, and the future is always changing in the sense that possibilities shift as changes eliminate some and open up others. Therefore we should say that, whereas we are conscious of existence only in the present, the reality of that of which we are conscious extends into the past and future, both of which can be completely out of mind and imagination.

A deeper issue of identity lies in this point. Who Hermann Deuser is at the present time includes moral consequences of who he was and what he did in the past. For instance, he is now bound by promises and commitments he made in the past. Of course, he does not have to keep them. But in that case his moral identity now would be that he is guilty of abandoning or rejecting those promises and commitments, and his moral identity is even more complex if there are good reasons for abandoning past commitments. In order for this moral identity to make sense, which is essential if we are responsible beings, it is necessary to acknowledge that his past moments of present promising and committing are real together with his present moments of deciding whether to keep them. This is to say, his present moment is together with his now past moment as it was when that past moment was present and he was making the promises. The past and present moments are not temporally together, since within time they do not occupy the same time as present. In the present the past is a fixed past, not a decisive present when Deuser was making the commitments. But they are eternally together in the sense defined above: they are together as both present, although there is no time when this is so.

Moreover, if there is anything in his present changing decisions that involves moral consequences, then there must be future moments when those consequences will occur that give meaning to his present decisions. If those future moments were not together as present occurrences with his present decisions, then his present decisions would not have moral meaning until later, and we would not have to worry ever about making moral decisions. Present decisions and their future consequences as present are not together temporally, since by definition they are not in the same time. Rather, they are together eternally in the sense defined above.

If this argument has merit, then there are two kinds of togetherness of temporal changes, the temporal togetherness that makes the present seem most real and the eternal togetherness in which all modes are equally real. Eternal togetherness is the most concrete identity, however, because its equal inclusion of the past and future with the present is what defines the moral (and other) identity of present changes. Our ordinary consciousness is aware only of abstract elements of our identity because it lets the past and future slip from mind. Nevertheless, in moments of serious moral reflection we force ourselves to bring to mind and acknowledge our past promises and commitments as present, responsible decisions, and we force ourselves to take seriously the future consequences as later present occurrences of what we do. This is to take responsibility for the fact that our true identity is our eternal one, in which our past moments, present moments, and future moments, are all together, though not temporally together.

So we should say, then, that our most concrete identity is the eternal togetherness of all our moments as future, all our moments as present, and all our moments as past. As a very young child, you had very little past save that derived from your family and living situation. Your present moments back then were filled with play that had little to live up to in terms of past commitments and little to worry about in terms of future moral consequences. By fifteen you realized that you were growing into a moral identity and so you set your mind on learning so that you could come to understand how to exist in a moral world. As you matured, more and more of your present life was fitted into a moral and ritual round of commitments as you became enmeshed in the rich texture of public life, and your past and present were very much with you. Should you reach middle age, like Hermann Deuser at 60, you might have so organized the inertial forces of your life—your heart's passions, your ritual commitments, your work of teaching, that you can trust that organized past to move effortlessly through your present decisions so that you can trust their future consequences to be in accord with that of which you approve. Who is the real you? The young child? The mature learning and teacher? The surely not yet old spiritual adept? We might be tempted to say that the real you is the person at the end of his or her life, as we sometimes think of other people's identity as most real in their last moments. But the truth is that the real you is the young boy, the mature teacher, and the future elderly adept all together. The real you is the eternal identity of all your moments as future, all those same moments as present, and all as past. Your biography would not treat all of your life as past relative to your last moments. It would treat all of your moments as you lived them in the present, all as past moments that influenced later present changes, and all as future possibilities to which you have had to respond or will have to respond that would come as surprises. A biography tells the story of a person as in the passages of time, as a series of changes, all of which involve the dynamic togetherness of past and future relative to each moment as present. Please excuse the fact that, for sake of simplicity, I have spoken of persons as if they were isolated individuals. Of course people are defined in reference to others and to their environments through their conditional features, and so biographies really are group biographies, or natural histories.

The kind of change typical of the present is the decisive actualization of possibilities for the potentials inherited from the past. The kind of change typical of the past is its growing edge of meaning and moral significance that results from decisions. The kind of change typical of the future is the shifting of possibilities because of decisions taken. So, our image of the eternal identity of a person, or community, or changing biological ecosystem, or nation, or cultural tradition, or world situation, ought to be one that entertains all their moments in their temporal modes of being present, of being past, and being future, with all those moments involving the kinds of changings appropriate to their temporal modes.

All of this is to say that change is not what meets the eye when we think only about things changing within time. Change in our lives is not merely the passage from one state of affairs to another as measured by forms of different structures. Rather, change, when understood in its eternal identity, is a complex of dynamisms in which the past, present, and future temporal dimensions of changes are eternally together. So a change needs to be understood partially in terms of how it adds to the actuality, meaning, and value of the past. It needs to be understood partially in terms of how it involves spontaneity and decision-making that selects among possibilities, actualizing some while excluding others. It needs to be understood partially in terms of how the actualization of some possibilities shifts the field of yet future possibilities, moment by moment. The togetherness of these three senses of dynamism, or modes of time, is not temporal, but is eternal in the ways I articulated earlier, and that is our true reality.

Our fundamental relation to the eternal living God, therefore, is as parts of the divine life. Moreover, because we are connected with one another, we are parts together of the divine life. Although we ordinarily are cognizant only of the temporal aspects of our lives, with spiritual consciousness, or aesthetic consciousness, or metaphysical consciousness, we can gain greater awareness of our eternal identity and our eternal home. As Alpha, God is our eternal creator. As Omega, God is our eternal destiny. The symbol of the Cosmic Christ points to the fact that we live all our lives within the divine eternal immensity, whether we know it or not. Jesus' parables about waking up to the immanence of the kingdom are spurs to greater spiritual awareness.

With regard to some of the eschatological options mentioned at the beginning, on the conception of our eternal identity within the eternal life of God everyone has eternal life in this sense. It is not a reward for good behavior. Moreover, everyone is under divine judgment because everyone has just the complex moral character achieved in his or her eternal identity, and that is part of God, allowing for the complexities of conjoint behavior with others. There is no gainsaying the ambiguities of our moral identity in God. By the same token, the symbols of God's love and mercy point to the fact that God is our creative ground and home all the while we work out our identity.

Salvation means wholeness in a variety of senses. For instance, some people feel isolated in the moment of present consciousness, and salvation means coming to recognize their eternal connections with their own past and future and with each other: we are who we are, not alone, but with others. These connections, nevertheless, still remain fragmentary: that is life. Many people also feel alienated from their life and its ground in God, and salvation means reconciliation in the classic Christian sense. Reconciliation, however, is not like peace between two parties but rather like the at-one-ment of parts of a product with the singular act of producing. The goal of religious seeking is not some future spiritual material reward, such as life in heaven with cushy rewards, no hellfire, and no trash to take out. Rather it is greater awareness and consciousness of the glory of the Creator, including the extent of creation and the depths of the singular creative act that is our common ground. Although you have suffered enough metaphysics for one day, perhaps you can imagine an aesthetic account, in the tradition of Jonathan Edwards, of the glory of so rich a harmony as includes the nine-fold dynamic of divine eternity, the many dimensions of space, and the infinitely rich variety of creatures within creatures. What bliss it is to catch a glimpse of that! And for those not given to such mystical yearnings, there is blessed comfort in knowing that there is nothing we can do and nowhere we can go that can separate us from the loving creation of God.

Notes

INTRODUCTION

1. See John F. Boler's *Charles Peirce and Scholastic Realism: A Study of Peirce's Relation to John Duns Scotus* (Seattle, WA: University of Washington Press, 1963).

2. Hans W. Frei, *The Eclipse of Biblical Narrative: A Study in Eighteenth and Nineteenth Century Hermeneutics* (New Haven, CT: Yale University Press, 1974).

CHAPTER ONE. THEOLOGIES OF IDENTITY AND TRUTH: LEGACIES OF BARTH AND TILLICH

1. An earlier draft of this chapter was the presidential address to the American Theological Society that I gave in April 2006. Since 1973 this Society has been one of the most influential instructors in my theological education. The address was more an expression of one of my concerns for our theological profession than a direct statement of my own theology, although of course these are intertwined.

2. Karl Barth, *The Doctrine of the Word of God, Church Dogmatics*, vol. 1, part 1, translated by G. T. Thomson (Edinburgh: T. & T. Clark, 1936), 1.

3. Paul Tillich, *Systematic Theology*, vol. 1 (Chicago: University of Chicago Press, 1951), 3.

4. See Karl Barth, *Dogmatics in Outline*, translated by G. T. Thomson (New York: Harper Torchbook, 1959), 5.

5. Barth, *Dogmatics*.

6. The premier book of Radical Orthodoxy is John Milbank's *Theology and Social Theory: Beyond Secular Reason* (Oxford: Blackwell, 1990). George Hunsinger's *How to Read Karl Barth* (Oxford: Oxford University Press, 1991) is a good introduction to Barth's theology. The historical position of Barth and his movement as a search for Christian identity in relation to liberalism is beautifully explored in Gary Dorrien's *The Barthian Revolt in Modern Theology* (Louisville: Westminster John Knox, 2000). One of the most sensitive defenders of identity Christian theology today is Stanley M.

Hauerwas; see, for instance, his *Christian Existence Today: Essays on Church, World and Living In Between* (Durham, NC: Labyrinth Press, 1988). For the very rich story of identity theology in the evangelical Christian right, see Dorrien's *The Remaking of Evangelical Theology* (Louisville: Westminster John Knox, 1998).

7. This was first elaborated in my *God the Creator: On the Transcendence and Presence of God* (Chicago: University of Chicago Press, 1968; reprinted with a new Preface, Albany: State University of New York Press, 1992).

8. See Wesley J. Wildman's "Ground of Being Theologies" in Philip Clayton, editor, *The Oxford Handbook of Religion and Science* (Oxford: Oxford University Press, 2006).

CHAPTER TWO. TRUTH IN THEOLOGY

1. See, for instance, Ernst Troeltsch's *Religion in History*, translated by James Luther Adams and Walter F. Bense, with an Introduction by Adams (Minneapolis: Fortress Press, 1991) or *The Christian Faith*, translated by Garrett E. Paul and edited by Gertrud von le Fort (Minneapolis: Fortress Press, 1991). For an acute study see Wesley J. Wildman's *Fidelity with Plausibility* (Albany: State University of New York Press, 1998), part 1.

2. See Schubert M. Ogden's *Christ without Myth* (New York: Harper & Row, 1961) for an account of Bultmann's work from the standpoint of process philosophy.

3. See, among his many works, *Systematic Theology*, vol. 1 (Chicago: University of Chicago Press, 1951).

4. For Peirce's semiotics, see Vincent Colapietro's *Peirce's Approach to the Self: A Semiotic Perspective on Human Subjectivity* (Albany: State University of New York Press, 1989), Robert Corrington's *An Introduction to C. S. Peirce: Philosopher, Semiotician, and Ecstatic Naturalist* (Lanham, MD: Rowen and Littlefield, 1993), and my *The Truth of Broken Symbols* (Albany: State University of New York Press, 1996). For the claim that classical salvific symbols can be recovered, see my *Symbols of Jesus: A Christology of Symbolic Engagement* (Cambridge: Cambridge University Press, 2001).

5. Gary Dorrien, *The Making of American Liberal Theology: Idealism, Realism, and Modernity: 1900–1950* (Louisville: Westminster/John Knox Press, 2003).

6. Dorrien discusses Niebuhr and Tillich under the head of Neo-liberalism, but not process theology which he left to the third volume of his series, *The Making of American Liberal Theology: 1950–2005* (Louisville, KY: Westminster/John Knox Press, 2006).

7. I have studied these four levels in detail in *On the Scope and Truth of Theology* (New York and London: T & T Clark International, 2006), and also in the trilogy called *Axiology of Thinking*, including *Reconstruction in Philosophy* (Albany: State University of New York Press, 1981) for imagination, *Recovery of the Measure* (Albany: State University of New York Press, 1989) for interpretation, and *Normative Cultures* (Albany: State University of New York Press, 1995) for theoretical and practical thinking. *On the Scope and Truth of Theology* is the first of a project four volume work

called collectively *Theology of Symbolic Engagement*; the other three volumes are intended to treat theology systematically, drawing on many world religions, the sciences, the arts, and practical disciplines.

CHAPTER THREE. REALISM AND CONTEXTUALIZATION

1. George A. Lindbeck, *The Nature of Doctrine: Religion and Theology in a Postliberal Age* (Philadelphia: Westminster, 1984).

2. He and his colleague Hans Frei sometimes characterize philosophy as self-description of the Christian community and therefore closer to cultural anthropology than to philosophy. See Frei's *Types of Christian Theology*, edited by George Hunsinger and William C. Placher (New Haven: Yale University Press, 1992).

3. In fact, it is close to what Frei characterizes as the "fifth" kind of Christian theology epitomized by D. Z. Phillips, ibid., 46–55. Lindbeck gives an extensive analysis of the conservative approach to doctrine which considers it to be given in propositions or verbal statements. He also analyzes the liberal tradition from Schleiermacher to Tillich which treats doctrine as the expression, whether propositional or not, of religious experience. Of course, his characterizations of these alternatives to his own postliberal theology are contested by thinkers holding to them. My own position shares with the conservative propositional tradition a strong realism of reference to religious realities. I am probably closer to the liberal experiential tradition in my claim that we experientially engage religious realities by means of religious symbols guiding action.

4. He says, in *The Nature of Doctrine*, p. 113, "The task of descriptive (dogmatic or systematic) theology is to give a normative explication of the meaning a religion has for its adherents." The question is whether there is a larger meaning of theology, normative with regard to truth.

5. See Peter Berger and Thomas Luckmann, *The Social Construction of Reality: a Treatise in the Sociology of Knowledge* (Garden City, N.Y.: Doubleday, 1966) and Peter Berger, *The Sacred Canopy: Elements of a Sociological Theory of Religion* (Garden City, N.Y.: Doubleday, 1967).

6. Peirce's theory of signs and interpretation is set forth at length in *The Collected Papers of Charles Sanders Peirce*, edited by Charles Hartshorne and Paul Weiss (Cambridge: Harvard University Press, 1931–36), vol. 2, book 2 "Speculative Grammar." The pragmatic theory of hypotheses is explained in many ways throughout volume 5. Hermann Deuser's *Gott: Geist und Natur* draws out many of the theological implications of Peirce's theory.

7. See Barth's "An Introductory Essay," translated by James Luther Adams, to Feuerbach's *The Essence of Christianity*, translated by George Eliot (New York: Harper and Brothers, 1957). I owe this point about Barth, Feuerbach, and the conception of religion as social constructs to Wesley J. Wildman's "Theological Literacy: Problem and Promise," in *Theological Literacy*, edited by Rodney Petersen (Grand Rapids: Erdmans, 2001).

8. See Barth, "An Introductory Essay," xxii–xxiv.

9. For a systematic defense of this claim, see my *Recovery of the Measure* (Albany: State University of New York Press, 1989), chapters 3–4.

10. In his *Varieties of Religious Experience* (New York: Longmans, Green, 1902), lectures 4–7.

11. I had the privilege to direct the Cross Cultural Comparative Religious Ideas Project at Boston University which engaged a collaborative team of scholars in a self-corrective process that ran from 1995 to 1999, the public results of which were published in three volumes: *The Human Condition*, with a foreword by Peter Berger, *Ultimate Realities*, with a foreword by Tu Wei-ming, and *Religious Truth*, with a foreword by Jonathan Z. Smith, all edited by myself (Albany: State University of New York Press, 2001). The team included six historical specialists in different traditions of world religions (Francis X. Clooney, S.J. on Hindu traditions, Malcolm David Eckel on Buddhist traditions, Paula Fredriksen on Christian traditions, S. Nomanul Haq on Islamic traditions, Livia Kohn on Chinese religion, and Anthony J. Saldarini on Jewish traditions), each chosen because of a penchant for particularity and suspicion of easy generalizations. Four generalists from different disciplines were included to push the discussion to comparative issues (Peter Berger, a sociologist of religion, John H. Berthrong, an historian of religions, Wesley J. Wildman, a philosophical theologian, and myself, a philosopher of religion and theologian). Graduate assistants participated vigorously in the collaboration, including Christopher Allen, Joseph Kanofsky, James Miller, Hugh Nicholson, Tina Shepardson, Celeste Sullivan, and John Thatamanil. Each year the group discussed one of the topics in the book titles (save the fourth year that was devoted to editing the publications). In the fall semester each of the historical specialists presented a paper on what their tradition or text had to say about the comparative topic. After much discussion each then rewrote the paper for the spring meetings so as to reflect comparative comments. In addition to revising the comparative points many times, the collaborative discussion also honed a theory of comparison, changing it as our experience and shared knowledge grew. The individual essays on a given tradition read across each of the volumes gives a good introduction to that tradition. The summary comparative and methodological chapters provide detailed philosophical reflections. A narrative of each year's discussion describes the existential aspects of collaboration. Many of the comparative points made in the present and subsequent chapters arose from that collaboration, and some are to be found in the publications. The experience of the collaboration goes beyond any particular comparison.

12. Frei, *Types of Christian Theology*, chapter 3.

13. Lindbeck, *The Nature of Doctrine*, 113ff.

14. See Samuel Hugh Moffett, *History of Christianity in Asia* (San Francisco: Harper, 1992), 169–170.

15. See Wesley J. Wildman, *Fidelity with Plausibility: Modest Christologies in the Twentieth Century* (Albany: State University of New York Press, 1998).

16. This understanding of comparison as analyzing the different ways religions specify the vague respects in which they engage reality and can be compared was explored at length in *The Human Condition, Ultimate Realities,* and *Religious Truth*.

CHAPTER FOUR. HOW TO READ SCRIPTURES FOR RELIGIOUS TRUTH

1. This chapter began as a contribution to a Festschrift honoring Anthony Saldarini, completed after his premature death. That context explains its rhetorical structure. My friendship with Tony Saldarini began over twenty years ago when he advised me on personnel for the Judaic Studies program I chaired at the State University of New York at Stony Brook. That neither of us was Jewish made it possible for that program to go forward in that political place. We reconnected in a much more intense way in the mid 1990s when Tony joined the collaborative Comparative Religious Ideas Project. Our principle of selection was to invite participation from historical scholars who were expert in religious traditions other than their own affiliation. Tony, a Christian, was our expert in Judaism while Paula Fredriksen, a Jew, was our expert in Christianity. Again, his being not Jewish was central to our discussions. That collaboration lasted four intense years. Tony participated with great vigor and wisdom, despite a continuing battle with cancer. His articles in our publications are among his last and best. Unlike most contributors to the memorial volume I am not a biblical scholar or a historian of Judaism or Christianity, but a theologian committed to a global public and the academic objectivity and responsibility of theology. I shall attempt to honor Tony in this chapter by addressing one of the main issues, if not the single most important issue, to surface in our collaborative comparative studies: how to read scriptures for religious truth.

2. See Karl Jaspers' *Way to Wisdom: An Introduction to Philosophy*, translated by Ralph Manheim (New Haven: Yale University Press, 1954).

3. See S. Nomanul Haq's "The Human Condition in Islam: Sharia and Obligation" in *The Human Condition*, edited by Robert Neville (Albany: State University of New York Press, 2000), chapter 7. Haq also points out that Islam disconnects living under obligation from accounts of the fall, stressing instead that people are created by Allah to live lives of continual moral choice.

4. See John Knoblock's *Xunzi: A Translation and Study of the Complete Works*, in three volumes (Stanford: Stanford University Press, 1988, 1990, and 1994 respectively). Book 19, in volume three, "Discourse on Ritual Principles," is a focused discussion, although Xunzi treats ritual through all his books. Xunzi was born around 310 BCE and lived perhaps a hundred years, into the Chin dynasty, commenting on the philosophers of Chinese antiquity including Confucius and Mencius.

5. Kant's argument about imagination is most important in the Transcendental Deduction of the A edition of the *Critique of Pure Reason*, and in the discussion of schematism in both A and B editions.

6. See Peter Berger, *The Sacred Canopy* (Garden City, N.Y.: Doubleday Anchor, 1967).

7. See Paul Tillich's *The Courage to Be* (New Haven: Yale University Press, 1952).

8. "Heaven and Earth are not humane (jen). They regard all things as straw dogs. The sage is not humane. He regards all people as straw dogs." *Daodejing*, stanza 5, Chan translation in *A Sourcebook in Chinese Philosophy*, edited by Wing-tsit Chan (Princeton: Princeton University Press, 1963).

CHAPTER FIVE. SYSTEMATIC THEOLOGY IN A GLOBAL PUBLIC

1. This chapter began as a contribution to a conference on "religious apologetics and philosophical argument"; hence the orientation of the topic.

2. See, for instance, David Tracy's *The Analogical Imagination: Christian Theology and the Culture of Pluralism* (New York: Crossroad, 1981), where he distinguishes systematic theology from "fundamental theology," which is philosophical, and from "practical theology."

3. In addition to Judaism, Christianity, and Islam, who claim special revelations in their scriptures, Hindus claim authoritative special revelation in the Vedas, and medieval Daoists claim special revelations to which their scriptures witness, for instance *The Scripture of Western Ascension*. On the last, see Livia Kohn's *Taoist Mystical Philosophy: The Scripture of Western Ascension* (Albany: State University of New York Press, 1991).

4. The philosophic basis of this attack derives from Charles S. Peirce's 1868 paper, "Questions concerning Certain Faculties Claimed for Man," originally in the *Journal of Speculative Philosophy* 2(1868) 103–114; it is in *The Collected Papers of Charles Sanders Peirce*, edited by Charles Hartshorne and Paul Weiss, vol. 5 (Cambridge: Harvard University Press, 1934) 135–155, and in most shorter anthologies of Peirce's works. Later European anti-foundationalism had different roots, arising from the collapse of Edmund Husserl's program to establish a phenomenological foundation for the sciences and deriving posthumous inspiration from Friedrich Nietzsche, Peirce's younger contemporary; both Peirce and Nietzsche were influenced by Ralph Waldo Emerson, a thoroughly non-foundationalist and non-modernist thinker.

5. See my "On the Complexity of Theological Literacy" in *Theological Literacy for the Twenty-First Century*, edited by Rodney L. Petersen with Nancy M. Rourke (Grand Rapids, MI: Eerdmans, 2002), 39–54. See also Wesley J. Wildman's essay in the same collection, "Theological Literacy: Problem and Promise," 335–351.

6. Interfaith dialogue is nothing new. Hindu and Buddhist scholars debated throughout the first millennium. The transfer of Aristotelian texts from the Muslim to the Christian world during the high middle ages created a Christian-Muslim dialogue. Matteo Ricci's work in China in the sixteenth and seventeenth centuries began a Confucian-Christian dialogue. In our time Christians have been in ongoing dialogues with Jews, Buddhists, Confucians, and Muslims.

7. Those labels are Whitehead's, elegantly explained in *Process and Reality*, corrected edition by Donald Sherburne and David Ray Griffin (New York: Macmillan/Free Press, 1978), chapter one.

CHAPTER SIX. A PEIRCEAN THEORY OF RELIGIOUS INTERPRETATION

1. References to Peirce are given in the *Collected Papers of Charles Sanders Peirce*, vols. 1–6, edited by Charles Hartshorne and Paul Weiss, vols. 7–8 edited by Arthur W. Burks

(Cambridge: Harvard University Press, vol. 1 1931, vol. 2 1932, vol. 3 1933, vol. 4 1933, vol. 5 1934, vol. 6 1935, vol. 7 1958, vol. 8 1958) (hereafter cited as CP); references are given by volume and paragraph number, e.g. 2.274 for the beginning of the discussion of reference in volume 2, paragraph 274. Although discussions of semiotics are spread throughout Peirce's works, the concentrated discussions are in volume two in the section the editors call "speculative grammar." A good general introduction to Peirce that focuses upon his semiotics is Robert S. Corrington's *An Introduction to C. S. Peirce: Philosopher, Semiotician, and Ecstatic Naturalist* (Lanham, MD: Rowman and Littlefield, 1993).

2. CP 5.358–410. Peirce's general idea of vulnerability as a virtue for hypotheses has been developed elaborately for religion, from many points of view and by many authors, in the three volumes of the Comparative Religious Ideas Project, *The Human Condition*, *Ultimate Realities*, and *Religious Truth*, edited by Robert Cummings Neville (Albany: State University of New York Press, 2001); see especially the jointly authored articles by Wildman and Neville.

3. See, for instance, CP 6.238–271, "Man's Glassy Essence." For an excellent study see Vincent M. Colapietro's *Peirce's Approach to the Self: A Semiotic Perspective on Human Subjectivity* (Albany: State University of New York Press, 1989).

4. CP 6.66–87, 102–163.

5. CP 1 entire!; CP 6.7–87. For good discussions of Peirce's system as arising from semiotics, see Douglas R. Anderson's *Creativity and the Philosophy of C. S. Peirce* (Boston: Nijhoff, 1987) and *Strands of System: The Philosophy of Charles Peirce* (West Lafayette, IN: Purdue University Press, 1995).

6. For Dewey on this point, see John E. Smith's discussion in "John Dewey: Experience, Experiment, and the Method of Intelligence," in his *The Spirit of American Philosophy* (revised edition; Albany: State University of New York Press, 1983). For an excellent comparison of Dewey with Peirce on the points made in the text here, see Smith's *Purpose and Thought: The Meaning of Pragmatism* (New Haven: Yale University Press, 1978), chapter 4.

7. In terms of his categories, signs are "firsts" which can be understood in terms of their own systems; reference is "secondness" which relates signs to their objects; interpretation is "thirdness" which connects the signs to objects by making an interpretation or giving rise to what he called an "interpretant."

8. CP 2.274–282.

9. Ludwig Wittgenstein, *Tractatus Logico-Philosophicus* (London: Routledge and Kegan Paul, 1922), propositions 6.41–7.00.

10. CP 2.283–291.

11. CP 2.292–308. I prefer "conventional" because in religion, nearly all signs are called symbols, and it should be said that there are three kinds of *symbolic* reference: iconic, indexical, and conventional.

12. CP 1.521–544.

13. CP 1.15–42; 6.619–624. This point was so important to Peirce that his editors, Hartshorne and Weiss, put his strong statements in the first and last paragraphs of their six-volume edition.

14. See Anderson's two books referred to in note 5 above for an exposition of the theory of signs.

15. On Peirce's approach to religion as such, see Michael L. Raposa's *Peirce's Philosophy of Religion* (Bloomington: Indiana University Press, 1989) and Hermann Deuser's *Gott: Geist und Natur: Theologische Konsequenzen aus Charles S. Peirce's Religionsphilosophie* (Berlin: Walter de Gruyter, 1993). Peirce's writings on religion have not been collected in English, except for those in the Hartshorne-Weiss-Burks *Collected Papers*, which contain only a small fragment of Peirce's writings. They have, however, been collected by Deuser in *Charles Sanders Peirce: Religionsphilosophische Schriften*, Uebersetzt unter Mitarbeit con Helmut Maassen, eingeleitet, kommentiert und herausgegeben von Hermann Deuser (Hamburg: Felix Meiner Verlag, 1995).

16. Charles W. Morris, *Foundations of the Theory of Signs*, in the *International Encyclopedia of Unified Science*, vols. 1–2 (Chicago: University of Chicago Press, 1938).

17. Several times it has been noted that the interpreter has to be of the right sort for a symbol to have effective reference. So, for instance, a Chinese Daoist would not have the culture to interpret symbols such as the blood of the lamb, unless learned anew. People with no feeling whatsoever for human sinfulness are not likely to be able to refer effectively, iconically, indexically, or conventionally, with atonement symbols. A person abused by their father as a child is not likely to be able to refer to God effectively as Father. The way to put this is to say that the objects of reference in the three modes are *primarily* the things referred to. But the *secondary* referents are the types of persons for whom the primary references can be actually engaging. So, God can be referred to by the symbol Father only for those secondary referents who have good connotations for father, atonement symbols can refer to God's saving work, the primary referent, only for those with a sense of sin, the secondary referents. Secondary reference is closely connected with the state of the interpreters, a point to which the argument will return shortly.

18. Peirce's main discussions of this are in CP 2.309–390, but are found in many other places, including CP 8.327–379. The defense of the irreducibility of the triadic relation to dyadic relations is part of Peirce's overall defense of the categories of Firstness, Secondness, and Thirdness, e.g. in CP 1.417–520.

19. For a very subtle and many-faceted discussion of these issues, see his "Philosophy in America: Recovery and Future Development," a reply to many commentators in a Festschrift in his honor, *The Recovery of Philosophy in America: Essays in Honor of John Edwin Smith*, edited by Thomas P. Kasulis and Robert Cummings Neville (Albany: State University of New York Press, 1997).

20. That form is a function of value, and not the other way around as usually thought, is the thesis of my *Reconstruction of Thinking* (Albany: State University Of New York Press, 1981), part 2. That nature can be conceived properly and in line with both science and aesthetic experience as processes of achievement of value is the overall thesis of *Recovery of the Measure*, which also indicates how interpretation is the particular achievement of value in experience through carryover.

21. The idea of "making a case" derives from Stephen Toulmin's discussion in *The Uses of Argument* (Cambridge: Cambridge University Press, 1958). It was applied particularly to theological argument by Van A. Harvey in *The Historian and the Believer* (New York: Macmillan, 1966).

CHAPTER SEVEN. THE CONTRIBUTIONS OF CHARLES S. PEIRCE TO PHILOSOPHY OF RELIGION

1. See *The Collected Papers of Charles Sanders Peirce*, edited by Charles Hartshorne and Paul Weiss, vols. 1–6 (Cambridge: Harvard University Press, 1931–1935), CP1.616 ff; or *The Essential Peirce*, edited by the Peirce Edition Project (Nathan Houser general editor), vol. 2, 27 ff.

2. CP 6.452 ff; *The Essential Peirce*, vol. 2, 434 ff.

3. CP 5.447–448; *The Essential Peirce*, 350–352.

CHAPTER EIGHT. INTUITION: A PLATONIZING OF PRAGMATISM

1. This chapter presents detailed dialectical arguments for many of the points in the theory of interpretation discussed in other chapters in this book. Originally written and published forty years ago, the arguments seem a bit obsessive now, but nevertheless have a force beyond the general attractiveness of the pragmatic theory of interpretation.

2. CP 5.123, note, and 5.264.

3. *Critique of Pure Reason*, A 19.

4. *Duns Scotus: Philosophical Writings*, edited and translated by Allan Wolter, O.F.M. (New York: Nelson, 1962), 9.

5. I have argued in *God the Creator* that the question is not meaningless and that its answer is that the harmonies are created by God, who is not a determinate being, without the employment of determinate principles of creation. That is, what things are harmonious and what things not is a matter of free, creative divine will.

6. *The Axiology of Thinking*, that is, *Reconstruction of Thinking* (Albany: State University of New York Press, 1981), *Recovery of the Measure* (Albany: State University of New York Press, 1989), and *Normative Cultures* (Albany: State University of New York Press, 1995), was the detailed working out of this point.

7. CP, 5.553.

8. CP, 2.228.

9. Pierce attempts to account for the respect or ground by identifying it with the abstractness in the predicate term (CP, 1.551). Thus the proposition "the stove is black" he says is equivalent to the proposition "there is blackness in the stove." The respect or ground he says would be "blackness." The difficulty with this is that the respect is identical with the predicate, and thus does not indicate the respect in which

the predicate interprets the subject's object. "Black" does not interpret the stove with respect to blackness but with respect to color or something of the sort.

10. A related example is found in art. A painter, for instance, after making some initial moves on the canvass in virtue of preconceived plans or preparatory drawings, assesses the elements given and attempts to determine the most ideal way of fulfilling and harmonizing them. As he proceeds, new elements get added as part of the harmonizing process and they too must be taken into account, and the conception of the ideal form changes. In the case of must painters, it is probably true that they do not think of the final version of the ideal form of their painting until the last stroke is finished and they recognize that the ideal and embodiment are exhibited together. The essential point is that the ideal form in this case varies with elements in the canvass that it should be the ideal for; each work of art has its own ideal and therefore should be judged according to its own standards. Since the stuff of art is experiential and since its elements are mostly sensual instead of mathematical, art should be placed on the second level of the divided line instead of higher. Still, the artist's judgment deals primarily with formal considerations of harmony. The formal elements are sensuous, but this makes their combination and integration into harmonies no less a formal matter. The formal elements of an artist's judgment make him more like a mathematician than a practical moralist.

CHAPTER NINE. WHITEHEAD AND PRAGMATISM

1. On Royce as a pragmatist and absolute idealist, see John E. Smith's *Royce's Social Infinite* (New York: Liberal Arts Press, 1950), 46–61 and *passim*. For Royce's own informal discussion of his relation to pragmatists, see his *Metaphysics*, the notes of his undergraduate course edited by Richard Hocking and Frank Oppenheim (Albany: State University of New York Press, 1998), especially the first several lectures.

2. See George R. Lucas, Jr., *The Genesis of Modern Process Thought* (Metuchen, N.J.: Scarecrow Press and ATLA, 1983) and *The Rehabilitation of Whitehead: An Analytic and Historical Assessment of Process Philosophy* (Albany: State University of New York Press, 1989). See also Whitehead's biographical remarks and Dewey's essay in *The Philosophy of Alfred North Whitehead*, edited by Paul Arthur Schilpp (Library of Living Philosophers, vol. 3; New York: Tudor, 1941). See the discussions of Whitehead, process philosophy, and pragmatism in *The Philosophy of Charles Hartshorne*, edited by Lewis Edwin Hahn (Library of Living Philosophers, vol. 20; LaSalle, Ill.: Open Court, 1991), especially in Hartshorne's Intellectual Biography and Donald Lee's article. See the same topics discussed in *The Philosophy of Paul Weiss*, edited by Lewis Edwin Hahn (Library of Living Philosophers, vol. 23; LaSalle, Ill.: Open Court, 1995), especially in Weiss's biographical remarks and in the essays by Sandra Rosenthal, Kevin Kennedy, and Jay Schulkin.

3. Whitehead, expressing appreciation for Bradley's notion of *feeling*, asks whether his own thought might not be "a transformation of some of the main doctrines of Absolute Idealism onto a realistic basis," *Process and Reality* corrected edition edited by Donald Sherburne and David Ray Griffin (New York: Free Press, 1978), xiii. See also Whitehead's discussion of idealism and realism in *Science and the Modern World* (New

York: Macmillan, 1926), 131 ff. Hartshorne might well be accused of idealism because of his panpsychism; nevertheless, he accepted Whitehead's argument that an actual occasion when finished is no longer conscious but a physical entity to be prehended as such, a realistic position. As to the pragmatists, Peirce did argue that the character of evolution behaves more like mind than like dead mechanical matter, and said that matter could be regarded as "frozen mind." See for instance *The Collected Papers of Charles Sanders Peirce*, vols. 1–6, edited by Charles Hartshorne and Paul Weiss (Cambridge: Harvard University Press, 1931–35; cited by volume and paragraph number), CP 6.238–286. But his complaint was with the mechanistic conception of matter and his own conception of mind was wholly naturalistic. His criticism of idealism focused on the fact that Hegel let Thirdness swallow Secondness, to use Peirce's categories, resulting in degenerate Secondness such that bumping real nature is not seen to be a corrective; see CP 6.218, 305; 1.521–529. Part of Peirce's Scotistic realism is his defense of the over-againstness of nature relative to mind, for which he cites Scotus' idea of haecceity (CP 1.405). On James against idealism see *Pragmatism* (New York: Longmans, Green, 1907), especially chapter 2, "On Some Hegelianisms," in *The Will to Believe* (New York: Henry Holt, 1912), and *A Pluralistic Universe* (New York: Longmans, Green, 1909), chapters 2–3. James' most effective rejection of idealism is shown in the photograph of him and Royce in which he cried "Royce, you're being photographed! Look out! I say *Damn the Absolute*" in *The Letters of William James*, edited by his son Henry James (Boston: Atlantic Monthly Press), vol. 2, opposite page 134. Dewey, of course, avowed idealism in his early period, but rejected it for pragmatic realism; see his "Experience and Objective Idealism" in *The Influence of Darwin on Philosophy* (New York: Henry Holt, 1910). George Herbert Mead set pragmatism and realism alongside one another as opponents of idealism in *Philosophy of the Act*, edited by Charles W. Morris (Chicago: University of Chicago Press, 1938), 360 ff. There were many kinds of realism in early twentieth century American philosophy besides the pragmatic, including neo-realism and critical realism; they agreed in affirming that nature can correct our views in ways that the rational coherence of thought cannot, and that this is because things somewhat are as they seem to be. For subtle interpretations of the ways pragmatism sought to be realistic without any kind of copy theory of knowledge, and how Royce appreciated this to some extent, see John E. Smith's *The Spirit of American Philosophy* revised edition (Albany: State University of New York Press, 1983), chapters 3–4. For a good survey of many of the kinds of realism and idealism in the heyday of classical pragmatism, see Andrew J. Reck's *Recent American Philosophy* (New York: Random House, 1964) which treats Ralph Barton Perry, William Ernest Hocking, George Herbert Mead, John Elof Boodin, Wilbur Marshall Urban, Dewitt H. Parker, Roy Wood Sellars, Arthur O. Lovejoy, Elijah Jordan, and Edgar Sheffield Brightman.

4. Whitehead was a strong Platonic realist in his defense of eternal objects; see *Science and the Modern World*, chapter 2, and *Process and Reality*, part 2, chapter 1. Peirce was a Scotistic realist in another sense from that in the previous note in defending the reality of what Scotus called "common natures" and Peirce called Thirdness or generals or vagues; see CP 1.337–415, 6.102–317. Peirce thought nominalism has been the root of all evils in modern philosophy; see CP 1.15–26, 6.619–624. Peirce's notion of habit, the embodiment of universals, is taken up and developed by James, Dewey, and Mead.

5. See Whitehead's discussion of civilized experience in the first chapter of *Process and Reality*, and throughout *Adventures of Ideas* (New York: Macmillan, 1933) and *Modes of Thought* (New York: Macmillan, 1938); see also his technical discussions of symbolic reference in *Symbolism* (New York: Macmillan, 1927) and the revised subjectivist principle in *Process and Reality*, part 2, chapter 7. James' *Essays in Radical Empiricism*, edited by R. B. Perry (New York: Longmans, Green, 1912) is the most polemical pragmatic critique of British empiricism, but all the pragmatists developed that critique and the pragmatic alternative. This point has been one of the chief themes of the work of John E. Smith in *The Spirit of American Philosophy, Religion and Empiricism* (Milwaukee: Marquette University Press, 1967), *Themes in American Philosophy* (New York: Harper, 1970), *Purpose and Thought: The Meaning of Pragmatism* (New Haven: Yale University Press, 1978), and *America's Philosophical Vision* (Chicago: University of Chicago Press, 1992).

6. Whitehead began *Process and Reality* with the following, which amounts to a rejection of the objections to metaphysics in the grand tradition:

> These lectures will be best understood by noting the following list of prevalent habits of thought, which are repudiated, in so far as concerns their influence on philosophy:
>
> (i)   The distrust of speculative philosophy.
> (ii)   The trust in language as an adequate expression of propositions.
> (iii) The mode of philosophical thought which implies, and is implied by, the faculty-opsychology.
> (iv)   The subject-predicate form of expression.
> (v)   The sensationalist doctrine of perception.
> (vi)   The doctrine of vacuous actuality.
> (vii) The Kantian doctrine of the objective world as a theoretical construct from purely subjective experience.
> (viii) Arbitrary deductions in *ex absurdo* arguments.
> (ix)   Belief that logical inconsistencies can indicate anything else than some antecedent errors.
>
> By reason of its ready acceptance of some or all of these nine myths and fallacious procedures, much nineteenth-century philosophy excludes itself from relevance to the ordinary stubborn facts of daily life. (*Process and Reality*, xiii)

Whitehead, of course, is the great speculative metaphysician of the twentieth century whose use of categoreal schemes as hypotheses gets around both the empiricist and Kantian objections to metaphysics. The method of hypothesis as a way around empiricism and Kant, of course, was invented by Charles Peirce much earlier; the neatest statement is in CP 6.452–493, and that whole volume illustrates it. James had little flair for metaphysics but he made a valiant effort in *Some Problems of Philosophy*, edited by Henry James, Jr. (New York: Longmans Green, 1911). Dewey's great metaphysical works are *Experience and Nature*, in volume 1 of *John Dewey: The Later Works*, edited by Jo Ann Boydston (Carbondale and Edwardsville: Southern Illinois University Press, 1981; first edition, 1925, second edition revised, 1929) and *The Quest for Certainty*, in volume 4 of *John Dewey: The Later Works*. Whitehead praised Dewey's metaphysics in "John Dewey and his Influence," in *Essays in Science and Philosophy* (New York: Philosophical Library, 1948). Of all the pragmatists, Dewey gave the most sustained criticism of the prior Western metaphysical tradition, in *Reconstruction in Philosophy* (New York: Henry Holt, 1920).

7. See Whitehead's *Science and the Modern World*, chapters 9, 12, and 13, and *The Function of Reason* (Boston: Beacon, 1929); Whitehead's influence in this regard has been extended directly to William M. Sullivan's *Reconstructing Public Philosophy* (Berkeley: University of California Press, 1982), a title also reflective of Dewey, and *Work and Integrity: The Crisis and Promise of Professionalism in America* (San Francisco: Harper, 1995); Sullivan analyzes Whitehead on the public use of philosophy in his "The Civilizing of Enterprise," in *New Essays in Metaphysics*, edited by Robert C. Neville (Albany: State University of New York Press, 1987). Of the pragmatists, Peirce was the least concerned with public roles for philosophy, though he responded to William James' advocacy of public philosophy with his subtle essay, "Vitally Important Topics," CP 1.616–677. James talked about vitally important topics all the time—see the essays collected together by Ralph Barton Perry in *Essays on Faith and Morals* (New York: Longman's Green, 1942). Dewey's great work on public philosophy was *The Public and Its Problems*, volume 2 of *John Dewey: The Later Works* (original edition; New York: Henry Holt, 1927).

8. For Whitehead truth is the correspondence of propositions with their objects through symbolic reference, defined technically in *Process and Reality*, part 2, chapter 8, and colloquially in chapter 1; in *Adventures of Ideas*, at the beginning of chapter 16, he says "Truth is the conformation of Appearance to Reality." For Peirce's discussion of truth as correspondence, see CP 5.549–573; his theory of truth was closely allied with his theory of signs, such that a sign is true or false of its indicated object as interpreted; his definition of reality was that it is the object of the representation or opinion that has been infinitely corrected (CP 5.405–410). Dewey defined truth as "warranted assertability," which was in fact to define it by its criteria; but the criteria he employed served to make our representations agree with reality so far as that is relevant to our purposes; he rejection the rhetoric of correspondence insofar as that meant an internal mirroring of reality; see his *Logic: The Theory of Inquiry* (New York: Henry Holt, 1938).

9. In his theory of truth as symbolic reference, Whitehead said, "Symbolism can be justified, or unjustified. The test of justification must always be pragmatic" (*Process and Reality*, 181); see also the chapter on truth in *Adventures of Ideas*. The pragmatists, of course, take the criteria of truth to be pragmatic. Some such as James do not distinguish very carefully between the meaning of truth and the criteria. Dewey has a fully developed theory of nature, within which are to be found truth-seeking human beings; so he defines truth in terms of its successful achievement as a natural phenomenon.

10. See Whitehead's famous discussion in chapter one of *Process and Reality*. See Peirce's attacks on intuition and defense of fallibilism in the several published papers in CP 5. 213–463.

11. See John E. Smith's "The New Need for a Recovery of Philosophy" in the revised edition of *The Spirit of American Philosophy*, and *The Recovery of Philosophy in*

America: Essays in Honor of John Edwin Smith, edited by Thomas P. Kasulis and Robert Cummings Neville (Albany: State University of New York Press, 1997).

12. Hartshorne expressed some bitterness at not being kept on at Harvard, but the University of Chicago where he spent the bulk of his career is itself about as Episcopalian as a Baptist university can get. See *The Philosophy of Charles Hartshorne*, 26.

13. See Sherburne's "Whitehead without God," in *Process Theology and Christian Thought*, edited by Delwin Brown, Ralph E. James, Jr., and Gene Reeves (Indianapolis: Bobbs-Merril, 1971), 305–328.

14. See the biography by Joseph Brent, *Charles Sanders Peirce: A Life* (Bloomington: Indiana University Press, 1993).

15. See Reck's *Recent American Philosophy*.

16. C.I. Lewis' *Mind and the World Order* (corrected edition; New York: Dover, 1956; original edition 1929) is about ordering knowledge of the world by epistemological elements of givenness, the apriori, and hypothesis.

17. John Dewey, *A Common Faith* (New Haven: Yale University Press, 1934). See Steven C. Rockefeller's *John Dewey: Religious Faith and Democratic Humanism* (New York: Columbia University Press, 1991).

18. Justus Buchler is a case in point. One of the great systematic metaphysicians of our time, he says very little about God except that God would have to fit within his system as a natural complex just like everything else; and he says less about religion. A recent set of essays about his work, *Nature's Perspectives: Prospects for Ordinal Metaphysics*, edited by Armen Marsoobian, Kathleen Wallace, and Robert S. Corrington (Albany: State University of New York Press, 1991), has about 20 articles on Buchler, only two of which deal at all with God. One, by John Ryder and Peter Hare, says it might not be too bad to be a natural complex and the other, by Robert S. Corrington, uses Buchler's categories to advance a theory of divinity within nature. The God of Aristotle, Plotinus, Augustine, Thomas, Spinoza, Hegel, or Peirce is not even a topic. Religion is not mentioned, as if it were not as important as art and politics which are Buchlerian topics.

19. Weiss' first book, *Reality* (Princeton: Princeton University Press, 1939), was an explicit argument against Whitehead's emphasis on process and in defense of substance, although it is dedicated to Mrs. Whitehead.

20. See Buchler's *Charles Peirce's Empiricism* (London: Kegan Paul, Trench, Trubner, 1939), *Metaphysics of Natural Complexes* (New York: Columbia University Press, 1966), and *The Main of Light* (New York: Oxford University Press, 1974).

21. *Being and Value* (Albany: State University of New York Press, 1996) and *Knowing and Value* (Albany: State University of New York Press, 1998).

22. *Importances of the Past* (Albany: State University of New York Press, 1986), *The Realizations of the Future* (Albany: State University of New York Press, 1990), and *The Patterns of the Present* (Albany: State University of New York Press, 2001).

23. *Nature: An Environmental Cosmology* (Albany: State University of New York Press, 1997) and *The City* (Albany: State University of New York Press, 1999).

24. *The Civilization of Experience* (New York: Fordham University Press, 1973) is his Whitehead book, and Whitehead's philosophy is apparent in *The Uncertain Phoenix* (New York: Fordham University Press, 1982) and *Eros and Irony* (Albany: State University of New York, 1982). His first three books with Roger T. Ames develop a philosophy of culture that enables him to contrast the Western with the Chinese tradition, with the latter looking somewhat Whiteheadean in its aesthetic emphases; see Thinking *Through Confucius, Anticipating China, and Thinking from the Han* (Albany: State University of New York Press, 1987, 1995, 1998). His recent book with Ames, *Democracy of the Dead* (LaSalle: Open Court, 1999) is a straightforward defense of pragmatism as the philosophy with which to engage China.

25. Her *The Metaphysics of Experience* (New York: Fordham University Press, 1979) is a commentary on Whitehead's *Process and Reality* but presents its own aesthetic interpretation of Whitehead.

26. See her *Intensity: An Essay in Whiteheadian Ontology* (Nashville: Vanderbilt University Press, 1998).

27. *Speculative Pragmatism* (Amherst: University of Massachusetts Press, 1986; reprint edition, Open Court).

28. See his *Philosophy and the Mirror of Nature* (Princeton: Princeton University Press, 1979), *Consequences of Pragmatism* (Minneapolis: The University of Minnesota Press, 1982), *Objectivity, Relativism, and Truth* (Cambridge: Cambridge University Press, 1991) and *Essays on Heidegger and Others* (Cambridge: Cambridge University Press, 1991). The best general study of Rorty is David L. Hall's *Richard Rorty: Prophet and Poet of the New Pragmatism* (Albany: State University of New York Press, 1994).

29. See Rorty's *Philosophy and the Mirror of Nature*, chapter 8.

30. See Hall's *Richard Rorty*, 202 ff.

31. *Philosophy and the Mirror of Nature*, chapters 6–8.

32. See Rorty's edited volume, *The Linguistic Turn: Recent Essays in Philosophical Method* (Chicago: University of Chicago Press, 1967), editor's introduction.

33. See the analysis in Hall's *Richard Rorty*, chapter 3.

34. See Rorty's powerful *Achieving Our Country: Leftist Thought in Twentieth Century America* (Cambridge: Harvard University Press, 1997).

35. See Dewey's *Reconstruction of Philosophy*.

36. *Consequences of Pragmatism*, 213 ff.

37. *Consequences of Pragmatism*, 161. Rorty's criticism of Peirce was that Peirce seemed to believe philosophy can find a foundationalist ahistorical context for philosophy. I have no idea how he can find that in Peirce unless he made the mistake of thinking that an hypothesis about basic things, *signs* according to Rorty, has to be itself foundational. Peirce and Whitehead agree that all metaphysical hypotheses are historically contextual, ideas adventuring.

38. *Process Metaphysics and Hua-Yen Buddhism* (Albany: State University of New York Press, 1982).

39. *The Social Self in Zen and American Pragmatism* (Albany: State University of New York Press, 1996).

40. See Weissman's *Eternal Possibilities* (Carbondale: Southern Illinois University Press, 1977) for the Wittgenstein roots, and then *Intuition and Ideality* (Albany: State University of New York Press, 1987), *Hypothesis and the Spiral of Reflection* (Albany: State University of New York Press, 1989), and *Truth's Debt to Value* (New Haven: Yale University Press, 1993) for his system that engages process philosophy and pragmatism.

41. See his *An Introduction to C. S. Peirce: Philosopher, Semiotician, and Ecstatic Naturalist* (Lanham, MD: Rowman and Littlefield, 1993), *Ecstatic Naturalism: Signs of the World* (Bloomington: Indiana University Press, 1994), *Nature and Spirit: An Essay in Ecstatic Naturalism* (New York: Fordham University Press, 1992), and *Nature's Self* (Lanham, MD: Rowman and Littlefield, 1996).

42. And what am I? I think of myself as a pragmatist, most others call me a process philosopher, and my critics blame my inadequacies in either allegiance on my teacher Paul Weiss. See the collection of essays in *Interpreting Neville*, edited by J. Harley Chapman and Nancy Frankenberry (Albany: State University of New York Press, 1999) and the collection in *Theology for a Global Public* (New York and London: T & T Clark International, 2005), edited by Amos Yong and Peter Heltzel.

43. George R. Lucas, Jr., "Outside the Camp: Recent Work on Whitehead's Philosophy," Part I in *Transactions of the Charles S. Peirce Society* 21/2 (Winter 1985) 49–75, and Part II in the same journal, 21/3 (Summer 1985) 327–382.

44. See John E. Smith's responses to the papers in *The Recovery of Philosophy in America*.

45. See her "Contemporary Process Metaphysics and Diverse Intuitions of Time: Can the Gap Be Bridged?" in *The Journal of Speculative Philosophy* (New Series) 12/4 (1998), 271–288, and "Neville and Pragmatism: Toward an Ongoing Dialogue," in *Interpreting Neville*, edited by J. Harley Chapman and Nancy K. Frankenberry (Albany: State University of New York Press, 1999) These essays contain some overlap of material, with the former analyzing Whitehead in more detail, and the latter pragmatism and my own work. See also her "Continuity, Contingency, and Time: The Divergent Intuitions of Whitehead and Pragmatism," in *Transactions of the Charles S. Peirce Society* 32 (1996) 542–567.

46. This conclusion is fully drawn by Harold H. Oliver, for instance, in his *Relatedness: Essays in Metaphysics and Theology* (Macon, GA: Mercer University Press, 1984). See also his essay in *Theology for a Global Public*.

47. See his *Whitehead's Metaphysics of Extension and Solidarity* (Albany: State University of New York Press, 1986).

48. The point is discussed throughout his work. The most extended discussion is probably in CP 6.101–213.

49. See Elizabeth Kraus' poignant essay on this, "God the Savior," in *New Essays in Metaphysics*, edited by Robert C. Neville (Albany: State University of New York Press, 1987).

50. The classic criticism of this view, in defense of novelty, is Paul Weiss's in *Modes of Being* (Carbondale: Southern Illinois University Press, 1958), chapter 3.

51. CP 6.452 ff.

52. This is much of the reason I think of myself as a pragmatist rather than a process philosopher, despite process commitments on continuity in time, because the theology is so central to much of process thinking.

53. Trivial things lose the details and the contrasts of the things they prehend, and hence most of their intrinsic value.

54. See his essay in *New Essays in Metaphysics*.

CHAPTER TEN. PHILOSOPHY OF NATURE IN AMERICAN THEOLOGY

1. Hermann Deuser is Europe's greatest expert in the topic of this chapter, and it is my great privilege to contribute an essay to a Festschrift in his honor. His principle contributions on this topic are, first, his translation into German (with his collaborator, Helmut Maassen) of Charles S. Peirce's writings on religion, making this originator of pragmatism accessible to a German audience that previously had thought of pragmatism through the casual lens of William James. See his *Charles Sanders Peirce: Religionsphilosophische Schrifte*, (Hamburg: Felix Meiner Verlag, 1995). On the basis of this translation work, Deuser then examined the theological significance of Peirce's pragmatic philosophy of nature, with special attention to its significance for German theology. Most recently, in *Gottesinstinkt: Semiotische Religionstheorie und Pragmatismus* (Teubingen, DE: Mohr Siebeck, 2004), he has broadened his theological analysis of the consequences of American (and other) philosophies of nature to include traditional theological loci such as the Trinity, and working from some post-Peircean pragmatists. My purpose in this brief chapter is to develop some of the background of American philosophy of nature for theology.

2. See Clarence H. Faust and Thomas H. Johnson's *Jonathan Edwards: Representative Selections, with Introduction, Bibliography, and Notes* (Revised edition; New York, NY: Hill and Wang, 1962). These are also in *The Works of Jonathan Edwards*, General Editor, John E. Smith, vol. 6, edited by Wallace E. Anderson, *Scientific and Philosophical Writings* (New Haven: Yale University Press, 1980).

3. See Leon Howard, "The Mind" of Jonathan Edwards: A Reconstructed Text (Berkeley: University of California Press, 1963). See also *The Works of Jonathan Edwards*, vol. 6.

4. See *The Nature of True Virtue*, with a Foreword by William K. Frankena (Ann Arbor, MI: The University of Michigan Press, 1960). See also volume 8 of the Yale Edition, *Ethical Works*, edited by Paul Ramsey (New Haven: Yale University Press, 1989).

5. I list these figures to indicate that there is indeed a community of thinkers that are living heirs to the American tradition as described here. See George Allan's trilogy, *The Importances of the Past: A Meditation on the Authority of Tradition* (Albany:

State University of New York Press, 1986), *The Realizations of the Future: An Inquiry into the Authority of Praxis* (Albany: State University of New York Press, 1990), and *The Patterns of the Present: Interpreting the Authority of Form* (Albany: State University of New York Press, 2001). See Frederick Ferre's *Being and Value: Toward a Constructive Postmodern Metaphysics* (Albany: State University of New York Press, 1996) and *Knowing and Value: Toward a Constructive Postmodern Epistemology* (Albany: State University of New York Press, 1998). See Joseph Grange's *Nature: An Environmental Cosmology* (Albany: State University of New York Press, 1997), *The City: An Urban Cosmology* (Albany: State University of New York Press, 1999), and *John Dewey, Confucius, and Global Philosophy* (Albany: State University of New York Press, 2004). See David Weissman's *Intuition and Ideality* (Albany: State University of New York Press, 1987), *Hypothesis and the Spiral of Reflection* (Albany: State University of New York Press, 1989), *Truth's Debt to Value* (New Haven: Yale University Press, 1993), and *A Social Ontology* (New Haven: Yale University Press, 2000). My own philosophy of nature is in *Recovery of the Measure* (Albany: State University of New York Press, 1989) and *Eternity and Time's Flow* (Albany: State University of New York Press, 1993).

6. For instance, he defended Calvinistic predestination in *Freedom of the Will*, vol. 1 in the Yale edition, edited by Paul Ramsey (New Haven: Yale University Press, 1957).

7. See his magnificent set of sermons, *A History of the Work of Redemption*, vol. 9 of the Yale edition, transcribed and edited by John F. Wilson (New Haven: Yale University Press, 1989), and vol. 4 of the Yale edition, *The Great Awakening*, edited by C. C. Goen (New Haven: Yale University Press, 1972).

8. See *A History of the Work of Redemption*, especially sermon one, which lays out the plot.

9. See *Religious Affections*, edited by John E. Smith, vol. 2 in the Yale Edition (New Haven: Yale University Press, 1959).

10. On the point of this continuity, see Warren G. Frisina's *The Unity of Knowledge and Action: Toward a Nonrepresentational Theory of Knowledge* (Albany: State University of New York Press, 2002). This book does not treat Edwards, but does focus on Dewey and Whitehead, and compares them fruitfully with the Confucian thinker, Wang Yangming.

11. John E. Smith, the General Editor of the Yale Edition of Edwards Works for twenty five years and the volume editor of *Religious Affections*, is the best exponent of this contrast between the American and European approaches to experience. See, among his numerous books, *The Spirit of American Philosophy* (New York: Oxford University Press, 1963; revised edition Albany: State University of New York Press, 1983), *Religion and Empiricism* (Milwaukee: Marquette University Press, 1967), *Experience and God* (New York: Oxford University Press, 1968), *Themes in American Philosophy: Purpose, Experience, and Community* (New York: Harper and Row, 1970), *Purpose and Thought: The Meaning of Pragmatism* (New Haven: Yale University Press, 1978), and *America's Philosophical Vision* (Chicago: University of Chicago Press, 1992). On a personal note I should say that as an undergraduate I

worked for Professor Smith and typed the introductory materials for his edition of Edwards' *Religious Affections*; he directed my dissertation a few years later and in the over forty years since my degree I have had very few ideas he did not plant in those early days.

12. Several modern editions of Emerson's essays exist, all with about the same selection of essays. A standard edition is edited with an introduction by Brooks Atkinson and a foreword by Tremaine McDowell, *Selected Writings of Emerson* (New York: The Modern Library, 1950). All the essays cited here can be found in this volume. On transcendentalism, see "The Transcendentalist."

13. See his essays, "Self Reliance" and "Compensation."

14. See "The Oversoul" and "Circles."

15. See his short book (in Atkinson) *Nature*.

16. Ibid.

17. See "Heroism," "Intellect," "Art," "The Poet," "Experience," and "Character."

18. From "Circles," in Atkinson, 286.

19. See "Experience."

20. See Deuser's translation in *Charles Sanders Peirce: Religionsphilosophische Schriften*, 170–208, and his analysis in *Gott: Geist und Natur*, chapter 2.

21. Deuser's *Religionsphilosophische Schriften*, 229–359.

22. For a good critical study on the topics of this essay, see David C. Lamberth's *William James and the Metaphysics of Experience* (Cambridge: Cambridge University Press, 1999).

23. *A Common Faith* (New Haven: Yale University Press, 1934). See his extraordinary book, *Experience and Nature* (Chicago: Open Court, 1925; revised edition New York: Norton, 1929). See Stephen C. Rockefeller's *John Dewey: Religious Faith and Democratic Humanism* (New York: Columbia University Press, 1991) for a fine study of Dewey on the topics of this essay.

24. *Science and the Modern World* (New York: Macmillan, 1925).

25. This account was in his major systematic book, *Process and Reality: An Essay in Philosophical Cosmology* (New York: Macmillan, 1929; corrected edition by David Griffin and Donald Sherburne, New York: Free Press, 1978). My remarks here are about the theory in *Process and Reality*.

26. In *Process and Reality*, part 5.

CHAPTER ELEVEN. CONCEPTS OF GOD IN COMPARATIVE THEOLOGY

1. Although some of the comparative points to be made in this chapter are in need of much justification, the expository points about individual religious or theological traditions are commonplaces. Encyclopedias or introductory text books can be

consulted if necessary, as well as the volumes of the Cross Cultural Comparative religious Ideas Project, *The Human Condition, Ultimate Realities, and Religious Truth*, all edited by Robert Neville (Albany: State University of New York Press, 2001).

2. Huston Smith is the most influential comparative historian of religions to employ the Perennial Philosophy. See his *The World's Religions: Our Great Wisdom Traditions* (San Francisco: Harper San Francisco, 1991; revised edition of *Religions of Man*, 1958).

3. On personification of the ultimate in religious symbols, see my *Religion in Late Modernity* (Albany: State University of New York Press, 2002), chapter 4.

4. See "Cooking the Last Fruit of Nihilism: Buddhist Approaches to Ultimate Reality" by Malcolm David Eckel with John J. Thatamanil in *Ultimate Realities*, chapter 6.

5. On this general theory of comparison, see chapter 1 of *The Human Condition* and chapter 8 of *Ultimate Realities*, both by Wesley J. Wildman and myself.

6. See "Religious Dimensions of the Human Condition in Judaism: Wrestling with God in an Imperfect World" in *The Human Condition* and "Ultimate Realities: Judaism: God as a Many-sided Ultimate Reality in Traditional Judaism" in *Ultimate Realities*, both by Anthony J. Saldarini with Joseph Kanofsky.

7. See Richard Rorty's edited book, *The Linguistic Turn: Recent Essays in Philosophical Method* (Chicago: University of Chicago Press, 1967), including his introduction.

8. On the proper vagueness of the notion of *ultimacy*, see the Introduction to *Ultimate Realities* by Wesley J. Wildman and myself.

9. On the spectrum of personification and abstraction, see "Comparative Conclusions about Ultimate Realities" by Wesley J. Wildman and myself in *Ultimate Realities*, chapter 7. On the Axial Age, see Karl Jaspers' *The Way to Wisdom*, translated by Ralph Mannheim (New Haven: Yale University Press, 1954).

10. See S. Nomanul Haq's "Ultimate Reality: Islam" in *Ultimate Realities*, chapter 4.

11. See his "The Two Types of Philosophy of Religion" in *Theology of Culture*, edited by Robert C. Kimball (New York: Oxford University Press, 1959), 10.

12. See the fine discussion in Livia Kohn's "Chinese Religion" in *The Human Condition*.

13. The position of George Lindbeck, for instance, in his *The Nature of Doctrine* (Philadelphia: Westminster, 1984).

14. On the idea of the sage or perfected one, see "Ultimate Reality: Chinese Religion" by Livia Kohn with James Miller in *Ultimate Realities*, chapter 1, and "Truth in Chinese Religion" by Livia Kohn and James Miller in *Religious Truth*, chapter 1.

15. See "Beginningless Ignorance: A Buddhist View of the Human Condition" by Malcolm David Eckel with John J. Thatamanil and "To be Heard and Done, But Never Quite Seen: The Human Condition According to the *Vivekacudamani*" by Francis X. Clooney, S.J., with Hugh Nicholson, in *The Human Condition*, chapters 3 and 4 respectively.

16. On this interpretation of prayer, see James P. Carse's brilliant *The Silence of God: Meditations on Prayer* (New York: Harper/Collins, 1985).

17. Peter Berger, *The Sacred Canopy: Elements of a Sociological Theory of Religion* (Garden City, N.Y.: Doubleday, 1967).

CHAPTER TWELVE. SOME CONTEMPORARY THEORIES OF DIVINE CREATION

1. The classification of theologies into determinate entity and ground of being conceptions has been developed recently in the terms used by Wesley J. Wildman; see his "Ground of Being Theologies" in Philip Clayton, editor, *The Oxford Handbook of Religion and Science* (Oxford: Oxford University Press, 2006). This distinction in my own way of thinking derives from my *God the Creator: On the Transcendence and Presence of God* (Chicago: University of Chicago Press, 1968; revised edition with a new introduction, Albany: State University of New York Press, 1992). That book divides theories of Being-itself into those that conceive being to be determinate and those that conceive it to be indeterminate. The popularity of the phrase "ground of being" derives from the extensive work of Paul Tillich.

2. Some Thomist scholars dispute the classification of Thomas as holding to the fullness-of-being type, arguing instead that he has a strong doctrine of creation *ex nihilo*. In light of Thomas' use of analogy, however, according to which God is eminently what finite things are partially, I stress the importance of the fullness-of-being element in his thought. In this I follow contemporary Thomists for whom finite things "participate" in the fullness of being of God's Act of Esse. In Buddhist rhetoric, the ontological ground is absolutely full nothingness. See, for instance, Keiji Nishitani's *Religion and Nothingness*, translated by Jan van Bragt (Berkeley: University of California Press, 1982).

3. One of the most exacting discussions of diremption or contraction is by the founder of this society, Paul Weiss, in his *Modes of Being* (Carbondale: Southern Illinois University Press, 1958), 505–506.

4. Scotus, of course, is far too subtle to be summarized adequately in a slogan about the priority of divine will or nature. He argues that God's will and nature are identical, but that the nature is of the character of an act of will intrinsically defined by a final cause. See, for instance, his *Opus oxoniensem* 1, dist. 2, question 1; this is translated by Allan Wolter, O.F.M. in his *Duns Scotus: Philosophical Writings* (London: Thomas Nelson, 1962), 35–81.

5. See John Milbank's *Theology and Social Theory: Beyond Secular Reason* (Oxford, UK: Blackwell, 1990), 14; 423–426.

6. See John Boler's *Charles Peirce and Scholastic Realism* (Seattle: University of Washington Press, 1963).

7. Whitehead's great work on God is *Process and Reality: An Essay in Philosophical Cosmology*, revised edition edited by David Ray Griffin and Donald Sherburne (New York: Free Press, 1978). See also his *Religion in the Making* (New York: Macmillan, 1926).

8. Whitehead's most succinct statement of his theology is in part 5 of *Process and Reality*, although the technical discussions of God's interactions with finite actual entities run throughout the book.

9. His classic statement is in *The Divine Relativity* (New Haven, CT: Yale University Press, 1948).

10. See *Process and Reality*, 24–26 and *passim*.

11. For the Category of the Ultimate, see *Process and Reality*, 21–22.

12. On the eternity of the ontological creative act, see my *Eternity and Time's Flow* (Albany: State University of New York Press, 1993).

13. This is an interesting reversal of the more common analogy drawn between human beings and God, elaborated splendidly by Keith Ward in his *Religion and Creation* (Oxford: Oxford University Press, 1996). I have discussed his analogy, and presented the one defended here, in *Symbols of Jesus: A Christology of Symbolic Engagement* (Cambridge: Cambridge University Press, 2001), chapter 1.

14. The debates discussed here occur widely in the literature of process thought. But see especially "Three Responses to Neville's *Creativity and God*" by Charles Hartshorne, John B. Cobb, Jr., and Lewis S. Ford in *Process Studies* 10/3–4 (Fall-Winter 1980), 73–88; see also my follow-up, "Concerning *Creativity and God*: A Response," in *Process Studies* 11/1 (Spring 1981), 1–10.

15. "Why is there anything at all rather that absolutely nothing" was the theme of the conference for which this chapter was written. It was the choice of Fr. John Wippel, President of the Metaphysical Society.

CHAPTER THIRTEEN. DESCARTES AND LEIBNIZ ON THE PRIORITY OF NATURE VERSUS WILL IN GOD

1. "These days" referred to the 1960s. Nevertheless, the interest in philosophical problems of transcendence and immanence remains today, refocused somewhat through the lens of the science and religion debates. See the references to Wildman's work in the previous chapter.

2. Descartes, *The Philosophical Works of Descartes*, translated by Elizabeth S. Haldane and G. R. T. Ross (2 vols.; New York: Dover Publications, 1955), II, 248.

3. Leibniz, Leibniz: *Philosophical Papers and Letters*, edited by L. Loemker (2 vols.; Chicago, University of Chicago Press, 1956), I, 586, n. 163.

4. Descartes, *Philosophical Works*, II, 248.

5. Leibniz, *Philosophical Papers*, I, 509.

6. Descartes, *Philosophical Works*, II, 248; italics mine.

7. Leibniz, *Discourse on Metaphysics*, translated by G. R. Montgomery (La Salle, Ill.: Open Court Publishing Co., 1953), p. 5.

8. Leibniz, *Leibniz*, II, 913.

9. Ibid., II, 912.

10. Leibniz, *Discourse*, p. 5.

11. Leibniz, *Leibniz*, I, 541.

12. Ibid., II, 793.

13. Ibid., II, 915.

14. Descartes, *Philosophical Works*, II, 248; italic mine.

15. Ibid., II, 249.

16. Ibid., II, 248.

17. Friedrich Schleiermacher, *The Christian Faith*, translated by H. R. Mackintosh and J. S. Stewart (Edinburgh: T. & T. Clark, 1928), 156.: "Now it is self-evident that He on Whom everything is absolutely dependent is absolutely free. But if we suppose that the free decision implies a prior deliberation followed by choice, or interpret freedom as meaning that God might equally well have not created the world (because we think that there must have been this possibility, otherwise God was compelled to create), we have then assumed an antithesis between freedom and necessity, and, by attributing this kind of freedom to God, have placed Him within the realm of contradictions."

18. See Carl G. Vaught, "The Nature of God and Its Relation to Certain Proofs for God's Existence" (unpublished Ph.D. dissertation, Yale University, 1966). Vaught argues, among other things, that Tillich's view of God as the ground or power of being should recognize the need for metaphysical arguments of the sort Hartshorne proposes; such a recognition, he claims, would require some alteration of Tillich's conception of God.

19. The original essay said "fifty years." Nevertheless the points made in the following still hold; see, for instance, chapter 1 above.

CHAPTER FOURTEEN. THE METAPHYSICAL SENSE IN WHICH LIFE IS ETERNAL

1. "Vaguely" in this sentence means that immortality embraces several versions of life in time without end, some of which are contradictory to others. This logical usage of vagueness derives from Charles Peirce.

2. See Whitehead's *Process and Reality* revised edition by David Griffin and Donald Sherburne (New York: Free Press, 1978), chapter 2.

3. This is a fundamental insight of Platonic, Confucian, Daoist, Buddhist, and certain contemporary process philosophies. Of course, others have argued that such "becoming" is not as real as static "being." Often these are disputes about words, and each philosophy has a model for representing its sense of change.

4. I say "for convenience's sake" because we know that contemporary physics describes the inner workings of time in ways that seem far from common sense.

5. On continuity and discontinuity, see chapter 9 above.

6. This is one of the powerful arguments in Paul Weiss's masterful *Modes of Being* (Carbondale: Southern Illinois University Press, 1958), chapter 3.

7. See the discussion of essential and conditional features in chapter 12 above.

8. If we were to speak in the language of modern physics we would have to add space as a mode of space-time reality with its own essential feature and conditional features from the three modes of time. But think only of the temporal modes for the moment.

9. That form is the organization of things formed to achieve value is defended at length in my *Reconstruction of Thinking* (Albany: State University of New York Press, 1981).

10. All these are controversial points I have defended at length elsewhere, in *God the Creator, Eternity and Time's Flow* (Albany: State University of New York Press, 1993) and *Symbols of Jesus* (Cambridge: Cambridge University Press, 2001).

11. With respect to the Christian doctrine of the incarnation, we should say that God in some way became wholly and plainly human in Jesus, not that God is a big human-like spirit.

Index

Abe Masao, 15
Abraham, 117, 213
Absolute dependence, 249
Absoluteness, of meaning and value, 66
Abstractions, 97–98
Abyss, 94
Act of Esse, 44, 46, 182, 247
Action, 168
Actual entity, 193–96. *See also* Occasion
Adepts, religious, 106
Adequacy, 85, 105
Advaita Vedanta, 81, 178, 183
Aesthetics, 4, 11, 110, 124, 129, 134, 168; in Edwards, 166–68
Affections, 167–68
Africa, 17; tribal religions in, 50
African-Americans, 104
Agapism, 90
Alfarabi, 73
Alghazali, 73
Alienation, 225
Allah, 181,183,231
Allan, George, 155, 167, 243–44
Allen, Christopher, 230
Alpha and Omega, 225
American Academy of Religion, 14
American Theological Society, xi
Ames, Roger T., 157, 241
Analogy, 130–31; of proportion and proper proportionality, 198
Anderson, Douglas R., 233–34
Angels, 25; and gender, 213

Anglicanism, 10, 13, 42
Anselm, 96, 213
Anthropology, 12, 14; as theology, 40, 82
Anthropomorphism, 73–74, 182–90
Anti-Semitism, 52
Apartheid, 165
Apollo, 182
Apologetics, 13, 31, 73–75
Apophaticism, 36, 80, 92–94
Applicability, 85, 105
Aquinas, Thomas, 5, 23, 32, 37, 73, 93, 117, 182, 191–92, 240, 247
Arbitrariness, 17, 75–77, 80–84, 133–34, 172, 195, 208, 238; in Barth, 10–11, 28
Architecture, 30
Argument, from *esse* to *posse*, 193; as rope not chain, 120–21
Aristotelianism, 93
Aristotle, 1, 31, 40, 73, 99, 128, 138, 155, 161–62, 185, 215, 240
Art, 27, 30, 32, 39, 62, 83–84, 129–30, 138, 141, 173, 236; criticism, 129–30; as experience, 4; in theology, 12
Ascent, to God, 211
Aseity, 207–10
Asian philosophy, for pragmatism, 156–57
Assertion, 136–37, 146; in theology, 81–83

Assessment, 86
Asymmetry, 197–99
Atheism, 12
Atkinson, Brooks, 235
Atonement, 59, 225; Day of, 96; symbols in, 98–99
Attunement, 91
Augustine, 18, 73, 160, 163, 213, 221, 240
Augustinians, 211
Authority, 17–20, 48; of scripture, 57–60
Avalokiteshvara, 183
Averroes, 73
Avicenna, 73, 128
Awe, 200
Axial Age, 55, 55–59, 90, 178, 182, 186–90

Balance, of obligations, 66–67
Baptism, 214
Barth, Karl, 2, 9–17, 20, 23, 27–30, 40, 49, 79, 165, 172, 227, 229; Society for, 14
Barthianism, 28–30, 33–34
Beauty, 166–72
Becoming, 197, 249
Being, 145–46; as first object of intellect, 136; of God, 204–207; -itself, in Tillich, 210
Belief, 4, 73–75, 111; in religious identity, 16–20
Berger, Peter, 37–38, 62, 229–31, 247
Bergson, Henri, 156
Berthrong, John H., 230
Bhagavad Gita, 73
Bhakti, 73
Bias, 115–18
Bible, 10–11, 23–24, 27, 32, 51, 68, 76, 98; imagery of, plausible for some non-elites, 63; interpretation of, 2;
Biblical literalism, 16
Biblical scholarship, 36
Biography, 224
Biology, 41, 84, 173
Bio-psychic dance, 41, 62, 102
BMW, 39

Bodhisattva, 65, 183
Boler, John F., 227, 247
Boodin, John Elof, 237
Boston University, 28
Boydston, Jo Ann, 238
Bracken, Joseph, S. J., 29, 193
Bradley, F. H., 236
Brahman, 189
Brahmins, 70; Boston, 154
Breadth, in interpretation, 106–107
Brent, Joseph, 240
Brightman, Edgar Sheffield, 237
Brown, Delwin, 29, 240
Buchler, Justus, 155, 157, 240
Buddha, the, 18, 26; -mind, 66; -nature, 181
Buddhism, 10, 12–13, 31, 33, 48, 57–60, 64–65, 73–74, 76, 79, 81–86, 117, 172, 178, 182–84, 187–89, 197, 214, 232, 247, 249; Hua-yen, 157; Korean, 52
Bultmann, Rudolf, 15, 26, 64–65

Caesar, 18
Calvin, John, 40, 97, 167
Calvinism, 165–68, 171, 244
Canaanites, 182
Cannibalism, in Eucharist, 97–98
Carryover, of value, 31, 102, 104, 114
Carse, James P., 247
Cartesianism, 123
Cassirer, Ernst, 119
Category of the Ultimate, 159, 194
Causation, 38, 142–43; in engagement, 78; in interpretation, 3–4, 90; in reference, 45–46
Certainty, 24–25, 146
Chan, Wing-tsit, 231
Change, ontological possibility of, 216–19
Chaos, 164, 220
Chapman, J. Harley, 242
Chemist, 169
Chicago, University of, 28, 33, 153
China, 17, 42, 50–51; Dewey in, 156
Christ, mind of, 24. *See also* Jesus Christ
Christendom, 26

Christian identity, 23
Christian realism, 29
Christianity, 29, 33, 57–60, 76, 79, 81, 83–86, 97, 116, 178, 182–85, 213–14, 232; Absolute, 179; as banal morality, 26; changed by Augustine, 18; as cross-cultural, 51–55; history of, how to read, 51–55; and other religions, 50–55; not a religion, 28–29; western and non-western, 49–54
Christocentrism, 29, 52, 172
Circles, in Emerson, 169
Civilization, 38, 154, 101
Claims, in theology, 81–83
Clarity, 107
Class distinctions, among pragmatists and process philosophers, 154
Classification, 115
Clayton, Philip, 247
Clod, aesthetic, 130
Clooney, Francis X., S.J., 230, 246
Cobb, John B., Jr., 29, 154, 248
Cobb-Abe Group, 15
Codes, of signs or symbols, 38–42, 91–93
Cohen, Hermann, 73
Coherence, 85, 105
Colapietro, Vincent, 228, 233
Collaboration, in reading scriptures, 70
Colonialism, 10, 17
Commentarial traditions, 59
Commitment, 17–19
Common natures, 78
Communion, of man and God, 10
Community, alienation from, 82; as context, 43–44; of investigators, 107; pre-reflective, 81–82; religious, 15, 18–19, 33, 35–37
Comparative categories, 49–55, 83–84, 116–18, 179–81
Comparative theology. *See* Theology
Comparison, xiii, 5, 37, 49–55, 83, 85–86; interfaith, 15; for the sake of identifying respects of interpretation, 54; theory of, 179–81
Complexity, 126–51; of symbols, 103–104

Components, of human society, 66
Composition, art, 130
Compossibility, 204
Conditional features. *See* Harmony
Confessional theology, 49, 82
Confessions, 11
Confucian-Americans, 53
Confucianism, 10, 21, 26, 50, 57–60, 65, 74, 157, 172, 179, 182–83, 187–89, 214, 249
Confucius, 26, 231
Consciousness, 168
Consistency, 85, 105
Content, of signs, 95–100
Context, 31; in interpretation, 113–14, 181; in religious symbols, 43–45; in theological assertions, 2–3, 103–104
Contextualization, 41–47, 75
Continental philosophy. *See* Philosophy
Contingency, 133–35
Continuity, 158–64
Convention, in religious symbols, 105
Conventional reference, 3, 45–47, 91
Copts, 42
Correlation, method of, 12
Correspondence, theory of truth, 41, 114; in perception, 142–43
Corrington, Robert S., 157, 228, 233, 240
Cosmic Christ, 30, 225
Cosmological creativity, 194–95
Cosmology, 134, 136; in Peirce, 90
Creation, divine, 20, 25, 29, 80, 203–12; act of, 199; *a deo*, 191–98; doctrine of, 165–68; *ex nihilo*, 5, 14, 157, 161–64, 194–96
Creative act, 199
Creativity, 164, 199; in imagination, 142; in pragmatism, 160
Creator, 46, 52, 59, 97–98, 114–15, 166–68, 177
Criteria, for biblical hermeneutics, 68–71; for system, 105; for truth, 104–107
Criticism, in the arts, 84, 142
Cross Cultural Comparative Religious Ideas Project, 230

Cross, as symbol, 43–44
Crucifixion, 90, 92
Cultural/linguistic theory, 2–3, 13, 35–37, 48–50, 82–83
Culture, 41; German, 12

Daly, Mary, 14
Dao, 59, 66, 178, 183, 189
Daoism, 10, 57–60, 74, 172, 182–83, 187–89, 234, 249
Daoist-Americans, 53
Death, 213
Decay, and immortality, 214
Decision-points, 194–96
Deconstruction, 77, 93
Deduction, 114–15, 145–46
Deep structure, 2
Definition, of signs, 95–100
Deism, 116
Delusion, 168
Demonic symbols, 60
Demonstration, 115
Demythologizing, 26–27
Depravity, 34
Depth, in interpretation, 106–107
Derrida, Jacques, 89
Descartes, Rene, 5, 84, 91, 119, 123, 203–204
Determinateness, 125–28, 131–35, 163–64, 196–99, 210
Determinism, 166–67
Deuser, Hermann, xii–xiv, 5, 222–23, 229, 234, 243, 245
Devil, 167–68, 206
Devotion, as context, 44
Dewey, John, 4, 15, 90, 100–101, 109, 153–57, 159, 167–68, 170–71, 233, 236–41, 244
Diagrams, 120–21
Dialectic, 83, 85, 144–45, 148–51, 208
Dialogue, ecumenical, 48
Diremption, 191, 200
Discernment, 69–70
Discrimination of imaginative worlds, protection against violence, 71
Discursiveness, 146
Dispensationalism, 10

Distributive justice, 53
Diversity, 161
Divided line, in Plato, 128–35, 140–51
Doctrine, 35–37, 48
Dorrien, Gary, xi, 28, 228
Dreams, 141
Driving, 78
Dyad, in continental semiotics, 100
Dyaus, 182
Dynamism, eternal, 199; in modes of time, 218; nine-fold in divine life, 221–22, 225

Eckel, Malcolm David, 230, 246
Ecology, 28
Economics, 30, 33
Ecstatic naturalism, 157
Education, in theology, 10
Edwards, Jonathan, 4, 149, 166–72, 225, 243
Egyptians, 182
Elegance, 134
Eliot, George, 229
Emergence, 193; in pragmatism, 159–60
Emerson, Ralph Waldo, 167–71, 232
Empiricism, 115; British, 119, 156, 168, 170; in hermeneutics, 68–70; in theology, 31
Emptiness, 184
Energy, 160
Engagement, xiii, 38–42, 47, 50–51, 78, 99, 116, 120, 169, 199; in Peirce, 89; and purpose, 101; of truth through scriptures, 58–61, symbolic, 2–3; tests of, 68–69
Enlightenment, European, 59–60, 76, 166; spiritual, 104, 186
Environment, 38
Equivocity, 95
Eros and mind, 147
Error, 146–47
Erudition, 109; in philosophy of religion, 119–21
Escapism, in biblical reading, 68
Eschatology, realized, 214–15
Essential features. *See* Harmony
Estrangement, 184

Eternal life, 214–25
Eternal objects, 158, 215
Eternity, 5, 157, 160–64, 194, 199; defined, 163–64, 218; defined by Plotinus, 215
Ethicists, 36
Ethics, 110
Eucharist, 37, 97–98, 111, 169
Evaluative judgments, 146–51
Evidence, in theology, 85–86
Evil, 135; and sacrifice, 98
Evolution, 39, 89, 99, 109, 170–71, 188; and religion, 111; of religion, 120
Evolutionary love, 170
Existence, 180; necessary, 209; of world, 80
Existential situation, a fundamental human issue, 65
Existentialism, 12, 26, 34, 160
Exodus story, 98
Exodus, 103–104
Experience, 101, 167–68, 185; religious, 211–12
Experimental religion, in Edwards, 167–68
Expertise, in reading scriptures, 70
Explanation, 114–15
Explication, 115
Extension, in interpretation, 77–78; 95–96

Faculty-psychology, 238
Faith, a fundamental human issue, 65; in Kant, 25; religious, 74; seeking understanding, 106–107
Fall, 167
Fallibilism, 154, 156; in intuition, 142–51
Falsity, 31
Family, 30
Farewell Discourse, 60, 215
Father, God as, 45–46
Faust, Clarence H., 243
Features, of harmony. *See* Harmony
Feedback, 30, 32
Feminism, 14–15, 60
Ferre, Frederick, 155, 167, 244

Feuerbach, Ludwig, 38–40, 78
Fideism, 49
Finite/infinite contrasts, 80
Finitude, of God, 171–72
Firstness, 90, 161, 233
Fitness, of things together, 124–25, 29–30
Folk psychology, 198
Ford, Lewis, 29, 164, 193, 248
Forgiveness, 214
Form, carryover of, 61; of harmony, 134; ideal, 147–51; in truth, 40–41
Foundationalism, xi, 24–25, 27, 76, 119–20
Four Noble Truths, 178
Fourthness, 4
Fragmentation, 225
Frankena, William K., 243
Frankenberry, Nancy, 242
Frankfurt University, xii–xiii
Fredriksen, Paula, 230–31
Freedom, 29
Frei, Hans W., 2–3, 13, 49–50, 227, 229–30
Freud, Sigmund, 38
Friendship, 30
Frisina, Warren G., 244
Fruits, 33, 105
Fundamentalism, 11, 16, 76
Future, 160–64, 199, 216–25

Generality, distinct from vagueness, 117
Generals, 78, 94
Genetic analysis, in Whitehead, 159
Genus, God not, or in, 93
Global public, 75–86
Globalization, and plausibility, 63–64
Glory, 166–68, 225
God, xiii, 18–19, 25, 28–29, 36–37, 40, 44, 55, 60–61, 66, 94, 97–98, 103–104, 114–15, 117–18, 158, 162, 164, 169, 180, 182–90; as agent, 198–201; being in, 5; beyond god, 14; classification of concepts of, 191–92; as common noun, 181; as comparative category, 116–18; concepts of, 177–90; as creator, 2; as cre-

God *(continued)*
  ator *ex nihilo*, 191–201. *See also* Creation *ex nihilo*; as determinate entity versus ground of being, 5, 15, 191–201; essence and existence in, 204–205; as explanation, 208; as father, 182, 234; as finite, 15; freedom of, 206–207; as fullness of being, 191–201; as future, 164; as ground of being, 191–201; immanence of, 107–109, 211; as immense, 171; as intentional, 115; as judge, 177, 180; as king, 187; life of as eternal togetherness of modes of time, 218–22; of the living, 213; nature of, 198–99, 203–12, 220–22; as One, 46; Peirce's argument for, 110, 114–15; not a person, 222; in process theology, 193–96; not prominent in all religions, 177–79; right hand of, 214; as rock, 113; in scriptures, 58; not a thing, 93–94; transcendence of, 207–209; Whitehead's compared with Creator *ex nihilo*, 164; will of, 203–12
Goen, C. C., 244–45
Good, form of, as creator, 150
Goodness, created, 205–206; in God, 191–92
Gospel, 51
Grammar, 35–37, 48, 77, 95–96
Grange, Joseph, 155, 167, 244
Grasp, of making, 162
Great Awakening, 167
Great Commandment, 91
Great Ultimate, 178
Greek philosophy, 59
Griffin, David Ray, 29, 232, 236, 245, 247
Ground of being, 14, 44, 46, 194–200, 210
Guanyin, 37, 183, 188
Guiding principles, 4

Habit, 59, 78, 102–103
Haecceity, 78
Hahn, Lewis Edwin, 236

Haldane, Elizabeth S., 248
Hall, David L., 155–57, 241
Haq, S. Nomanul, 230–31, 246
Hare, Peter, 240
Harmonies of harmonies, all the way down, 131–32
Harmonization, in process philosophy, 158–60
Harmony, 104, 123–51, 161–62, 171–72, 186, 219–22; as bad, 133; conditional features of, 163, 195–96; of intrinsic composition and conformity, 125; defining being, 166–68; in Edwards, 166–68; essential features of, 131, 163, 195–96; features of, 131–35; of modes of time, 216–18; semiotic, 138–40; subjective, 193–96; theory of, 128–35
Harnack, Adolf von, 28
Hartshorne, Charles, 29, 153–54, 171, 193, 196, 203, 205, 209–10, 229, 232–33, 235–37, 240, 248
Harvard University, 153–54, 170
Hauerwas, Stanley, 13, 227–28
Heaven, 25–26, 183, 213–15, 225; and Earth, 178, 185
Hegel, G. W. F., 39, 74, 78–79, 115–16, 119, 128, 179, 197, 240
Heidegger, Martin, 62, 157
Hell, 213–14
Hermeneutical circle, 63–68
Hermeneutics, 24–27, 33, 63–68, 89
Highlands Institute for American Religious and Philosophic Thought, xi
Hindu-Americans, 52–53
Hinduism, 10, 21, 57–60, 73, 76, 79, 81, 172, 177–78, 183–85,
Historical criticism, 57–58
Historicism, 2
Historicity, of Jesus, 29
History, 52, 79; philosophy of, 12; scripture as, 60
Hocking, Richard, 236
Hocking, William Ernest, 153–54, 237
Holy Spirit, 52, 165, 215; procession of, 105

Homosexuality, 18
Honesty, 38
Hook, Sidney, 154
Hope, as fundamental human issue, 66
Howard, Leon, 243
Humanity, ideal, 134
Hume, David, 77, 111, 116, 119, 168
Husserl, Edmund, 156, 160, 168, 232
Hypothesis, 38–39, 43–47, 89, 94, 114–15, 142, 184; in comparison, 65–58; in metaphysics, 25–27; method of, 154, 238; in theology, 76–77; theoretical, evidentiary, and historical, 85–86

Iconic reference, 3, 45–47; 61; 80; 90–94
Idealism, 1, 77, 153–54, 169; German, 12; in personalism, 28–29
Ideals, 134, 143–45
Identity, 17–20; in Hinduism, Buddhism, Confucianism, Daoism, 17; moral, 222–23; ontological, 20–21; religious, 2, 12–14, 19–20, 76; theology, 9, 23, 29
Idolatry, 59, 94
Images, in Plato, 141–51
Imagination, 12, 27–28, 30–34, 141–51; in art, 32; biblical, versus modern, 90, 96; in cultures, 61–64; metaphysical, 221
Imaginative worlds, 61–64, 67–68
Immanence, 66
Immediacy, 124, 127–28
Immensity, divine, 199, 225
Immortality, 213–15
Importance, 102, 144
Incarnation, 250
Inconsistencies, 238
Indeterminateness, 132, 163–64, 219
Indexical reference, 3, 45–46, 61, 68, 78, 90–94, 113
India, 50, 178
Indifference, divine, 204, 206
Indigenization, 50
Individuality, 59
Indra, 182
Induction, 114–15, 145–46

Infinite, actual, 127; God as, 29, 93–94
Ingression, 164
Initial aims, 193–96
Inquiry, 3–4, 81–83, 115, 170; modes of, 15–20; as piety, 200; in theology, 9, 12, 107
Instinct, 110
Instrumentalism, 170–71
Integrity, 129–30
Intellect, as guide, 33–34
Intelligibility, created, 209; harmony in, 140
Intention, in interpretation, 77–78; of signs, 95–96
Intentionality, in God, 115, 117; levels of, in theology, 81–83
Interaction, in Dewey, 90, 168
Internal relations, 208
Interpretant, 100
Interpretation, xiii, 30–34, 77–80, 95–107, 135–40, 180–81; for Peirce, 112; theory of, 3–4, 39–47; triadic, 100–104
Interpreter, and value, 103–107
Intuition, xii, 4, 119, 123–51; defined by Peirce, 123; defined by Kant, 124; imaginative, 142
Inwardness, in reading scripture, 69–70
Isaac, 213
Isaiah, 182
Islam, 10, 17, 31, 33, 37, 57–60, 64, 73, 76, 79, 81, 172, 178, 185, 188–89, 231–32
Israel, 185
Israelite exceptionalism, 75–76

Jacob, 213
James, Henry, Jr., 238
James, Ralph E., Jr., 240
James, William, 41, 47, 100, 109, 153–55, 159, 167, 170–72, 237–39
Jaspers, Karl, 55, 59, 178, 231, 246
Jesus Christ, 13, 26, 29–30, 37, 43, 45, 50–52, 55, 59–60, 75–76, 79, 90–93, 96, 97, 112, 187, 213–15; the historical, 28; as Lord, 17–18; two natures of, 82

Jews, 23
Job, 102
John the Baptist, 18
John, Gospel of, 60–61, 182, 215
Johnson, Thomas H., 243
Jones, Judith, 155
Jordan, Elijah, 237
Judaism, 10, 16–17, 25, 31, 33, 52, 57–60, 76, 81, 104, 178, 182–83, 185; and pragmatism, 154–55
Judge, God as, 177, 180
Judgment, 130, 135–40; as final, 66; as discursive harmony, 137–38; as normative, 145–51; prudential, 137; as sign, 136–37
Judgments, of formal cohesion and evaluation, 145–51
Just seeing, 124, 128–35, 140
Justice, 59, 65–66, 200; divine, 96–97

Kabbala, 94
Kanofsky, Joseph, 230, 246
Kant, Immanuel, xi, 4, 24–25, 27, 42, 62, 65, 109, 111, 116, 119, 123–24, 128, 135, 138, 140, 165, 168–69, 192, 220, 231, 238
Kantianism, 136
Kasulis, Thomas P., 234, 240
Kataphaticism, 80
Kennedy, Kevin, 236
Kerygma, 12, 29
Kierkegaard, Søren, 12, 106
Kimball, Robert C., 246
Kindness, 38
Kingdom of God, 27–29
Knoblock, John, 231
Knowledge, divine and eternal, 99; of norms, 148–51
Kohn, Livia, 230, 232, 246
Kraus, Elizabeth, 155, 242
Krishna, 73

Ladder, in Plato, 150
Lamb, of God, 96; sacrificial, 59
Lamberth, David C., 245
Language, 2, 77–78, 91–93, 118, 238; private, 92; of religions, 2–4

Law, 32–33, 125; of nature, 78
Leakiness, in Tillich's system, 12
Leibniz, Gottfried, 5, 203–12, 248
Levels of harmony, 138
Lewis, C. I., 153, 240
Liberalism, 26–29, 30, 34, 212; in theology, 2
Liberation theology, 49–50, 64
Light, 102; of nature, 211
Lindbeck, 2, 13, 35–37, 45, 48–50, 82–83, 229–30, 246
Linguistic turn, xi, 180
Literacy, 24
Locke, John, 116, 166
Loemker, L., 248
Logic, 110, 115
Logos, 220
Love, 52, 59, 94, 102, 104, 185; divine, 96–97; as fundamental human issue, 66.
Lovejoy, Arthur O., 237
Lover, God as, 44
Loyalty, 20
Lucas, George R., Jr., 153, 157, 236, 242
Luckmann, Thomas, 38, 229
Luther, Martin, 40
Lutherans, 48

Maassen, Helmut, 234
Mackintosh, H. R., 249
Madhyamika, 178, 183, 189
Mahayana, 37, 178
Maimonides, 73
Making, 198–200, 219–20
Mandate of Heaven, 188
Manifold, 126–28
Marginalization, 49, 79–80
Marsoobian, Armen, 240
Martyr, Justin, 42, 73
Marx, Karl, 38
Materialism, 166
Mathematicians, 129
Mathematics, 120–21, 145, 147; in science, 167
Mead, George Herbert, 100, 109, 153–57, 159, 239
Meaning, 42–43, 66, 94–100, 114

INDEX

Mechanism, 166
Memory, 77, 141
Mencius, 231
Mercy, 59
"Mere wouldings," 168
Messiah, 92
Metaphor, 80–81
Metaphysical Society of America, xii
Metaphysics, 2, 15, 24–27, 32, 51, 81, 111, 131–34, 136, 138, 141, 153–57, 177, 188, 193; as answer to Kant, 25–26; in comparison, 67; as hypothesis, 1, 67–68; in Peirce, 89–90; speculative, 171; suffering from, 225; of time and eternity, 215–25; and violence, 71
Method, 33
Methodism, 12
Might makes right, 206
Milbank, John, 10, 13, 192, 227, 247
Miller, James E., 230. 246
Mind, frozen, 90
Modernism, 28–29
Modernity, 84
Modes of time, 216–25
Moffett, Samuel Hugh, 230
Mohammed, 26
Moltmann, Jurgen, 165
Monotheism, 66, 177–79, 181–82, 190
Montgomery, G. R., 248
Morality, 106, 134, 177, 222–23
Morris, Charles W., 95–96, 234, 237
Moses, 26, 61, 117
Mozart, 10
Musement, 141
Music, 39
Muslim-Americans, 52–53
Muslims, 23. *See* Islam
Mysticism, 80, 94, 119, 200, 225
Myth, 45, 70, 90

Nagel, Ernst, 154
Narrative, 13, 20, 93–94, 165, 172; creation, 182; master, 7–9; as nominalistic, 1–2, 78–79; in theology, 10–12, 91
Native American religions, 50

Natural theology, 119
Naturalism, 37, 154–55
Nature, 30, 62–63; 204; in American theology, 165–73; divine, 203–12; God's, 5, 15; orders of, 165; in romanticism, 169; as value-free, 166
Nazism, 27, 30, 60
Negations, as making determinateness, 197–98
Neo-Confucianism, 74
Neo-liberalism, 29–30
Neo-Orthodoxy, 27, 52, 212
Neo-Platonism, 14, 117–18, 178, 182, 184, 191, 197
Neo-pragmatism, 155–57
Neo-Thomism, 156
Nervous system, 38–42
Nestorianism, 42, 50–51
Nests, of signs, 97–100, 103–104
Networks, of signs, 97–100, 103–104
Neuroscience, 173
Neville, Beth, xiv
New being, 29
Newton, Isaac, 166
Nicholson, Hugh, 230, 246
Niebuhr, Reinhold, 29, 34, 228
Nietzsche, Friedrich, 38, 232
Nishitani Keiji, 197, 247
Nobo, Jorge, 158
Nominalism, 1–4, 78–80, 94, 111, 153, 192; default, 155; in narrative thinking, 78–79
Non-being, 197
Non-dualism, 184
Normative judgments, 146–51
Normative measure, 123, 143–44
Normativeness, 5; in future, 216–17; in theology, 35–37
Norms, 160; intuited, 143–45
Nothingness, 219
Novelty, 161–64; 194–96; 216–18; ontological, 220
Nyaya, 73, 157

Object, of judgment, 136; of reference, 94
Objectivity, 110, 238

Obligation, 59
Occasion, in process philosophy, 158–62, 172
Odin, Steve, 157
Ogden, Schubert, 29, 228
Oliver, Harold H., 242
Omnipotence, 208
Omnipresence, 169
One, as God, 46; and many, 184–85, 188, 193–96, 219–20; in Neo-Platonism, 182
Ontological, argument, 209–11; creative act, 194–96; principle, 194; shock, 160
Ontology, 11–12, 15
Oppenheim, Frank, 236
Order, 164; needs explanation, 220
Orientation, 105, 111
Origen, 163
Orthodoxy, 16, 82–83; Eastern, 10, 42, 97, 105
Otherness, 160
Otto, Rudolf, 119
Oversoul, 169
Own-being, 189

Paideia, theological, 83
Paleo-pragmatism, 156
Pannenberg, Wolfhart, 165
Pantheons, 177–78
Parker, Dewitt H., 237
Participation, through symbols, 26
Particulars, 1–2, 78–79
Past, 100, 160–64, 216–25; for Whitehead, 158–60
Pastoral care and counseling, 14
Patristic theology, 51
Pattern, 132–35; of life, 59–60
Paul, St., 50, 105
Peace, religions of, 69
Peirce, Charles Sanders, 1–4, 15, 25–27, 37–39, 42, 44, 46, 49, 61, 93–95, 99, 104, 107, 109–21, 123–24, 129, 136–40, 146, 153–57, 159–61, 164, 167, 170–71, 179–80, 192, 228–29, 232–35, 237–41, 243, 249; on argument as a rope, not a chain, xiii; as Platonist, xii; theory of interpretation, 100–107; theory for interpreting religion, 89–107
Perception, 41, 141–43
Perennial philosophy, 178, 1184, 197, 246
Performative, religious belief as, 17–18
Perry, Ralph Barton, 153, 154, 237–39
Personalism, Boston, 12, 28–29, 212
Personification, 42, 45–46, 98–99, 178, 182–83, 188–89
Perspective, ultimate, 66
Petersen, Rodney, 229, 232
Pharisees, 213
Phenomenology, 115, 119, 123, 168; in Peirce, 90
Philip, the Apostle, 50
Phillips, D. Z., 229
Philology, 74
Philosophy, 83; analytic, xi, 154–56; Continental, xi, 154, 156; Eastern, in West, 74; empirical, 119; of nature, 165–73; process, 4–5, 25–26, 29, 33, 153–60, 171–72, 249; of religion, 36–37, 109–11, 118–21; split from theology, 24; in theology, 11–12, 75–86
Pietism, 12
Piety, 166; as engaging God with symbols, 200–201; as a fundamental human issue, 65–66
Plantinga, Alvin, 119
Plato, 1, 4, 73, 83, 110, 123, 128, 134, 128, 141–51, 155, 215, 237
Platonism, 33, 123, 167, 171, 249
Plausibility conditions, 15, 18–19, 63
Plotinus, 200, 215, 240
Pluralism, 48
Plurality, 125–51
Poetry, 39
Poets, 129
Politics, 30
Polysemy, 95
Popcorn, 177
Positivism, 91
Possibility, 216–18
Postliberalism, 35–37, 49–50

Postmodernism, 93
Potentiality, 217–18, 220
Power, 18
Practical reason, 32–34
Practice, 41, 48, 111, 106; religious, 36–37
Pragmatic criteria, 154; as tests in reading scriptures, 67–68
Pragmatics, 95, 139
Pragmatism, xi, 1, 25–26, 33, 38–42, 77–80, 101, 109, 153–60, 170–71; in Edwards, 168
Pratitya samutpada, 184–85, 189, 214
Prayer, 61, 188, 221; and personification, 46
Precariousness, 171
Prehension, 158–64, 193–96
Pre-reflective theology, 81–83
Present, 160–64, 199, 216–25; for Whitehead, 159–60
Princeton University, 166
Principle, 125; (li), 178, 185, 189; general or specific, 126
Probationary induction, 115, 145–46
Process philosophy. *See* Philosophy
Process theology. *See* Theology
Process, versus substance, 158
Progressivism, 28–29
Projections, in religion, 38–42
Propositions, 102–103; Peirce's definition of, 136
Protention, in Husserl, 160
Protestantism, 42, 97
Providence, 167
Prudential judgments, 143–44, 147–48
Psychoanalysis, 12, 14
Psychology, 12
Public, global, 3, 34; life for philosophy, 153; for theology, 10–12, 48–49, 83–86, 116–21
Purgatory, 213
Purpose, 31, 41–42, 101–107, 139, 170, 189; in comparison, 179–81; divine, 200–201; in interpretation, 96–100; most worth having, 109
Purva Mimamsa, 73
Pythagorean theorem, 146

Quadratic interpretation, 137
Quest, 117; religious, as a fundamental human issue, 66–67
Quine, Willard, 153
Qur'an, 59

Radical Orthodoxy, 13, 16, 192
Rahner, Karl, 74
Ramanuja, 183
Raposa, Michael, 234
Rational, as real, 78–79
Rationalism, 12, 194
Reaction, 160
Reading strategies, comparative, metaphysical, and pragmatic, 64–68
Realism, 77–80, 111, 153, 180–81, 237; in epistemology, xi; in metaphysics, xi, xiii; Platonic, 237; Scotistic, 1–5
Reality, 1, 89; as anything about which one might be mistaken, 77; external, 77; human, 111; in reference, 50–55; religious, 91
Reason, 110
Reck, Andrew J., 237
Reconstruction, of symbols, 31
Redemption, 25, 96, 165
Reductionism, 135–36
Reeves, Gene, 240
Reference, 3, 42, 44–47, 61, 68, 80–81, 112–13; conventional, 91–93; God as beyond, 94; iconic, 102–107; indexical, 102–107; ontological, 178; Peirce's theory of, 90–94; of religious symbols, 38; secondary, 46–47, 68–69; theory of, 75
Reform Judaism, 17
Reformation, Protestant, 23–24, 32; theology, 29, 183
Reformed Christianity, 24
Reichenbach, Hans, 156
Reincarnation, 213
Relations, 158
Religion, 2–5; and the arts, 14; history of, 83; as normative, 38
Religious experience, 41
Religious truth, and ultimacy, 60–61
Representation, 118, 143

Resonances, 95–96
Respect, of comparison, 65, 117–18, 179–81; contextualized and cross cultural, 53–54; of interpretation, 41–47, 96–100, 137–38
Resurrection, 44, 213–15
Retroduction, 114–15
Revelation, 10, 12, 33; general and specific, 75–76
Rhetoric, 155
Ricci, Matteo, 232
Richard of St. Victor, 211
Righteousness, 186; as evil, 79–80; as fundamental human issue, 65
Ritschl, F., 27–28
Ritual, 59–60, 169
Roman Catholicism, 10, 16, 42, 28, 97
Romanticism, 168–69
Rorty, Richard, xi, 155–57, 241, 246
Rosenbaum, Stuart, xii
Rosenthal, Sandra, 155, 158–64, 236
Ross, G. R. T., 248
Rourke, Nancy M., 232
Rowling, J. K., 11
Royce, Josiah, 153–54, 236–37
Ruether, Rosemary, 14
Rules, 82, 125
Russell, Bertrand, 171
Ryder, John, 240

Sacred canopy, 62, 188
Sacrifice, blood, 98
Sadducees, 213
Sages, 65, 105
Saints, 105
Saldarini, Anthony J., xii, 230–31, 246
Salvation, 15, 24, 52, 60, 76, 104, 167–68; as the result of belief, 17–18
Samhkya, 73
Samsara, 66
Sartre, Jean-Paul, 12
Satan, 96. See also Devil
Satisfaction, in Whitehead, 159, 161–62
Saussure, F. de, 89
Schematism, 126, 131, 143–44
Schilpp, Paul Arthur, 236

Schleiermacher, Friedrich, 27, 40, 89, 229, 249
Scholasticism, 23
Schulkin, Jay, xiii, 236
Science, 27, 29, 32–33, 83–84, 100, 111, 138, 141, 166, 168, 171–73; and imaginative worlds, 62–63; in Kant, 165; as myth, 90–91; as paradigm for hermeneutics, 89; in philosophy of religion, 120; and religion, 14–15, 167; scripture as, 61; and supernaturalism, 25–26; theology as, 28
Scotistic realism, 237. See also Realism
Scotus, Duns, 5, 78, 80, 191–92, 235, 237, 247
Scriptures, 23–24, 81; how to read, 57–71; spiritual meaning of, 3
Second intention, 136
Second Temple Judaism, 60, 213
Second Vatican Council, 16
Secondness, 90, 129, 160–61, 233
Secularism, 29, 50, 84, 189
Self, 157; -contradiction, 204–207; as a living sign, 89–90; new, 215
Sellars, Roy Wood, 237
Semantics, 95, 139
Semiotics, 15, 26, 30, 33, 38–43, 53, 62, 77–78, 99; Continental, 100; harmony in, 139; for Peirce, 112, 118, 189–97
Sensationalist perception, 238
Sense perception, 135
Septuagint, 60
Sermons, 20
Shamanism, 50, 74, 172
Shangdi, 182
Shepardson, Tina, 230
Sherburne, Donald, 154, 232, 236, 240, 245, 247
Significance, ultimate, 185–90
Signs, 42, 112–14, 136–40; of gracious affections, 169; in Peirce, 89–107, 137
Sin, 15, 25, 28
Singularity, 1, 194; of creative act, 220
Singulars, 78
Siva, 73

Slavery, biblically justified, 64
Smith, Huston, 246
Smith, John E., 101, 233–34, 236–39, 242, 244, 246
Smith, Jonathan Z., 230
Social construction, 37–42
Social reform, 154
Social sciences, 36–37, 111; theology like, 2, 13
Society, in process philosophy, 193
Socrates, 26
Sola Scriptura, 23–24, 27
Soteriology, 91
Soul, 15, 169; created, 213
Specification, of vague categories, 117–18
Specious present, 159–60
Speculation, 105, 129, 136, 238
Spinoza, Baruch, 64, 89, 240
Spontaneity, 163, 196, 216–18
Standards, external or internal to God, 205–207
Stewart, J. W., 249
Straw dogs, 66
Strong misreadings, 156
Structuralism, 111
Structure, 125
Subjective unity, in Whitehead, 159
Subjectivity, 85
Subject-predicate, 238
Substance, 93
Suchocki, Marjorie, 29
Suffering, 183, 187
Sullivan, Celeste, 230
Sullivan, William M., 239
Supercessionism, 52
Superficiality, in philosophy, 110
Supernaturalism, 25–26, 28, 33, 63, 155
Superstition, 73–74, 182
Surprise, 200
Syllogism, 128
Symbolic, engagement, 30–34; forms, 111; reference, 90–94
Symbolism, 26, 239; participation through, 14–15; religious, 39–42; in Tillich, 210

Symbols, 37–40, 83–84; as engagement, 38–42; gripping versus indifferent, 97–99; networks of, 68; as rules, 42–43; as substitutes, 37–39; as true or false, 31
Symmetry, 197–99; versus asymmetry in God, 192
Synechism, 90
Syntactics, 95, 139
System, as analysis from many angles, 85–86; criteria of, 85; in philosophy, defined, xiii; of pragmatism, 109; of signs, 95–100; in symbolic engagement, 30–34; in theological inquiry, 83; as true, 105–107
Systematic theology, 75–77

Temporality, as abstraction within eternity, 222–25
Terminus, of creative act, 220–21
Text, 180
Thatamanil, John, 230, 246
Theism, 154–55, 162, 178, 220
Theologians, male versus female, 48
Theology, 109; American, 165–73; apophatic, 36, 80, 92–94; comparative, 15, 83, 109, 116–19, 177–90; as contextual, 76; for the church, 10; as description, 50; as empirical, 31; as experiential/expressive, 35–37; as inquiry, 36–37; liberal, 23; liberation, 49; making a case in, 83–96; non-Christian, 52–54; in Peirce, 111–16, 170; versus philosophy, 24; process, 4–5, 14, 34, 192–97, 200; as professional, 84; propositional, 35–37; reformed, 165–67; of religions, 12; defined by symbolic engagement, 30–34, 78; as system, 2, 11–12, 74–75
Theory, 115; as symbol, 98
Theravada, 178, 189
Third term, 124–25, 127
Thirdness, 90, 159, 161, 233; creeping, 164
Thomas, the Apostle, 50
Thomism, 10, 13, 191, 127

Thought, as real, 77
Thrasymachus, 206
Tillich Society, 14
Tillich, Paul, 2, 9–17, 20, 23, 26, 29–31, 34, 48–49, 60, 65, 74, 79, 84, 184, 203, 205, 209–12, 227–29, 231, 247, 249
Time, 5, 157–64, 194, 197–98; flow of, 219; possibility of, 215–18
Togetherness, 125–51, 223–25; immediate, 127–28; of modes of time, 163–64
Tolkien, J. R. R., 11, 27
Torah, 59, 76
Totality, 220
Totum simul, 158
Touch, in Aristotle, 99
Toulmin, Stephen, 235
Tracy, David, 232
Tradition, rabbinic, 94
Tragedy, 161
Transaction, in Dewey, 90, 168
Transcendence, 66, 188–89
Transcendentalism, 168–69
Transcendentals, 131
Translation, 50–51
Triadic interpretation, 137
Trinity, 30, 51, 193
Triumphalism, 29
Troeltsch, Ernst, 228
Truth, xiii, 16, 17–20, 77–883, 95–100, 114–16; assessing, 46–49; as carry-over, 40–47, 60, 99–100; as contextualized, 41–47, 50, 113; as correspondence, 140, 154; created and uncreated, 204–205; in engagement, 30–32, 58, 69–71; and form, 31; of hypotheses, 43–47; as inquiry, 47–49; living in the, 104; in metaphor, 80–81; for Peirce, 112; in perspectives, 55; presuppositions of, 187; question of, 50–55; in religion, 40–47, 120; in scriptures, 57–71; in theology, 2, 23–32; and value, 31, 75–77
Tu Wei-ming, 230
Tychism, 90

Ugliness, 138
Ultimacy, xiii, 4, 15, 30, 34, 53, 58–59, 80, 106–107; as anthropological, 183–85; in Buddhism, 117; interpreted, 185–90; as non-personal, 15; as ontological, 183–85; defining religion, 36
Ultimate concern, 15, 184, 186–90
Ultimate, the, 33, 98–99; Category of, 159
Understanding, divine, 204
Unification, of manifold, 42–43
Union Theological Seminary in New York, 28
Unitarianism, 16, 169
Unity, 125–51; formal, 217–18
University of Chicago. *See* Chicago, University of
Univocity, 95
Upanisads, 73
Urban, Wilbur Marshall, 237

Vacuous actuality, 238
Vagueness, 110–11, 136–37, 249; in comparative categories, 85–86, 116–19
Vaisheshika, 73
Value, 31–34, 66, 102, 114, 139, 169–73, 187–90, 217–18; in God, 197–200; in harmony, 133–35; in nature, 166–67; as objective, 172–73; of person, 103; in truth, 40–41
Values, codes of, 144; in Plato, 149–51
Van Bragt, Jan, 247
Vaught, Carl G., 249
Vedanta, 73
Vedas, 58, 61, 66, 73, 81, 182–83
Violence, 71
Virtue, in Edwards, 166–67
Vishnu, 182
Visisthadvaita Vedanta, 183
Voluntarism, 205–207
Vulnerability, to correction, 19, 32–34, 41, 65, 76, 83–86, 93, 107, 116, 119–21, 190, 233

Wallace, Kathleen, 240
Wang, Yang-ming, 185, 244

INDEX

Wangbi, 74
Ward, Keith, 248
Wars, 18; religious, 65
Weimar Republic, 12
Weiss, Paul, 153, 155, 157, 167, 171, 229, 232–33, 235, 237, 240, 242–43, 247, 249
Weissman, David, 157, 167, 242, 244
Wesleyan Quadrilateral, 19
Whitehead, Alfred North, xii, 1, 4, 14, 25, 29, 84, 147, 153–60, 167, 171–72, 192–96, 215–16, 232, 236–41, 244, 247–49
Wieman, Henry Nelson, 28
Wildman, Wesley, J., xiii, 14, 228–30, 232, 246–48
Will, 168; divine, 5, 191–92, 203–12; in error, 146
Wilson, John F., 244
Wippel, John, 200, 248
Wisdom, 38
Witness, 33
Wittgenstein, Ludwig, 90, 92, 157, 233, 242
Wolter, Allan, 235, 247

Wolterstorff, Nicholas, 119
Women, abuse of, 18
Wonder, 200
World Wars, 28
World, -definition, 80; as dependent, 207–209; possible, 204–207
Worldliness, 62
Worship, 190, 198
Wrath, divine, 96

Xenophanes, 73
Xunzi, 60, 74, 231

Yahweh, 182, 185, 220
Yale School of Theology, 2–3, 13, 16, 77
Yale University, 166
Yin-yang, 186
Yoga, 73, 81

Zeus, 182
Zhuxi, 185
Zionism, 64
Zizioulis, 74
Zoroastrianism, 59